Matsumoto Ki
薬
JAYRO
JAYRO
館
元!!
URL: http://w
まくらや
ミシン
カメラ館
こちらです
全品15%
ポイント還元中!!
6Fにて取り扱い中!
ようこそ新宿
21
世紀
MEN'S PLAZA
AOKI
ようこそ新
KFC
KFC
SALE
SALE
SALE

TOKYOLIFE
ART AND DESIGN

IAN LUNA · LAUREN A. GOULD · TOM MES · JASPER SHARP · YOSHIDA MIKA · DAVID G. IMBER

PROJECT COORDINATION: KAWANISHI KANA · APRIL HUOT · JEAN SNOW

TOKYOLIFE

ESSAYS BY: MORI TOSHIKO · KAWAMURA YUNIYA · HAYASHI FUMIHIRO

RIZZOLI
NEW YORK

ACKNOWLEDGMENTS

Recording the cultural output of any major metropolis for any length of time is a significant undertaking. This task is magnified exponentially when the city is the largest conurbation in the planet, and one that for the last decade has been undergoing a crucial generational transition in art, architecture, design, fashion, film, photography and other allied fields. However selective a document this volume ultimately is, its creation involved the participation of hundreds of individuals. Much gratitude is owed to every person who contributed time and energy in this endeavor.

Tokyolife is dedicated to the many esteemed artists, architects, industrial designers, fashion designers, photographers and filmmakers whose work made this anthology possible.

My heartfelt appreciation goes out to my co-authors, without whose painstaking research, editorial concision and all manner of intellectual support, this book would simply not exist. To Tom Mes and Jasper Sharp, for being such fantastic commentators and friends, and for being our astute eyes and ears in Europe; To Yoshida Mika and David G. Imber for their invaluable perspective on the major and minor arcana of *nihonjinron*, and their unflagging good humor and support; and to Lauren A. Gould, whose ever-timely editorial contribution and creative direction were matched by her singular patience, extreme generosity, and an unshakable, infectious enthusiasm. You all have my total and lasting gratitude.

I wish to also express deep appreciation to Mori Toshiko, whose encouragement is, as ever, never taken for granted; Kawamura Yuniya, whose knowledge of the role fashion plays in Japanese society has few peers; and Hayashi "Charlie" Fumihiro, for his charm and unstinting critical resolve.

The vital role of Kawanishi Kana deserves to be singled out, as her hours of toil allowed for the seamless transfer of information from dozens of sources; Jean Snow, for his oh-so timely, down-in-the trenches insight; and to April Huot, whose late-inning heroics as a matchless editorial interlocutor on this often unwieldy project was nothing short of a rescue.

The co-authors and project coordinators would also like to thank the untiring support of Rizzoli International Publications: Publisher Charles Miers; Managing Editor Ellen Nidy; Senior Editor David Morton; Production Manager Maria Pia Gramaglia; Editors Dung Ngo, Jessica Fuller, Julie DiFilippo, Klaus Kirshbaum and Meera Deean; and to Jennifer Pierson, Alan Rutsky, Pam Sommers, Jerry Hoffnagle, Gerard Nudo, Jill Su, Julie Schumacher, Gloria Ahn, Joshua Machat, Walter de la Vega, Paul Alwill, Jose Vazquez, Paul Richards, Raquel Camacho and Previn Allen.

As ever, Chip Kidd, Mark Melnick, Geoff Spear and Eugene Lee provided inestimable assitance towards the physical form of this title. A special thanks to Ninagawa Mika, Kanaya Hidetaka, Honjo Naoki and Nozaki Takeo.

I would also like to cite the support of the following individuals: Takeda Chigako, Namba Hitomi, Joshua Weeks, Sakamoto Nobuko, Watanabe Gen, Toby Feltwell, Takuma Yuko, Furumi Hikaru, Iida Akio, Saito Munenori, Kaneko Nobutaka, Muroga Hiroshi, Ito Daisuke, Murayama Satoko, Matsumoto Miho, Shimizu Yumiko, Yoshioka Ai Elena, Ikegami Shikiko, Takeda Mikiko, Yukari Tai, Mizuno Eiko, Maeda Ryosuke, Sakaguchi Hiroyasu & Ori, Kimura Asako, Awata Erika, Katsuno Hiroko, Yokoyama Yuko, Kuroda Tomoko, Ajima Junko, Terada Reiko, Fujibayashi Tomoko, Aude Mary, Watanabe Taichi, Kashiwabara Takatomo, Ozaki Jun, Suzuki Kenichiro, Yamada Ayumi, Nagae Aoi, Naoko Jansen, Lok Jansen, Shimizu Naomi, Ikeda Ayako, Takei Masakazu, Okazaki Jun, Iida Yumiko, Kubo Naomi, Kato Haruyuki, Sasaki Aya, Ibe Chikako, Florian Idenburg, Yamada Yumiko, Yoshii Etsuko, Fujisawa Kenichi, Takarada Mariko, Maru Ryugo, Sawa Kato, Kodaira Chisato, Araki Hiroshi, Ray LeMoine, MacKenzie Lewis, Allene Kim, Linda Trujillo, Ibi Maiko, Eva Prinz, Kato Kotaro & Okamoto Noe—*Ian Luna*

First published in the United States of America by Rizzoli International Publications, Inc. 300 Park Avenue South, New York, NY 10010 www.rizzoliusa.com

Copyright Foreword © 2007 Mori Toshiko
Copyright Essays © 2007 Kawamura Yuniya, Hayashi Fumihiro, Ian Luna, Tom Mes & Jasper Sharp

Editor: Ian Luna
Project Coordination: Kana Kawanishi, April Huot & Jean Snow
Editorial Assistants: Leah Whisler, Henry Casey, Claire L. Gierczak, Josh D. Jones & Moraiah Luna
Art Direction: Ian Luna & Lauren A. Gould
Book Design: Ian Luna & Eugene Lee
Cover Design: Chip Kidd & Mark Melnick
Production: Maria Pia Gramaglia, Kaija Markoe, Colin Hough Trapp & Usula Damm

Printed in China

2007 2008 2009 2010 / 10 9 8 7 6 5 4 3 2 1
Library of Congress Control Number: 2007933612
ISBN-10: 0-8478-2925-1

CONTENTS

FOREWORD
BY MORI TOSHIKO

Opposite page: Mikimoto Ginza 2, Chuo Ward, by Ito Toyo (2006).

In comparison to cities like Paris, London, New York and Rome, Tokyo lacks romance. Nor does it have an architectural icon. Tokyo Tower never quite made it, nor do the Towers at Roppongi Hills. Tokyo City Hall and Yoyogi Olympic Stadium are squalid civic structures that have no photogenic allure. Even compared with Asian cities like Beijing and Shanghai, Tokyo is a monochromatic blur. Its amorphous sprawl divides the city into distinct districts surrounding the void of the Imperial Palace. One has to take circuitous routes to travel through the city. It is a strangely indeterminate journey through the city. To add to it, the rate of rebuilding in the city is so rapid that its features are in a constant state of change. Because of this, the impact and vitality of the city, the experience of being in it and the powerful visceral attraction of Tokyo has no equal.

Its charisma is much different from the cities that have retained their historical character. The featureless, orderly business city of the day explodes into chaotic micro-shards of the lively city of the night. It is a city in constant and frenetic motion of metabolic life, transforming every minute and second as it sharpens its instinct for cultural life. More than any other city, Tokyo demonstrates that "city" is a verb and not a noun. One identifies Tokyo with its cultural production more than anything else. This book, *TokyoLife*, suggests this essential quality of this City by compiling a body of work by artists, fashion designers, industrial designers, photographers, film makers and architects. Ian Luna realizes that compartmentalization of disciplines can only represent a very limited spectrum of each one of the *métiers*. By combining them together in this volume, one field can refer to another, creating a synthetic and cohesive cultural tapestry and urban landscape that unfolds in the readers' mind.

One can also propose Tokyo to be a perfect example of a dystopia where everything is pushed to its limit. Instead of bursting open at its seams, it barely binds all of these discords and imbalances together. The senses are heightened; in this city, places where peace and safety do exist, but danger and transgression reside largely in the psychological domain. Because of its own history of continuous destruction through earthquakes, fires, and bombing during the war, the precarious nature of life behind its safe façade is real. Contrasts between the extremely ancient and cutting-edge contemporary culture literally coexist side by side. Dense high-tech commercial developments are around the corner from the spacious and serene Shinto precincts. There, the primitives and the sophisticates practice with an equal degree of panache and passion, balancing polar opposite cultural heritages. Fast and slow, rough and refined, brutal and elegant qualities are not mutually exclusive. The attraction for Tokyo is in its tolerance of pushing the limit of its cultural production. Beauty stops right at the edge of turning grotesque. Ugly and ordinary, with learned observation, become transcendental and enlightening. Poverty becomes a state of grace; violence is ritualized, excessive materiality and consumerism turned into an ethereal aesthetic. Cuteness coexists easily with the monstrous and the terrible.

It is the city of the moment, where one can live out virtual reality on its streets and in its public places. Traditionally, Japanese culture always had a spiritual life along with its mundane everyday life. Compounding this, there is the belief in the presence of spirits in multiple forms, deriving from the pantheism of Shinto and the multiple cyclical lives in Buddhism. Adding to this is the Christian idea of resurrection. In its tolerant and inclusive culture, ancient belief and spirituality can readily align themselves with the contemporary digital culture of virtual hyper-reality and simulation.

The relentless, repetitious and amorphous cityscape contributes to the desire of its citizens to cultivate a richer imaginary landscape. Citizens are never reconciled with living in their actual environment, but are always in search of places and objects that are extensions of their imagination. Tokyo can be said to be a city of the imagination, its cultural and artistic production so prolific and vital that it establishes a state of mind that churns out myth after myth: which is Tokyo Life.

THE STATE OF PLAY
ESSAY BY IAN LUNA

I. The Spirit of the City

In the most recent filmic adaptation of the novelist and futurist Komatsu Sakyo's *The Sinking of Japan*, (*Nihon Chinbotsu*, 2006) Tokyo is again at the mercy of a marine subduction zone that also threatens to swallow whole the entire archipelago. The movie does away with the pessimistic ending of the densely plotted 1973 book, and in fighting form, yet another member of the J-pop supergroup SMAP, Kusanagi Tsuyoshi, saves the country from a slow, watery death at the cost of his own life. And as the film opens with his own dramatic rescue from fire by the svelte, para-jumping female lead, passages of heroic self-sacrifice (and there are many) can be the only appropriate frames for the extended, CGI-addled panorama of destruction that is naturally the red meat of the story

Beyond its mix of speculative hard science, easy (if well-wrought) metaphor and cautionary messages—including an inflammatory broadside declaiming the abiding hostility of Japan's immediate neighbors and allies—this is firmly a disaster flick, and like the shrill blonde that invariably comes to a gruesome end in American slasher films, one visual staple of the genre is the demolition of the iconic building of the moment, lovingly depicted in a fury of cascading steel and broken glass. Almost always a structure of great height, this time it is the Roppongi Hills Tower, a massive 58-story mixed-use building from 2003, designed by New York-based Kohn Pedersen Fox (KPF), that crumples into the sinkhole with historic landmarks like the National Diet Building and Tange Kenzo's Tokyo Metropolitan Government Offices in downtown Shinjuku.

Onward and Upward

As conceived, the Roppongi Hills tower is notable more for its width than its height, and with a curtain wall formally inspired by the segmented, lacquered armor of medieval Japan, the skyscraper is furnished with some of the largest office floorplates in Asia—each a staggering 5,000 square meters. Perched on a battlement, an extruded reincarnation of a feudal castle lording over the pleasure district from whence it takes its name, the Roppongi Hills complex is the brainchild of Mori Minoru, the scion of a pioneering real-estate speculator, who along with his brother Akira, is one of the all-powerful *daimyo* of Japanese industry. Mori is also something of a theorist. Through an integrated publishing program in print and online, he bemoaned Tokyo's alleged lack of urbanistic character.[1] Looking to Manhattan as a model for land use, he advocated the creation of self-contained, self-sustaining nodes in the metropolis that could act as city-making attractors—or at the very least, connectors to an infamously decentralized city. Long-term, the greater Mori agenda is to add a live/work dimensionality to what he sees as Tokyo's Old Economy-model, where the industrial core was at some distance from the bedroom communities of the laborers that propped it up. Not incidentally, this is an urban remedy he is also exporting to Shanghai, Dalian and other cities on China's gold coast.

Ever the savvy globalist, Mori drafted Murakami Takashi, Bruce Mau and Jonathan Barnbrook to devise the corporate identity and environmental graphics for the $4 billion, 27-acre project, in concert with the stable of American and Japanese architects and landscape designers who transformed the site. Attracting high-visibility commercial uses and charging maximum rents, Roppongi Hills was plainly conceived as an agent of gentrification, maximizing land-use and creating a streetscape that in theory encouraged foot traffic in a city not particularly associated with leisurely, purposeless strolls.

With the centerpiece tower reserved for leasable Class-A office space, supplicating at its feet is a cluster of mid- to low-rise structures of differing programs. These include Maki Fumihiro's headquarters for Asahi Television (2003), Aoki Jun's crystalline Louis Vuitton boutique (2004) and the swank Tokyo Grand Hyatt. However, the developer's intention of a pedestrian-friendly zone was tempered by the project's proximity to the elevated span of the Shuto Expressway, a disruptive, many-tentacled presence that tears at the city fabric from street level on up, posing an irritating challenge to intrepid day-trippers making their way to either the shopping mall and movie theaters at the base of the tower, or the contemporary art museum on its crown.

Problems with access notwithstanding, the centerpiece tower became an instant icon before it was even completed, surrounded as it is by low-rise residential and commercial structures and not hemmed in by other competing skyscrapers. But its physical remove from other tall buildings tells only half the story. Arriving as it did midway through the Koizumi Junichiro premiership, Roppongi Hills became a psychic marker of Japan's slow but steady recovery from the *ushinawareta junen*, or the "lost decade" that followed the collapse of the asset price bubble in 1991. In era of newfound optimism, the tower complex confidently announced a period of incremental but sustainable national growth, its tornado-like

Previous page: Prada Epicenter Aoyama, Minato Ward, by Herzog & de Meuron (2003). Above: Murakami Takashi, Roppongi Hills Spiral Flowers *(2003), featuring the 66 seijin (l-r) Myan Myan, Yoshiko, Syacho, Cherry, Masamune, Spica, Poyoyon and Pi-Chan).*

heft a negation of the deflationary death-spiral that came very close to really sinking Japan. Indeed, some of the tower's New Economy tenants (Yahoo Japan, Konami, Goldman Sachs Japan and the online retailer Rakuten) peddle a more aggressive American-style entrepreneurialism, despite the recent, spectacular fall of one of its more flamboyant practitioners, Horie Takafumi of the internet portal Livedoor, who once leased both office and residential space at the 'Hills. (Prior to his controversial arrest and 2007 conviction for stock-price manipulation, Horie's cowboy approach was seen as a vigorous alternative to the glacial conservatism of the prevailing Japanese business model and its old-boy guardians.)

Mecha-Godzilla vs Mecha-Godzilla

But the non-celluloid, real-time threat to the Roppongi Hills tower is no less grave. Only now it is in the form of a rival development, the slightly taller Tokyo Midtown tower half a kilometer away. A Rockefeller Center manqué clad in a humorless variant of American corporate modernism, and with an identical program of office, retail and cultural uses as the Mori building, the Skidmore Owings & Merrill-designed Midtown complex opened in the spring of 2007.

This skyscraper contest—commanding opposite sides of the Shuto Expressway separating the worlds of Roppongi and Minami-Aoyama—is only the latest episode in an ongoing feud between the Mori brothers and their rivals in the ancient Mitsui clan, the operators of Tokyo Midtown and another of Tokyo's corporate and real-estate dynasties. On an explicitly sec-

ondary stage, this is also a proxy war between American modernism's preeminent skyscraper builders, with Gene Kohn and William Pedersen of KPF in one corner, and SOM's David Childs (he of the stolid World Trade Center Freedom Tower) in the other. Cast to the side the predictable nativist and anti-intellectual hand-wringing about cultural imposition, and this showdown actually says less about the American postwar settlement—and the macroeconomic and geopolitical order that remains its most crucial consequence— than it does about the rise of Tokyo as an expanding arena for postmodern exchange and competition in architecture, interior design and most every other form of creative production.

But this competitive mania for large office floor plates and structures with heights in excess of 300 meters are but one aspect of a densely layered and ever-unfolding urban saga. Any cursory reading of the city's topography and demography reveals that tall buildings are hardly the salient feature of Tokyo's present condition. The four central *ku* or wards making up the center of Tokyo—Chuo, Chiyoda, Minato, and Shinjuku—are generally low-rise in character. Moreover, these districts

Roppongi Hills Tower, Minato Ward, Kohn Pedersen Fox/Mori Building Company Architects & Engineers (2003). Several buildings erected as part of the Roppongi Hills redevelopment project are visible in the foreground, including the TV Asahi Headquarters by Maki Fumihiko (center left).

actually have a smaller population density than Manhattan, as the city is (in)famously given to unchecked horizontal expansion, and in direct, inverse proportion to its vertical underdevelopment.

And the average Tokyo city block measures a thousand square meters, only a tenth of the size of a block in New York City, and is further divided into small, privately owned parcels. Rarely in neat, marketable grids, and often in irregular shapes, these blocks remain an impediment to a model of "intensive land utilization"—in this case a euphemism for vertical mega-development—long advocated by the real-estate combines and quite a few urban sociologists since the immediate postwar period.

Thriving on entropy, the implied resistance to aggregation is a reflexive trait shared among urban residents and their relations in the countryside. In a society often criticized for its lack of subjectivity, property rights in Japan are sacrosanct, and in Tokyo, this hallowed status is often credited with maintaining the pedestrian character of the city, with its warren of narrow streets and extemporized zoning regulations.

Making and Unmaking

As a contemporary episode in this tug of war between competing notions of the city, the event-character of Roppongi Hill's brief but spectacular cameo in *The Sinking of Japan* is instructive. The unmaking of the tower in the film directly contrasts with the story of its making. In a process that took decades, the Mori Building Company required the patient acquisition of over 400 small plots before the project could commence, buying off the holdouts with gilded carrots—and virtually none of the sticks that once characterized old-school construction schemes.

These cycles of conflict, negotiation, accommodation and renewed conflict; between interests large and small, is played out on 10,000 square-kilometers of what is still a hilly, alluvial floodplain. In absolute terms, Tokyo is still the most expensive patch of real estate in the planet, where only two decades ago it was notoriously estimated that the value of the land under the Imperial Palace was equal to the entire land mass of Canada, and squabbles over land-use remains a central preoccupation. In the words of the architect and writer Tajima Noriyuki, modern Tokyo is after all a city "on the move and on the spend."[2] Constantly sloughing off its skin, the avenues of old Edo designed to take in views of the hills surrounding the Yamanote plateau defining the city have long been occluded by rising development.

This continuity of urban destruction, resurrection and commodification is *the* principal Tokyo narrative. Throughout the history of the modern city, the stimulus for change is often catastrophic and heart-rending. Profoundly transformed by the apocalypses of the twentieth century: the great Kanto Earthquake, the fascist interregnum, and the conflagration of General Curtis LeMay's 20th Air Force, these tragedies were themselves preceded by major earthquakes in 1855, 1812, 1782 and 1703. Crucially, the great Meireki fire of 1657—that like the fire-bombings of March 1945 claimed well over 100,000 lives—necessitated the first modern plan of Edo.[3]

Post-disaster planning proved a boon to adopting other people's models. Goto Shinpei, the visionary Taisho-era mayor of Tokyo City (and later Home Minister), was instrumental in the promulgation of the city's first truly "rational" planning law, in 1919. He modeled his think-tank after the contemporaneous New York Bureau of Municipal Research, diverging from the imperial and impractical Parisian ambitions of his Meiji-era predecessors, and would see tentative application in the aftermath of the 1923 quake. The National Capital Region plan that was forcefully implemented in the 1960s grew out of the devastation of the Second World War and the subsequent Postwar Recovery City Plan set in motion by the Allied Occupation—which naturally took after Goto Shinpei's American formulation.

No other capital has been so devastated so often and so spectacularly in any national cinema, from the gleeful abandon wrought by Godzilla and his winged pals in Honda's Ishiro's three-decade run of monster movies, to the post-apocalyptic nightmares of Otomo Katsuhiro's animated epic, *Akira* (1988). No other city has been so urgently cast and recast as the preeminent vision of the future either, and in Tokyo's star turns—both as utopia and dystopia—it is very nearly the principal player in many a film, novel or *manga* serial. The frequency of disaster movies in Japan is a five-decades-long, pop-culture phenomenon without precedent. Generatively attributed to the residual, psychic effects of the atom bomb and the other city-leveling events elaborated above, this cultural trend is rather inversely and indisputably linked to other latent and unsated appetites, and have, taken together, assumed the heft of an extended polemic.

Specifically, it is a canny urbanistic and social critique empowered by the high modality of film, its animus directed as it ever was to the physical city and its various psychosocial discontents. Not coincidentally, much of the scorn is heaped on the authors of redevelopment. The surges in postwar rebuilding never fail to resurrect the specter of the *doken kokka*—the "construction state"—that nefarious tangle of high government officials, financiers and real-estate bigwigs that arose out of the shadows of the Postwar Recovery City Plan. Effectively set up in the late 1940s by the American occupation authorities, who were at the time busy combating hyperinflation and micro-managing political ideology, the *doken kokka*, and the *zaito*, the public-private loan program that financed it, flourished to become an irresistible, rebarbative force in contemporary life.

This politico-industrial cabal was a staple of popular discourse in the heady decades of the Japanese "economic miracle," the villains of many a potboiler. Their machinations—real and imagined—were instrumental in the creation of the overblown city plan that went tandem with the 1964 Olympiad. Always radiating from Tokyo, the subsequent orgy of construction peaked under the graft-ridden Tanaka Kakuei and Nakasone Yasuhiro premierships of the 1970s and 1980s.[4] In a complot ominously dubbed "Restructuring the Archipelago" politicians empowered general contractors and their parasite *gumi*—guilds—to erect hundreds of white elephants in an unprecedented and sustained building program that ultimately saddled Japan with the largest public-sector debt in the industrialized world.

The lot of developers, as bearers of a economic growth and cultural uplift as well as authors and perpetuators of social inequity is at the heart of an irresolvable contradiction of Tokyo life, between the common desire for a landscape scalable to individuals and a city that serves as a mature vessel of municipal and corporate aspirations. The recent mêlée over the extension of a stretch of highway into the heart of the compact and self-consciously boho neighborhood of Shimokitazawa in the western ward of Setagaya assays only the latest episode in this attempt to define the "public interest," that in a capital city like Tokyo, often assumes national implications.

For all its causes, courses and tribulations, these oppositional forces stoke the furnace the modern metropolis and drive its contradictory, irrepressible ambitions. Indeed, it is the Shuto Expressway itself, its inaugural five-kilometer span between Chuo and Minato wards in 1963 now expanded to over 350 kilometers, which is indubitably the city's defining monument. A true monster, it required filling in the rivers and estuaries that defined the character of the city in Hokusai's *One Hundred Famous Views of Edo,* and divided once distinct neighborhoods in "riverbeds of concrete." Marking the perimeter of the city in its formidable headlock as it radiates outward, the road network consigns the streetscape in perpetual shadow, alternately containing, managing and dissipating its manifold energies. As Tajima Noriyuki notes, "the city's inhabitants are indifferent to the spectacular feat of engineering on their doorstep,"[5] which for all its frustrations, trumpeted the arrival of a Japan fully risen from the ashes of the Pacific War. A memorable affirmation of this is bestowed by a key scene in Andrei Tarkovsky's *Solaris* (1972). In the film, 1971 Tokyo stands in for a speculative Moscow or Leningrad, viewed from a car speeding on the same levitating stretches of the Shuto Expressway that mega-projects like Roppongi Hills now overlook—the undisputed once-and-future city.

The Fantasy of (Post) Modern Life

Quite unlike the nationalistic demands of the developmental state in Mainland China or India, the added value appended to engineering or designing Tokyo approximates more than just technological modernization, which the Japanese achieved decades ago. But the dystopic juxtaposition of Tokyo's medieval, labyrinthine street grid and its soaring American freeways also suggests something of the unfinished work of modernism.

While the totalitarian attempt to "overcome" expressions of modernity in all is guises in the 1930s and 40s proved untenable,[6] the same could also be said about the radical attempts to rid the cultural scene of all traditional forms and motivations. This is especially true in the Japanese context, where a modernism devoted to the rejection of "all that came before" had not itself metastasized into the oppressive tradition it became in the West, and where the gap between "high" and "low" forms of creative production had never been as pronounced as it was in the West—at least since the late Edo period.

And in contrast to the dislocations of modernism, the advent of philosophical postmodernism—with its preference for contradiction, chance, ambiguity, complexity and diversity—was embraced with open arms as it easily found corollaries in more ancient Japanese tendencies anyway. Chief of these is the phenomenology of *honne* and *tatemae*, the bifurcation of the Japanese soul into a "true self" and a "public self." The split between the private and the perceived, and the general inability of most Japanese to meet its unremitting demands, have for a millennium supplied all of the dramas of Japanese life. The tacit imperative to reconcile one's *honne* and *tatemae* had inculcated a pervasive weariness that eagerly welcomed the seductive, foreign alternatives that tore into Japan like a torrent after the forcible opening of its market by American gunboat diplomacy in the mid-nineteenth century.

As evidenced by the modalities covered in this book, contact with external stimuli can engender any number of responses. Architecture and urbanism, first among equals as the material expression of a civilization's achievements, could never really persist in a hermetic context. With much of traditional Japanese forms derived chiefly from Chinese antecedents, the story of modern architecture in Japan provides a uniquely empirical understanding of how the impositions of history—from within and without, from well before the days of the Meiji Restoration to the present—are either accepted, rejected, reimposed, and/or assimilated.

This putative confrontation between the modernist, utopian desire to remake the world and the horizontal values of postmodernity, which preoccupied Western thought for half a century, did not need to be refought in postwar Japan. An intellectual accommodation, to correct modernism's excesses without invalidating the nobility of its more idealistic intentions, seemed rather a *fait accompli*. Even more apt is the revisionist stance that postmodernity and modernity are not warring conditions, but as reconciled by the art critic Robert Hughes, merely aspects of the selfsame movement.

With this flexible intellectual framework, the self-referential nature of Japanese expression could then exist without remonstrance or apology, while it indulges a fetish for Western tropes. This is especially true in the Tokyo way of architecture and urbanism, since form-making and "style" on the one hand, and a valorization of space and tectonics on the other can both be seen as essential and ineluctable components of the same anarchic story. Indeed, the multiplicity of its forms and spaces, both metropolitan and peripheral, holds up a vast, multifaceted mirror of the society it supports, that for all its alleged homogeneity, is glittering and squalid, reflexively modern, and on occasion, ridiculously feudal and irrational. As evidenced by the photography of Homma Takashi and Hatakeyama Naoya, Tokyo's built-up areas are profoundly ambivalent sites that are as much the expressions of creative freedom as they attest to a of lack of social mobility, and a sense of detachment, alienation and suffocating loneliness—a condition typified by a species of depressed youth, the *hikikomori*, who elect to withdraw from society by never leaving their apartments. And whereas surveillance, self-policing [and the fear of technology] are vital rudiments of urban space in cities like contemporary Beijing and post-9/11 New York and London,[7] Tokyo's residents had always been subject to a measure of largely self-imposed social constraints (which had again acquired a public security dimension more than a decade ago, in the wake of the 1995 subway gas attack by members of the apocalyptic Aum Shinrikyu cult).

But a city whose visual chaos was once described by the architect Isozaki Arata as "dumb and irrelevant,"[8] can straightaway be comforting, even beautiful, to many others. Tokyo in the first decade of the 21st century is after all, is nothing but buoyant, and its inhabitants draw affirmative inferences from its peculiar charms, both old and new.

In passages, this is still the timeless, languid Tokyo of Ozu Yasujiro and Naruse Mikio and the brittle preserve of oversized, fire-breathing lizards. It is also the Tokyo of Mori Minoru's and Goto Shinpei's frustrations, scandalously unplanned and unrepentant of the fact, aware of its material complexity and moral uncertainties, a feral organism that the novelist Murakami Haruki, that great chronicler of urban anomie and estrangement, described in 2004's *After Dark* as a "single gigantic creature—or more like a single collective entity created by many intertwining organisms. Countless arteries stretch to the ends of its illusive body... to the rhythm of its pulsing, all parts of the body flicker and flare up and squirm."

Above: Tama Art University Library, Hachioji Campus, Western Tokyo, by Ito Toyo (2007).Opposite page, clockwise from top left: C-1 House/Curiosity Studio, Shibuya Ward, by Milligram Studio and Gwenaël Nicholas (2006); Midtown Tower, Minato Ward, by Skidmore Owings & Merrill (SOM)/Nikken Sekkei (2007); Omotesando Hills shopping complex, Shibuya Ward, by Ando Tadao (2006). National Art Center, Minato Ward, by Kurokawa Kisho (2007)

Space + Movement + Time

Tokyo is simply the toponym of an extraordinary locale that exists as resolutely in the real world as it does in the imagination. Ancient, Asian and firmly in the global North, it is as mesmeric to visiting anime *otaku* from St. Petersburg or Paris today as it must have been to parvenu second and third sons migrating from rural Japan in 1920s, or indeed to Frank Lloyd Wright, who glimpsed the frenetic Yokohama waterfront for the very first time from the deck of the *SS Empress of China* in 1905. In repudiating a purely material and static formulation of the city, the sociologist Sandra Buckley affirms a coruscating, living entity "constituted in and of movement."[9] Summoning popular images of nocturnal Tokyo and its frenetic commuter-scape, she also improves on a mere anthromorphosizing of inanimate forms, imputing the city's febrile character precisely on the motivations and activities of its inhabitants. "We don't have to return to Proust, Joyce, Tanizaki, or Kawabata to be reminded that the scopic quality is the least significant constituitive element of our experience and memory of the city. Our personal memories of cities, buildings and rooms are so often locked in the bodily traces of sound, taste, texture, smell, and the sensations of movement."[10]

Buckley's treatment of the city as a "complex, spacio-temporal configuration" can then apply to its varied, constituent parts. The Shibuya-based architect Aoki Jun sees architecture space only in correlation to physical movement, as organic, even non-rational "circulatory bodies" dependent "on the persons that live therein and on the ineluctable human 'nature' of desires that drive the body. In other words, architecture as object opens towards possession, as dictated by human 'nature.'"[11]

If this reductive stance, wholly rooted in the body of the "doer," is applied liberally, retrospectively and taken as a framework for making sense of the city and its hybrid texts, Tokyo's radical charms are then as much about the interaction of flesh, and its compromise with the rational articulation and manipulation of steel, concrete, glass and man-made light. The city's spaces and buildings become the most suitable venues for the enactment of individual dramas, multiplied in the tens of millions. The properties of its architecture are then necessarily scenographic, uniquely suited armatures and carapaces that give meaning to movement. These constructions are not ends in and of themselves, but are at once purposed and incidental—and as ever, full of incident and accident.

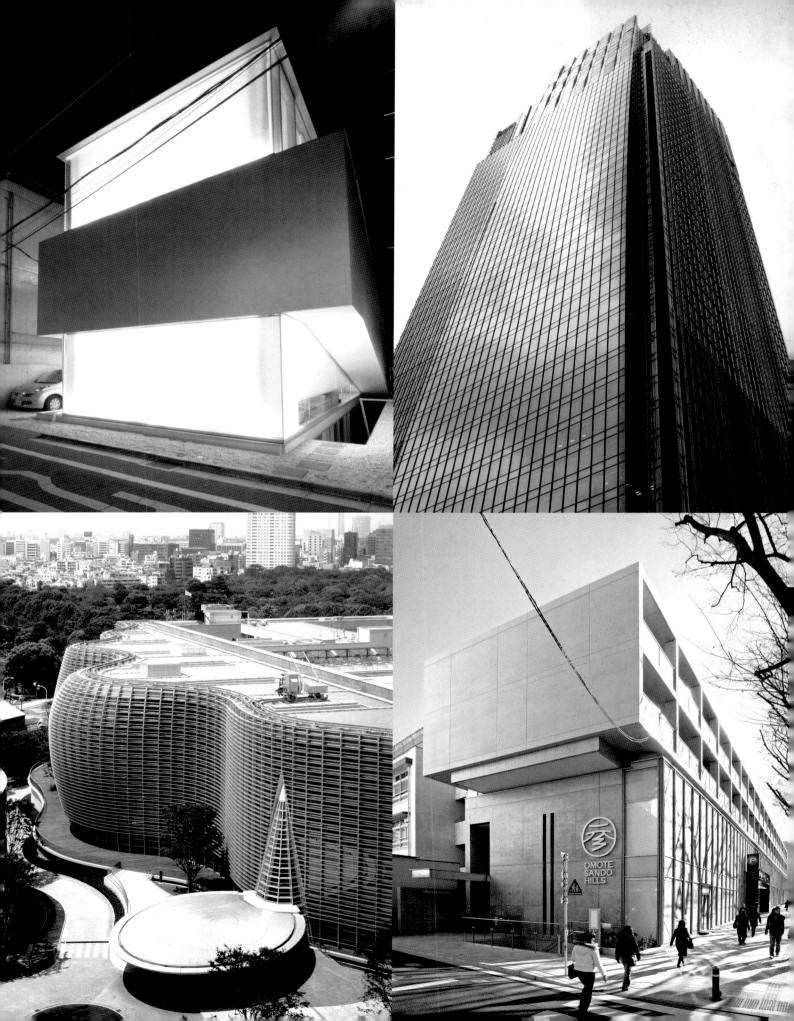

II. The Shape of the City

A city constantly on the move, reducible to containing movement, but not nearly as full an expression of the energies it is capable of unleashing, the contemporary metropolis is made up of three distinct administrative elements that together form the prefecture of Tokyo-to. In order of magnitude, these include the 23 Special Wards and the reclaimed waterfront—colloquially the *nijusan-ku*—that once comprised the old city prior to the reforms of 1943; followed by Western Tokyo or the Tama Area, a collection of small cities and municipalities that were gradually merged with the special wards; and lastly, two small island chains—the Ogasawaras and the Izus—that dangle south from Tokyo Bay for hundreds of kilometers.

Governed from Nishi-Shinjuku by novelist and right-wing ideologue Ishihara Shintaro but effectively operating as autonomous towns, the *nijusan-ku* is the city of history and memory. Traditionally centered around the *kokyo*, the Imperial Palace, and the *shitamachi*—the densely packed "lower town" of old Edo—the postwar economic miracle shifted Tokyo's center of gravity from the east to its western and southern wards. All told, over twelve million souls inhabit Tokyo-to. And if the sprawling prefectural suburbs of Kanagawa to the southwest, Saitama to the north and Chiba to the east are factored in this census, Metropolitan Tokyo is easily the most populous urban agglomeration in the known universe.

Befitting the political, economic and cultural engine of what is by a wide margin, and in real terms, still the world's second largest economy—with a small trade *surplus* with China to boot—the physical manifestations of this creative tumult demand and consume vast amounts of wealth. The locus of development, which in the late 1990s seemed to be preoccupied with salvaging Odaiba, a reclaimed island in Tokyo Bay ruled by the all-seeing eye of Tange Kenzo's Fuji TV Headquarters (1996), has now shifted to several key zones in the *nijusan-ku*. To date, the most active sites are the Marunouchi and Tokyo Station area in Chiyoda ward, the southern wards of Meguro and Shinagawa, and in Minato and Shibuya wards, the districts of Shiodome, Minami Aoyama, "flagship row" on Omotesando, and of course, Roppongi.

Trafficking as it does in a formal exuberance, Tokyo's varied architectures, with their sheer tectonic qualities and exacting detail, exist in one of the most fertile and sophisticated urban laboratories in the developed world. The city's elite architects invariably preface their attitude to designing for the city by first declaring fealty to planning space, with fashioning building envelopes a subordinate concern. But a sensory acquisition of the landscape belies an unregenerate addiction to form-making, arguably stemming from a historic continuity where an "awareness of physical objects long predated any conscious notion of space."[12] But the overwhelming desire to react to visual disorder can also accommodate the depth, order and fluidity of spaces that characterize the traditional programming of Japanese buildings. It is the conscious accommodation of form with ergonomics that propel the best of Japanese contemporary design, and the provision in traditional arts and crafts for objects that are at once ceremonial or decorative—*jotemono*—and fully functional—*getemono*—find special resonances in the variety of contemporary architectural forms.

Modern Japanese buildings are the product of a very particular theory for practice as well, and one that adapted well to architecture's transition from craft to profession in the last two centuries. The way know-how is transferred from university, the approach to forming professional teams, the general attitude to collaboration between architects, consultants and fabricators, the relative paucity of lawyers, and the near unanimous acquiescence to an oligopolistic system of subcontractor trades, are all specific to the Japanese context.[13]

Skins of the Nation

In an attempt to catalogue recent tendencies in Japanese architecture, the editors of *Japan Architect* proffered an urban taxonomy, complete with a cladogram of sorts, detailing lines of ascent and descent and charting the courses of recombinant hybridization and mutation. Tracing the arc of a number of movements that first saw physical expression in the 1970s and 1980s, this system of classification provides an admittedly limited reading of the current state of play but is nonetheless a readily accessible and expandable primer on the Herculean effort of designing for such a vast and unruly conurbation.[14]

Experiential and visual, orthogonal or blob, dark and light, heavy and weightless, monochromatic or luridly hued, the shapes of the city grow like crystals in a dish, rising in quick succession in the temporal hyperdrive of Ura-Harajuku, and at more measured rates in Tokyo's older quarters. Fully engaged, flitting between modernist orthodoxy, apostasy and a dozen points in between, there can be no common formal vocabulary or material palette now. The relative unity achieved by the late '80s heyday of a referential, narrowly defined architectural postmodernism in the bubble years has given way to a truly ecumenical condition. Functionalism *ad absurdum* and the fetish for ornament and extreme gesture exist side-by-side; philosophical and stylistic attitudes once held as gospel within some ateliers have been either moderated, restated or abandoned altogether.

Show and Tell

Kuma Kengo, who had once devised a showroom for Mazda capped with a single, monumental Ionic column (M2 Building, Setagaya ward, 1989), now specializes in structures that maximize natural light, devising a variety of screens to modulate its entry into space. Professing a shift from fragmentary compositions to "erasing architecture,"[15] his present work ranges from the glazed promontory of the Baiso-in Temple (2003) in Aoyama to the objective delicacy of the Murai Masanari Art Museum in a quiet corner of Setagaya ward (2004). A collagist mise-en-scène of found architecture and scoured white surfaces, the two-story structure is conceived as reliquary for the work of a pioneer of Japanese mid-century abstraction, and elements of Murai's old house are preserved within and without. Chief of these is the late painter's small studio in the middle of the site, combining a modern gallery program with the intimate domesticity that surrounded Murai in life.

But the worldwide museum boom impacted other parts of Tokyo with far less modesty. Yanagisawa Takahiko's sprawling Tokyo Museum of Contemporary Art (1995) in the working class neighborhood of Koto-ku set a bombastic precedent, incorporating some of the largest exhibition spaces—totaling 24,000 m²—in a city where dedicated gallery space is often spirited high up office buildings or else confined to the aging and cramped national museums dotting Ueno Park. Expansive museum and exhibition uses transformed a number of underutilized plots in 2007, including a number of key sites in and around Roppongi. Across from the 21_21 Design Sight museum by Ando Tadao bundled with the Mitsui conglomerate's Tokyo Midtown development is the glazed, giant wave of Kurokawa Kisho's National Art Center north of Roppongi, affording some 45,000 m² of dedicated gallery space, making it the biggest of its type in Japan. The opening of Gluckman Mayner's Mori Art Museum (2003), located as it is on top of the Roppongi Hills office tower is the apotheosis of the corporate galleries of the 1980s. Approached through a memorable sequence of ascent through a glass cocoon at the base of the skyscraper, the large galleries reserved for revolving shows empty into a 360-degree observation deck, expanding the exhibition program notionally to encompass the pulsating city below.

The impenetrable granite facades of Mario Botta's landmark Watari-um Museum (1990) in Shibuya have given way to a blinding porosity, typified but not limited to the ascetic minimalism of Taniguchi Yoshio's Gallery of Horyu-ji Treasures at the Tokyo National Museum (1999)—and other steel-and-glass boxes. This desire for transparency and material delicacy gravitate easily to other functions. The postmodern fortresses of Tange Kenzo's United Nations University (1992), Tokyo Metropolitan Government Offices (1991), and the grey, gargantuan bulk of Hara Hiroshi's appropriately named Yamato International Building in Ota ward (1986) would be supplanted by new icons that trade bulk for light. In Marunouchi, the oblanceolate plan of Rafael Viñoly's Tokyo International Forum (1997) extrudes to create one of the largest atria in the city, its curved, supporting girders suspended from the roof in a feat of engineering bravado, like the iron ribs lining the keel of a capsized, glass-bottomed boat.

Dimensionality

Critically, the heirs to Deconstruction have fared much better. The shifting planes of Peter Eisenman's experiments in "textual geology," the Koizumi Lighting Showroom in Kanda (1990) and the positively tectonic NC/Nunotani Corporation Building in Edogawa ward (1992) find further articulation in the shifting, subducting wood-plank dunes of Foreign Office Architects' Osanbashi International Passenger Terminal (2002) in Yokohama Bay. The progress of an indigenous Decon alternatively finds full expression and refutation in the work of Tokyo stalwart Watanabe Sei Makoto's radical experiments in "form-generating algorithms." His Aoyama Technical College (1990) in Shibuya verily bursts as it ascends vertically, like a building halfway to its transformation into a bipedal robot. A similar unease afflicts the entrance to the Iidabashi stop on the Oedo subway line (2000), where rings of stainless steel and glass disks barely contain the energy of a violent expulsive event seemingly frozen in time. His K-Museum in Ariake (1997) projects horizontal movement like the slide and barrel assembly of a massive sci-fi handgun forever aimed at Tokyo Bay.

Triangles and wedges—in elevation and plan—are a major fixation, and in the 1980s they found objective vitality in the pyramids of the National Noh Theater in Sendagaya by Ohe Hiroshi (1983), in Kitagawara Atsushi's Metrotour in Marunouchi (1989), and in the constituent surface elements of Mito Art Tower (1990) by Isozaki Arata in nearby Ibaraki and Rokakku Kijo's Budokan (1989) in Adachi ward. Their contemporary application, monumentally affirmed by the inverted pyramids of the Tokyo Big Sight convention center in Odaiba (1996), derive considerable drama from much smaller forms and irregular sites. Endoh Masaki and the structural engineer Ikeda Masahiro's Natural Wedge in Suginami (2003) maximizes the provision for natural light by devising a generously glazed, south-facing, four-story townhouse where the exposed diagonal trusses of the steel structure intersect with vertical supports to form right triangles on the exterior and interior.

Grids and their derivative forms also provide an inexhaustible supply of internal and external narratives. The facades of Yamamoto Riken and Ito Toyo's Shinonome Canal Court (2003) apartments in Ariake break up a tight grid of squares with recessed diagonal sequences of even larger squares. The glass-block tower of Renzo Piano's Ginza flagship (2001), echoing as it does Pierre Charreau and Bernard Bijvoet's Maison de Verre, is the controlled variable to Herzog & de Meuron's asymmetric polyhedron for Prada in Minami-Aoyama (2003). Rotating an equilateral grid of 840 glass lozenges at roughly forty-five degrees, this glass fishnet is tacked on a peripheral steel frame that supplies the retail and show-room program with column-free space. Away from Omotesando, the new headquarters building (2003) for Nikken Sekkei—the giant architectural firm that practically built modern Tokyo—employs columns on the periphery to support expansive open-plan floors within a no-frills, 13-story box. Endoh Masaki and the structural engineer Ikeda Masahiro's sublime Natural Illuminance (2002) in Edogawa utilizes insulated steel squares on its east-facing elevation, with the tolerances between panels introducing natural light into the residential interiors.

The All-Consumer

And as this is Tokyo, shops, boutique hotels and bar/lounges provide the most seductive examples of infill where added value is motivation enough for good design. Relatively small commercial interventions, many of which incorporate a number of programs beyond their principal use, have become major touristic draws, must-see stops on a new and glitzy Tokaido Road. With nearly sixty percent of all foreign visitors to Japan spending their entire time and currency in Tokyo,[16] the opportunity to work with highly visible clientele fueled a sense of healthy competition among the city's eminent designers. Moreover, the emancipation of shopping as a proper cultural activity—with its own meaningful forms—has elevated the flagships of luxury brands into city-making agents.[17] The credit for this retailing and hang-out boom is shared equally between architects from near and abroad—including Ito Toyo, SANAA, Ando Tadao, Aoki Jun, Klein Dytham, Future Systems, Herzog & de Meuron, Peter Marino—and a key group of interior and industrial designers—Katayama Masamichi of Wonderwall, Morita Yasumichi, Sato Oki of Nendo, Tei Shuwa of Intentionallies—and shows little sign of abating.

In a shopping-crazed metropolis, critical engagement with the retail type takes a multiplicity of guises, and in some instances, the insistent demands of novelty transform signature formal and material vocabularies. The familiar polished concrete and intersecting cylinders of Ando Tadao's Collezione mall (1990) at the foot of the Aoyama-Omotesando shopping stretch have given way to the steel shell of the furniture retailer hhstyle's new Cat Dori home for Armani Casa and other lifestyle brands (2005). Playing off of the cultivated minimalism of SANAA/Sejima Kazuyo and Nishizawa Ryue's flagship for the same client next door (2001), Ando's two-story shop is hewn out of an armor of polished trapezoidal and triangular panels 16mm thick, the resulting anthracite mass a textural counterpoint to the corrugated steel walls of its white interior.

The opening of another Ando, the luxe Omotesando Hills (2006) shopping mall imparts a contrast in scale and material. With its internal circulation dominated by an impossibly deep atrium, the mall is particularly notable for its 250-meter frontage along an avenue lined by Zelkova trees, that sets back to form a ziggurat-like roofline along the side street defining the eastern boundary of the complex. The offspring of a contentious "regeneration" scheme by the Mori Building Company, Omotesando Hills elicited a significant, if ultimately toothless nostalgia for the Dojunkai Apartments that once stood on the site. A relic of the interwar years and a much-idealized age, the developer engaged a clever—or cynical, depending on one's perspective—strategy of accommodation. In the end, a compromise of sorts was reached. Two of the southernmost apartments were restored to their prewar Art Deco grandeur, painted a warm cream and reprogrammed as a visitors' center and gift shop for the complex, an incipient, corporate modernity supplanted by its diffuse, corporate 21st-century iteration.

Ando's incidental dialogue of heavy and light with SANAA cuts across the avenue from Omotesando Hills as well, as the main Tokyo home of Christian Dior en face intimates a parallel but altogether distinct set of generative motivations. "SANAA appears to have channeled the programmatic energies of Sejima Kazuyo's early-1990s work on Pachinko parlors to create a destination that is once sublime and whimsical."[18] With the varying floor heights of the 2003 building contributing to the illusion of a much taller structure, the architects advance the curtain wall metaphor with maximum with by effectively creating a double glazed-wall. Behind the clear vision glass, a second layer of fritted acrylic is gently bent and puckered to resemble billowing fabric.

Further afield, the traditional shopping quarter of the Ginza and the evolving retail zones in Marounouchi and Otemachi engage a neighborhood a world away from the quiet residential districts of Aoyama and Daikanyama. Subverting the banal forms of the Ginza's department-store vernacular, the concrete facades of Aoki Jun's flagship for Louis Vuitton on Namiki Dori (2004) is cast with white alabaster inserts, transforming what appears to be a blank grey box in the day into a delightful, kaleidoscopic lantern at dusk.

On the intersection of Marrionier and Nakimiki Dori stands Ito Toyo's suitably iridescent store for the inventor of cultured pearls, Mikimoto. With the site of Mikimoto Kokichi's original outpost also nearby, Mikimoto Ginza 2 (2006) provides a striking focal point for a shopping district once dominated by boxy, windowless department stores. Each of the tower's four walls are clad in 12 mm steel plate and coated in a nacreous pale pink, and like Ito's Omotesando flagship for Tod's (2004), the asymmetrical windows punctuating the hide of the building play with conventions of scale, obscuring any conception of individual floor heights. But its true delicacy lies in its structure and materials. Concrete was poured between a 20 cm gap separating the 57-meter-high steel panels that make up the nine-story tower, projecting a sleek, structural heft as maximizes the provision for a well-appointed interior that culminates in a 4-story spiral staircase.

The Faith that Moves Houses

The three historic typologies of Japan—shrines, temples and residences—have all had significant play in the last decade, but single-family homes, as ever, get the most attention. The constricted "eel-shaped" sites of Tokyo's landed have furnished amazing strategies for urban infill. The alphabet soup of houses designed by established firms and young practices, including Aoki Jun, Kishi Waro, SANAA, Atelier Bow-Wow, Yokomizo Makoto, Endoh Masaki, Milligram Architectural Studio, Yamashita Yasuhiro and Fukushima Katsuya, dot the city like randomly sprinkled gems, often with programs crammed into a total floor area that rarely exceeds 100 square meters.

Milligram Architectural studio, a small firm based in Ota ward helmed by Utsumi Tomoyuki offers archetypal solutions to frequently encountered site constraints. The House in Senzoku, Meguro ward (2002) maximizes the narrow exposures of a plot horizontally and vertically, distributing its programs with an arrangement of mezzanine floors as it boldly announces the presence of the house with a belfrylike gesture. In Kita ward, the six-story Towered Flats (2004), with its beefy perpendicular supports restricted to the periphery, provide the most efficient use of a corner site fragmented from a once larger allotment by public works and dominated by the approaches of an elevated highway. Intended as a residence, the option to contain a number of other potential uses was integral to the client brief, "allowing the building to transcend the category of dwelling and remain functional even beyond the continuity of the family."

Achieving comfort and programmatic flexibility in Tokyo's tight squeeze are fundamental to the design of contemporary housing. A veteran of Ito Toyo's studio, the residential work of Shinjuku-based Yokomizo Makoto is ever predisposed to messing with spatial configurations. The TEM House (2004) in Taito, halfway between Asakusa and Ueno, assumes an abstract, domestic presence at variance with its messy neighbors. Handed a straightforward brief for a three-story building with three studio apartments, the architect was not keen on having all the living functions on a single level. He instead partitioned the building vertically, distributing the qualities of every level to each of the three-story "town houses," all under a skylight of weatherproofed industrial fabric. Recalling the accessible form of one of his early domiciles—aptly called the House on the Hill in Kanagawa from 1989—the pitched roof of TEM mimics the idealized iconography of a one-family house, providing a witty object lesson in the manipulation of scale and space.

Occupying an aerie atop one of the waterfront warehouses of Shinagawa, the three-part firm of SANAA—formally distinguished between Sejima's practice, Office Nishizawa and SANAA proper—furnishes Tokyo and its environs with studies in nimble planning and spatial subversion. The Moriyama House (2006) by Office Nishizawa individuates the programs of a "house" into several autonomous structures. Objectively one residence and five separate apartments, with even smaller outbuildings, the white steel boxes are strewn atop a rectangular compound in a configuration that simulates in miniature the specificity of the Tokyo street. This particular arrangement freed the architects to "determine the size and shape of each individual room freely and to provide every home with a small garden. Various characteristics were given to the units such as a three-story unit with a broad sky view, a squared shaped unit half buried in the ground, a unit with a very high ceiling, or a unit surrounded by gardens in all directions."

The earlier House in a Plum Grove (2003) by Sejima Kazuyo condenses the rejection of spatial hierarchies within a single 78 m^2 cube. Conceived for a writer, her advertising producer-husband, their children, and their grandmother, the dwelling proposes a "refuge for the mind and spirit" devoid of many conventional domestic attributes. With a rooftop teahouse concealed by the thin steel skin, and ample provision for the clients to enjoy a copse of flowering plum trees, the three-level house forbids any external reading of all other programs, the seemingly random placement of windows logical only from the inside.

The functions within the house are encouraged by the open plan to expand, commingle and mutate, advancing a true fluidity of uses in a multiroom house that behaves like a one-room studio or loft.

Situated in the same ward as the Tokyo Dome and Tokyo University, the House in Bunkyo (2000) by Yokohama-born and Kyoto-based Kishi Waro evidences a spiritual kinship with Sejima's Plum Grove House. The application of corrugated panels on the exterior and steel supports mask what is essentially a wooden, one-story domicile. Built also for a couple, two children, and their grandmother, the house presents the dense vertical adjacencies with an anachronism as it is organized around a courtyard plan now rare in Tokyo. As in traditional courtyard homes, the open space unites the larger allocation for the young family and the single parent, nurturing the familial bond between three generations under one roof. A creature of his generation, Kishi is a deliberate modernist and refutes the existence of a typical, contemporary Japanese "style." But in the Bunkyo house, he nonetheless acknowledges a desire to address a unique—sometimes even insular—set of objective, material and affective concerns.

Shigeru Ban, whose use of cardboard tubes famously necessitated a change in Japanese building codes in the early 1990s, designed a number of small residential and commercial structures in Tokyo in the first decade of the 21st century, furthering his unique explorations on the nature of materials. The Glass Shutter House (2003) in Setagaya, with its automated storefront shutters, endows the three-story restaurant and residence of a culinary scholar with a programmatic flexibility that a static curtain wall system would not have permitted. Mimetic of changes in dress demanded by the seasons or particular events, this notion of architecture as clothing is further augmented by a spatial arrangement that can either link or separate a the private third-floor loft from the public ground floor through the mixed-use interstitial zone of the second floor.

Irie Keiichi, a disciple of the late Shinohara Kazuo and principal of Shibuya-based Power Unit Studio, practices a "relational architecture" that seeks to connect rather than sever the functions of a building with its immediate and often chaotic surround. He devised his O-House (2004) in Meguro as a heptahedron intersecting with open-ended concrete tube. Faced with constraints on three sides of a compact site, Irie avoids hermetically sealing the interior off from the outside. The combination of generous apertures and intersecting volumes allow for permeation and outward spatial expansion, liberating the thickset concrete of some of its weight as it creates a relational whole in a sea of accumulated and discontinuous fragments.

Aoki Jun's Tokyo portfolio imparts the discrimination of a native, and accordingly presents a thorough understanding of the urban fabric. Operating from the upper floors of a courtyard apartment on Shibuya's Killer Dori, the sizable number of residential projects undertaken by the firm in the city is unified only by their diversity. The G House (2004), secluded in a quiet area of Meguro ward, weds a reinforced concrete podium with a robust timber frame structure—complete with mortise-and-tenon joinery—familiar to traditional, wooden Japanese homes in both rural and urban areas. The public program of kitchen, living and dinning room are squarely within the massive concrete beams of the lower strata, while the

private spaces are set apart, garretlike on the upper floor. Skylights and windows are framed in prefabricated wood sash, and as there is no roof in the classical sense, the walls of the concrete skin built around the wood frame converge to form a sharp pitch. Inside, the distance between the internal wooden structure and the white walls amplify the effect of natural light within the house. In typical Aoki fashion, the exterior shell of the house does not neatly express the internal program. They do however correspond to Aoki's essential conception of design as "architecturing,"[19] namely the manipulation of space until it achieves something like architecture. In appearing to build around a void, the suggestion of incidental form is reinforced by the staggered placement of windows that only hint at the spatial arrangement of floors and interior walls, denying any assumption of structural redundancy.

The team of Tsukamoto Yoshiharu and Kaijima Momoyo of Atelier Bow-Wow is plenty capable of confronting any design challenge posed by the city, having published a number of handy treatises on "pet buildings," the sort of ad-hoc, shoebox-sized interventions that inhabit any leasable plot in Tokyo. A duo of houses within Setagaya ward describe the variability of site conditions within a specific locale, and the eminent utility of an open plan to support the contamination of programs that have become a key feature of modern living. The Juicy House (2005) is an unabashed homage to Luis Barragán's instruction to let color "occupy" space, a feeling of occupation that the architects believe is conferred to the inhabitants once they activate the steel hull of the house with their habituated movements and the shuffling of furniture and other possessions. GAK House (2005), situated in a part of town only slightly removed from a true agrarian condition, pursues a brief not too different from that of the Juicy House. Built largely out of wood and on a timber-frame structure, the house is divided into ten "rooms" that have the inherent flexibility for its occupants "to open books, notes, and personal computer to study wherever they like. Commissioned by a busy professional couple with an infant, the clients expressed a desire at the outset to have "a lot of small rooms rather than one big room because living materials will be scattered easily."

Superfuturecity

The informal approach to programming suggested by Atelier Bow-Wow at the GAK House can only allude to even more extreme design agendas at work. The ongoing effort at undermining the basic definition of a building, enshrined in Article 2 of the Building Standard Law of Japan as "any structure fixed to the ground and has a roof and either columns or walls," continues to generate new varieties of formal and spatial excitement. Endoh Masaki's Natural Ellipse (2003), the upended, habitable cousin to Ito Toyo's "Egg of Winds" from 1991, utilizes treated fiberglass stretched over a frame of 24 steel rings to contain a dwelling in jam-packed Shibuya. Again devised with Ikeda Masahiro, the milk-white enclosure is very much still anchored to earth, employs a recognizable residential configuration, but is at once other-worldly. At home in neon playground of its sur-roundings, Endoh's ellipse occupies physical space even as it suggest a Tokyo of the mind, the secret, amorphous components of an alternate city that is both familiar and fantastic.

Endoh and Ikeda's adventures—dubbed "soft architecture" by the architect and planner Baba Masataka[20]—is perhaps exemplified by the air-filled silver balloons of Pika Pika Pretzel (1999), erected by the Shibuya firm of Astrid Klein and Mark Dytham. Not a building but a temporary hoarding for a construction site in Harajuku, the near-weightless and alien form seemed forever on the verge of breaking the laws of gravity during its brief life. Pika Pika and the metaphoric and physical deviation from fixed concepts of structure and materiality that it embodied portend one direction out of many possible futures for design. The work of two English expatriates now com-fortably ensconced in the Tokyo architectural scene, the remarkable success in Japan of its authors also suggests an impending heterogeneity in the creative sources of architectural production, an objective befitting a workshop for 21st century global culture.

Notes

[1] Mori Minoru, Mau, Bruce and Yamagata Hiroo. *New Tokyo Life Style Think Zone.* Tokyo: Mori Building Company, 2002, np.

[2] Tajima Noriyuki, *Tokyo: A Guide to Recent Architecture.* Cologne: Köneman/Ellipsis, 1996. p 10

[3] See Suzuki Masao. *Edo no Toshikeikaku (City planning of Edo).* Tokyo: Sanseido, 1988; Fujimori Terunobu. *Meiji no Tokyo keikaku (Meiji Tokyo city planning).* Tokyo: Iwanami Shoten, 1990; —*Tokyo ko shi (History of Tokyo Harbor)* Volume 1. Tokyo: Tokyo Metropolitan Government, 1994.

[4] McCormack, Gavan. "Breaking the Iron Triangle," *New Left Review,* Issue 13. London: New Left Review, January/February 2002, np.

[5] Tajima Noriyuki, *Tokyo: A Guide to Recent Architecture.* Cologne: Köneman/Ellipsis, 1996. p 16

[6] Harootunian, Harry. *Overcoming Modernity: History, Culture and Community in Interwar Japan.* Princeton NJ: Princeton University Press, 2000, pp. 34-37

[7] Luna, Ian in "Structural Contradictions." Luna, Ian et al. *On the Edge: Ten Architects from China.* New York: Rizzoli, 2006, p. 32; cf, Virilio, Paul. *Ground Zero (Ce Qui Arrive).* London: Verso, 2002, np.

[8] Hagenberg, Roland. *14 Japanese Architects: Interviews.* Tokyo: Kashiwa Shobo, 2004, p. 74

[9] Buckley, Sandra in "Contagion," Davidson, Cynthia ed. *Anywise.* Cambridge, MA: MIT Press, 1996, pp. 82-83; cf, Virilio, Paul. *Speed and Politics: An Essay on Dromology* (1986 edition). New York: Columbia University Press, 1986, pp. 3-12

[10] Ibid.

[11] Hosaka Kenjiro, quoted in Aoki Jun et al. *Aoki Jun Works,* Volume I. Tokyo: Inax Shuppan, 2004, pp. 39-40

[12] Nute, Kevin. *Place, Time and Being in Japanese Architecture.* New York/London: Routledge, 2004, p. 11

[13] See Buntrock, Dana. *Japanese Architecture As a Collaborative Process: Opportunities in a Flexible Construction Culture.* London/New York: Taylor and Francis/Spon Press, 2002, pp.31, 47-51, 93 ff.

[14] Kobayashi Hiroto in "Cycle of City." Ogura Kazuo et al. *JA 65: Parallel Nippon— Contemporary Japanese Architecture 1996-2006.* Tokyo: Shinkenchiku-sha, 2007, np.

[15] Bognar, Botond. *Kuma Kengo: Selected Works.* New York: Princeton Architectural Press, 2005, p. 15, 28

[16] 1999-2000 data, from the Japanese National Tourism Office "Survey of Foreign Visitors to Japan, "p 55. More than half of all American, French, Hong Kong, British and Taiwanese respondents interviewed indicated shopping as a principal motivation for visiting Japan.

[17] Luna, Ian. *Retail: Architecture and Shopping.* New York: Rizzoli, 2005, p. 29

[18] Ibid., p. 237

[19] Aoki Jun. "Monthly Review," *Shinkenchiku,* May 1998, p. 282

[20] Baba Masataka. "Ten Architects Freed from the 20th Century," *Art It,* Vol. 3, No. 2, Tokyo: Realcities Publishing, Spring/Summer 2005, p. 72

This spread: hhstyle Armani Casa, Shibuya Ward, by Ando Tadao (2005).

This page and opposite: Mikimoto Ginza 2, Chuo Ward, by Ito Toyo (2006).

This page: House in Senzoku, Meguro Ward, by Milligram Architectural Studio (2002).

This spread and following spread: Murai Masanari Art Museum, Setagaya Ward, by Kuma Kengo (2004).

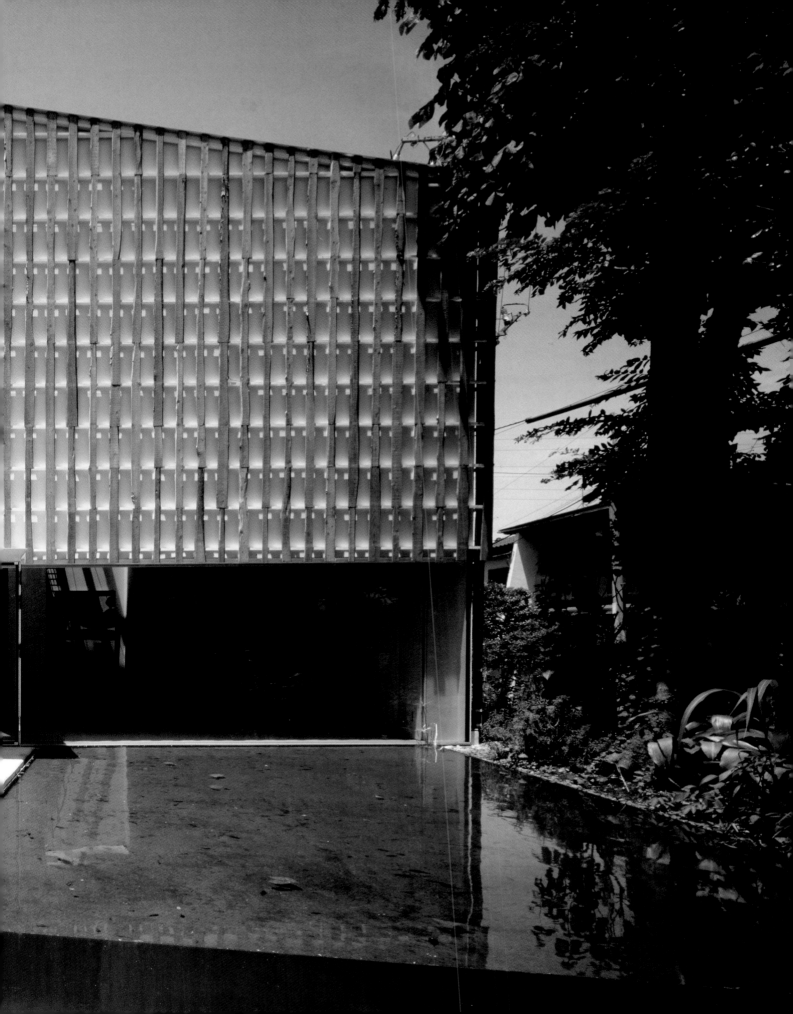

This spread and following spread: TEM House, Taito Ward, by Yokomizo Makoto (2004).

TEM House: (left to right), site plan, ground to third floor plans and section looking east

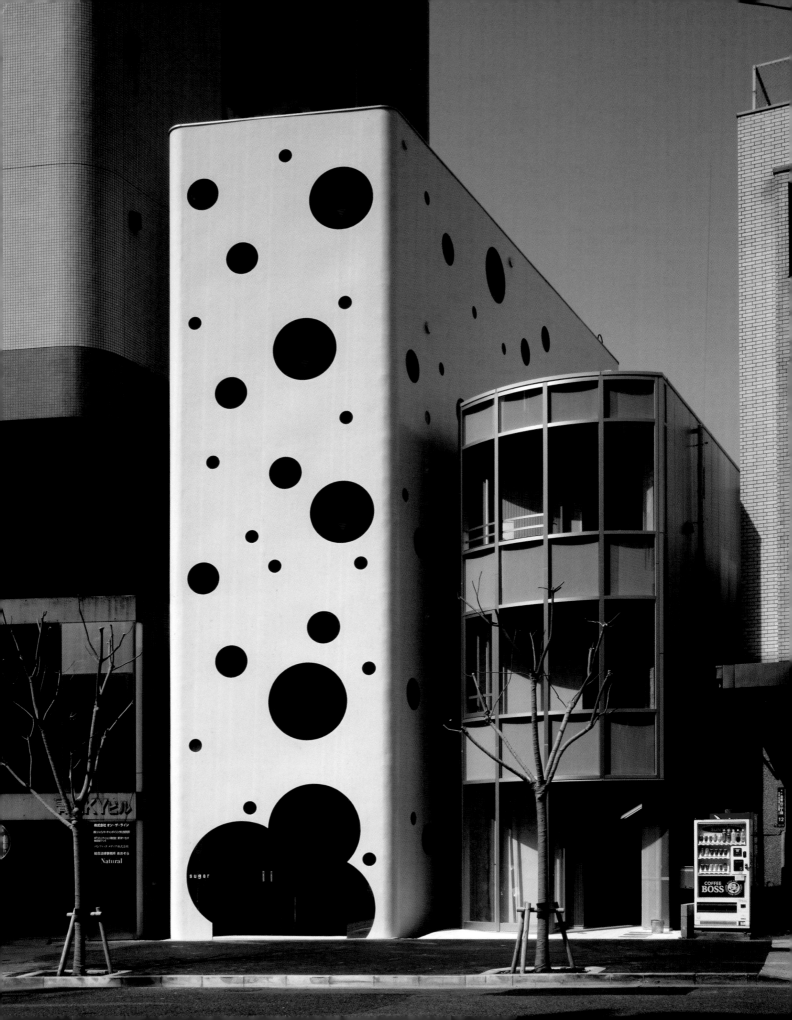

This spread: GSH House, Shibuya Ward, by Yokomizo Makoto (2006).

This spread: Natural Ellipse, Shibuya Ward, by Endoh Masaki and Ikeda Masahiro (2003).

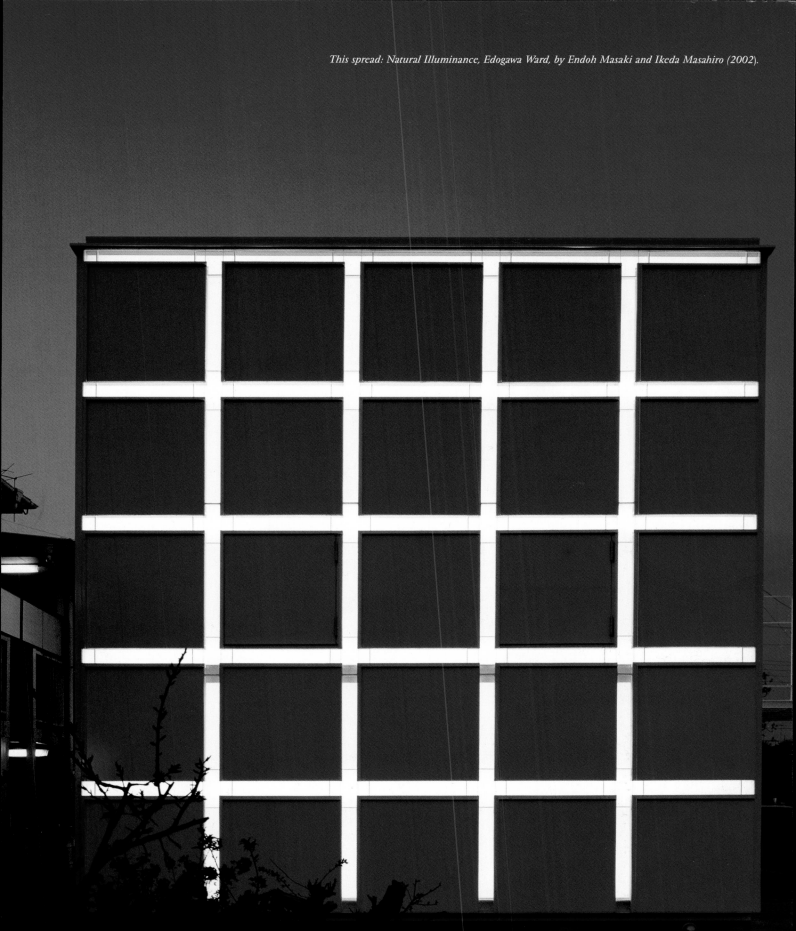

This spread: Natural Illuminance, Edogawa Ward, by Endoh Masaki and Ikeda Masahiro (2002).

This spread: Moriyama House, Tokyo-to, by Nishizawa Ryue (2006).

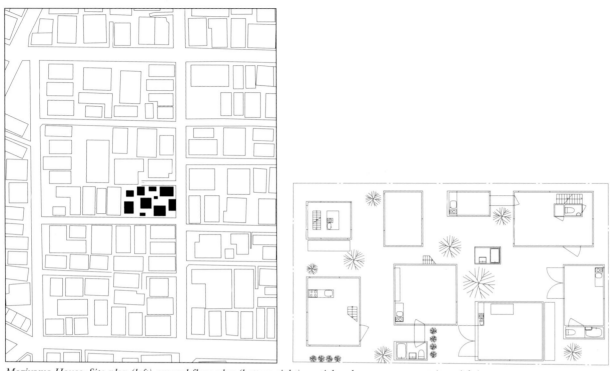

Moriyama House: Site plan (left), ground floor plan (bottom right), spatial and program concept (top right).

This spread: House in a Plum Grove, Tokyo-to, by Sejima Kazuyo (2003).

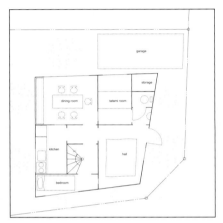  

House in a Plum Grove: Ground floor plan, second floor plan, third floor plan (left to right).

This spread and following spread: House in Bunkyo, Bunkyo Ward, by Kishi Waro (2000).

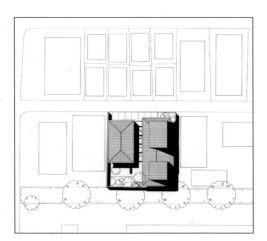 

House in Bunkyo: Site plan and ground floor plan (left to right).

This spread: O House, by Irie Keiichi/Power Unit Studio (2004).

This spread and following spread: Juicy House, Setagaya Ward, by Atelier Bow-Wow (2005).

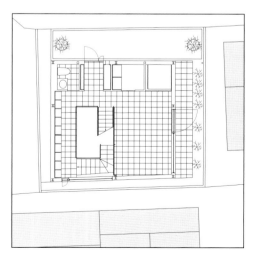

Juicy House: view from the southeast, ground floor plan and second floor plan (left to right).

This spread: GAK House, Setagaya Ward, by Atelier Bow-Wow (2005).

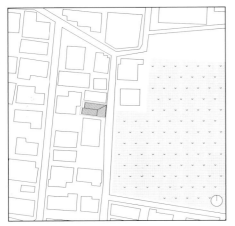 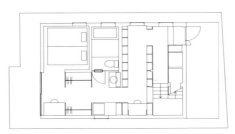 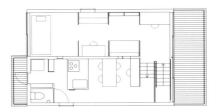

GAK House: site plan, ground floor plan and second floor plan (left to right).

KLEIN DYTHAM

Above: Astrid Klein and Mark Dytham; opposite page: Pika Pika Pretzel (1999), Harajuku, Shibuya Ward.

Every second book on architecture invokes the three conditions Vitruvius set down for good building: "firmness, commodity, delight." Check the inscription on the Pritzker Prize medallion and there they are. But no thinker in the two millennia since this prescription was uttered has laid out anything like a formula for the proportions in which each of the constituent parts are employed to best effect. From the evidence, Japanese designers offer a conclusive argument by example: "delight, first and foremost." In a 2003 Japanese magazine interview, Paola Antonelli of the Museum of Modern Art said that to her, Japanese design "[Is] a matter of continuous excitement...about the unexpected nature of some of the choices...a matter of delight, independently of whether it's 'good' or 'bad'...that comes later. I'm always fascinated!"

An abundance of the "good" naturally leads to attrition in the field, and among the few and the great, perhaps none have taken this exhortation to delight more seriously than two than two expatriates of Old Blighty, Mark Dytham and Astrid Klein. The two met at the Royal College of Art in London, and went together on six-month scholarships to the Tokyo office of architect Ito Toyo in 1988, where their tenure extended to two years. In 1991 they opened their own Tokyo office, a move decidedly daunting to those more intimately acquainted with the exclusivity of Japanese professional society. Their playfulness and willingness to assume high-profile, high-pay commercial projects that might be dismissed by others puts them at some distance from the mainstream Japanese design community, and they nurture that distinction as a liberating factor in their work. It is work in which the intentionality is explicit, serving the dual purpose of fostering delight among non-architects and discouraging more intimate inquiry into their motives, which, considering their status, would be ultimately self-defeating. Though Dytham is typically the more voluble of the duo, it is Astrid Klein who declared to *ICON Magazine* that their interest is in "the chaos and the crap" of Japanese life.

Their claim to legitimacy in their adopted home came early in 1993 when they won the Kajima Space Design Award for best young practice in Japan. Later that year they were commissioned to build the Idée Workstation in Shimouma by design impresario Kurasaki Tetsuo, garnering them both the Asahi Glass Design Award and the National Panasonic Design Award. From that point forward they've continuously juggled concurrent high-profile projects, despite a national economic flame-out in the early nineties.

Part of what fuels their prolific output is an affinity for what critic Deyan Sudjic terms an "ability to combine London's scavenging instincts with Tokyo's technological abundance." Typical of this is their Foret project in fashionable Harajuku, nicknamed "Cats Eyes." KDa enrobed the building in ordinary road reflectors. The reflectors shimmer colorfully in bright daylight. At night they reflect back the bustling activity of the street. Every neon sign, every car that passes changes the facade's seemingly electrified skin pattern. The apron of concrete that draws visitors into the store is covered by glass bead paint, the sort used for reflective road striping. Whether out of propriety or parochial thinking, these are materials that the Japanese design establishment would leave in the supply bin. Klein and Dytham revel in their undeniably attractive effect on the average passerby, who has no such compunctions about their use.

Undercover Lab (2001), Harajuku, Shibuya Ward.

Similarly, KDa has become the go-to company for construction hoarding in Tokyo. Unfazed by the temporary nature of such work, they imbue it with conscientiousness and considerable wit. While Ando Tadao was working on his tony, austere Omotesando Hills project behind it, Klein-Dytham took on the task of placing a protective barrier in front. They called the project their Green Green Screen (the nomenclature of KDa projects offers a parallel experience of delight). The 250-meter hoarding, festooned with 13 varieties of living plants, tapped into the aspect of Japanese national character that reveres seasonal change. It commented wryly on the growth and anticipation of the highly publicized project it concealed. To the architects, it was of great importance that the screen smelled nice to passersby. Critics be damned, the hit of transient olfactory pleasure was what ordinary people would cherish.

Other construction covers include the iFly Virgin Wonderwall. Also in Harajuku, the hoarding homed in on Japan's obsession with mobile phones. The design was minimal—a red LED tickertape embedded in a red acrylic plane. The LED posed one general-knowledge question an hour that pedestrians could answer by connecting to the project's mobile web site through their cell phone. They were notified within the hour if they got the question right, and if they won a prize. Japan's highly advanced cellular technology notwithstanding, an interactive campaign on this order had never before been seen in 2000. Less conceptual and more sensual was their Pika Pika Pretzel. The hoarding was made of shiny (literally: *pikapika*) inflated abstract forms, strung together with webbing. It was a firm rebuff to the notion that construction hoarding fills the role of an absence, a practical

invisibility, until what it hides is realized. People smiled ceaselessly. People feel joy when they look at shiny balloons—who would've thought it?

A wall of a different sort stands as a veritable landmark in Harjuku, and is characteristic of everything the firm holds dear. Tagged by esteemed, youth-oriented department store LaForet to revivify its image for a new century, Klein and Dytham took their cue from the plane trees that line the main street and confer a bucolic air upon the amped-up atmosphere of this commercial mecca. They erected a group of freestanding sculptures, formal outlines of trees that echo miniature die-cuts in the facade of the building. Each tree is a wildly fanciful graphic design sheathed in a frame of high-gloss metal. When approached from the side, the thick "trees," which resemble blow-molded toys, appear to vanish due to their reflective surface. Their opacity presents the image of a suitably distinguishing wall, sheltering the shop from the rest of the street. When viewed from across the street the trees appear as happy sentinels, providing a uniquely welcoming gateway in. The store's name, LaForet, is a take on the owner's. Mori means "forest" in

Rin-Rin(2001), Harajuku, Shibuya Ward.

Japanese. Klein Dytham named their installation Rin Rin or Little Forest.

The firm's forays into full-blown architecture extend their playful literalness and feel for unorthodox materials. Heidi House is essentially a thin-skinned shack, built of plywood. From inside there is a sense of architectural nakedness—although many Japanese houses are built of wood, making them impermeable to rain and fire requires that they be covered in thick, unattractive siding. Heidi House escapes fire regulations by being set back three meters from its nearest neighbor. Instead of covering the wood, as no further structural bolstering was required, KDa simply encased it in a simple glass and steel prism. Cutouts in the plywood offer the appearance of a solid wall when viewed from the side, but stream light in and out when viewed straight on.

KDa's other residential and commercial structures also capitalize on the odd zoning conditions of Tokyo's residential neighborhoods. None more so than the Billboard Building. The architects were challenged to build a retail store in an impossibly odd space: 2 stories high, 11 meters

long, 2.5 meters deep at one edge, tapering off to just 60 centimeters at the other. It was immediately clear to the team that this weird wedge was a billboard more than an edifice. They reiterated the dye-cut light source concept with a stenciled bamboo stand affixed upon the wide glass front. The wall not far behind it is painted forest green. As with LaForet and Heidi House, the building's illumination by day is distinctly different by night, but in either case the building acts as a sign, from within which one can obtain what is advertised—a unique retail proposition.

The Undercover Lab in Harajuku, built for Takahashi Jun's fashion label, addresses the dilemma of having one's cake and eating it. The building needed a driveway for five cars, but the architects didn't want to set it so far off the street that it lost contact with the flow of humanity. So they rhymed the asphalt driveway with a prismatic black tube that they cantilevered above it. This gives the humble studio a magisterial presence when one enters its ground space, but is modest in its impact on the street front.

The Museum Café in the super-luxe Roppongi Hills tower is so audaciously childlike in its use of materials that it difficult to decide whether the architects are ingenious or just impudent. Knowing that the astonishing 52nd floor vistas would serve as a distraction to even the most devoted dining partner, KDa chose to make them more inevitable. Floor elevations pile up toward the center of the café so that the innermost guests have a clear view through the windows. Convex mirrors of the sort used as safety devices on tiny, twisty residential streets are set in strategic positions throughout

how to play

ヴァージン アトランティック航空
i-modeでクイズに答えて、ロンドンへ行こう!
12月1日 → 12月31日 / 8:00am → 10:00pm

design and co-ordination
+ www.klein-dytham.com
+ www.namaiki.com
+ www.gomagoma.com
site co-operation
+ veloqx city investment limited

quiz

デジタルスクリーンで1時間ごとにクイズを出題。
答えがわかったら、i-modeでアクセス。
1人1時間1回のチャンス。当選者の発表はi-modeにてメールでご連絡します!

prize

the café so that diners can snatch a glimpse of landscape without moving a muscle, from almost any position.

Klein-Dytham's most enduring contribution to the field of architecture to date might not be a building at all, but an event space and the activity it birthed. Initially designated as an after-office pub for the firm's employees and friends, the SuperDeluxe event space became a place for fun and experimentation, a place, as Mark Dytham put it, to "think and drink." It rapidly evolved into a cinematheque, a library, a studio and finally into the first home for "Pecha Kucha Nights." Pecha Kucha, meaning "chit chat," began by inviting architects from competing firms, allied firms, schools, cultural institutions, and any and all interested in architecture to talk about their latest project. Klein and Dytham's formal bent expresses itself here in the structure of the presentation. One day a month, presenters show twenty slides, spending twenty seconds on each. Each presentation is over in 6 minutes 40 seconds, and the constraints are reportedly liberating. Pecha Kucha has now spread to nearly 25 cities across the globe, and the founders strive to make occasional appearances at all of them. They're fast becoming a premier venue for the cross-pollination of design concerns that will come to embody the era. Pecha Kucha is not an edifice, but it is a form of building, offering delight through fellowship and discovery—*David G. Imber/Yoshida Mika*

Above: iFly Virgin Wonderwall (2000) Harajuku, Shibuya Ward.

Opposite page, top: Pecha Kucha night at SuperDeluxe, Nishi Azabu, Minato Ward; below: TWBA\Hakuhodo Offices (2007), Shibaura, Minato Ward.

Page 74: Exterior views of Heidi House (2005), Uehara, Shibuya Ward.

Page 75: Exterior views of Billboard Building (2005), Moto Azabu, Minato Ward.

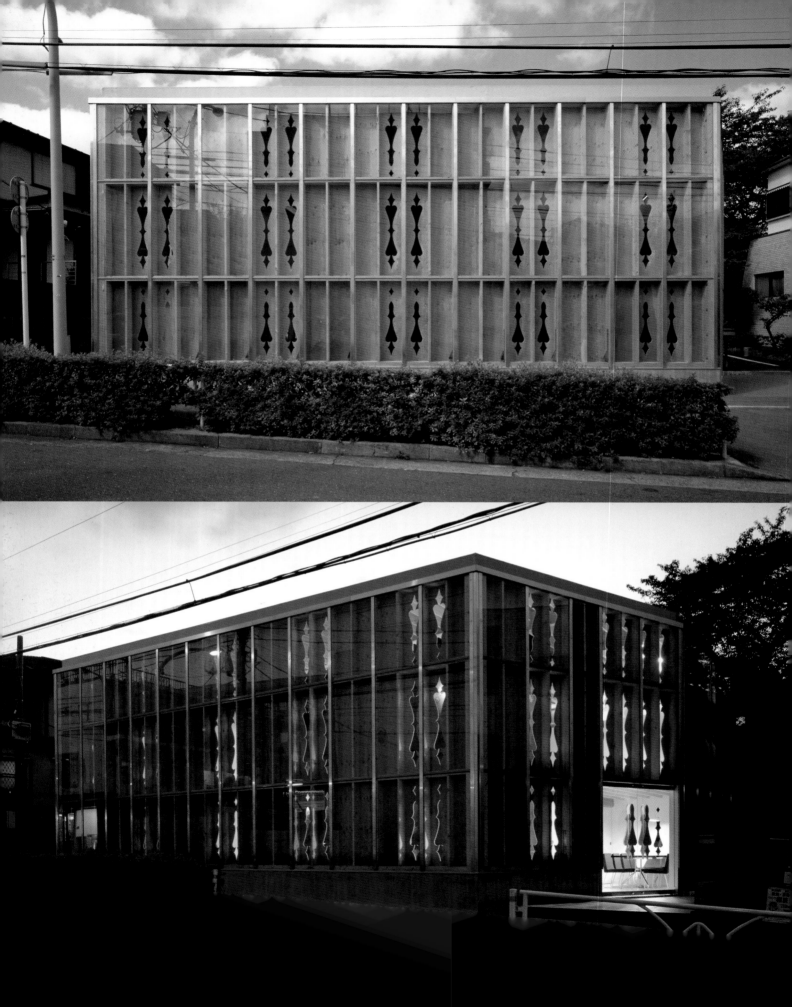

SATO OKI
NENDO

Opposite page: Book House, Shikinejima, Niijima-mura, Tokyo Prefecture (2005).

In 2002 Sato Oki, founder of the nine-person design office Nendo, took his degree in architecture from Tokyo's Waseda University. In 2003 he took Tokyo. More precisely, he took the TDB award at Tokyo Designer's Block, the annual five-day, freewheeling, citywide stage for everything new in design that since 2000 has consistently brought the best young creators from around the world to make their case in a lighthearted, non-parochial setting. Though only a year out of school, Sato was positioning himself to be the foremost preceptor of a unique direction in Japanese design, a barely explored dominion in which associative boundaries between technology and nature melded, and practical magic and theatricality composed the terrain. This was the realm of technological poetics, and Nendo would be its Lyceum. Its method, an amalgamation of two qualities Nendo refers to as "vividness" and "substance," which translate roughly to beauty, aestheticism, and allure on one hand; cost, practicality, and performance on the other. There's no better early illustration of this than the piece that won the TDB that year, the Rakuyo Bench.

The bench itself is utterly unassuming. But when it's occupied, images of green leaves begin to appear as if having fallen beneath it. Over time the leaves will turn yellow, then red. And when the occupants leave the bench, all traces of the fallen leaves—*rakuyo*—vanish. The cycle of nature insinuates itself into all aspects of Japanese activity. Its gradual changes are anticipated, celebrated, and revered throughout life as the objective correlative of the cycle of existence, the signposts of ongoing human consciousness. The Rakuyo Bench hints that our socialization and communication give purpose and meaning to this inescapable course of nature.

Not all of Nendo's designs weigh in as heavily on the poetic side of the equation. Sato's first major work of architecture, a home for his family designed while he was still in school, is a study in practicality. The Drawer House functions just as the name implies. Everything in the house, entire rooms, can be moved in and out of the walls to provide greater floor space when needed. Even the bath sits on a track, so that it can be moved outside when better weather beckons. But it is the golden mean between what is needed and what is desired that Nendo seeks to achieve in its prolific and far-ranging array of designs.

Theatricality comes easily to Sato Oki. He is known among his colleagues to favor the limelight, to genially hold court when others would withdraw to the studio. Like other contemporary Japanese architects and designers, Sato entered the field expecting celebrity. Japanese popular interest in matters of design is such that even older generation architects like Maki and Ando tend to turn up on daily talk shows. One of Sato/Nendo's favored means of addressing an audience is through pure stagecraft. For the hundredth anniversary of Lipton Tea in Japan, the group contributed a room of radically distorted proportions and furniture of progressively varying size, based upon the Mad Hatter's tea party in "Alice's Adventures in Wonderland," an effect so thorough that entrants experienced dissonance between what they were seeing and what they knew about the physical reality of the space. For an installation at "100% Design Tokyo" for a fashion conglomerate, Nendo constructed a series of rooms connected by flatly symbolic overhanging "roots." The message being that while the brands

Left to Right: Canvas Restaurant (2003), Minami-Oi, Shinagawa Ward.

are clearly connected, each grows and expands in a different direction. Again culturally cognizant of the fall season, Nendo placed spring fashions beneath the roots, in the designers' words, to gather "strength in the ground before they flower." For "Sinking About Furniture," Nendo fabricated objects that appear to literally sink into the ground. Though they clearly partake of the structure of ordinary chairs, tables and bookshelves, Nendo releases them from the bounds of their common utility, and by re-purposing them as objects of contemplation instead of accommodation, asks the viewer to question the form and nature of everyday trappings. In considering Wilde's famous declaration that "all art is quite useless," this environment, created to prompt rethinking and discussion, expresses itself somewhere outside the realms of both pure and applied art.

Theatricality is put in the service of play with the Karaoke Tub. Karaoke culture in Japan is completely unique. A feature of the strong social contract dictates that to release true emotion, desires, and motives—*honne*, meaning underlying truth—license may be granted by an external agent or circumstance, and vulnerability shared. Karaoke embodies this complicated interchange in one fell swoop; drinking lowers inhibition and singing aloud exposes the individual fully to the group (for better or worse). Yet the traditional "Karaoke Box" set-up is a stage/audience relationship. Japan has a long tradition of group bathing, another experience, like karaoke, that exposes the individual by means of the external agent of the bath. The bathing experience is shared and mutual, however, and doesn't separate the individual from the group. Nendo brilliantly overlaid one experience upon the other to delightful effect. As with so many Nendo designs, the Karaoke Tub is an imaginative contemporary revision of a conventional experience.

Repetition is another favored theme, seen in the table titled Snow, and in a design for the urban culture-inflected fashion boutique Seesway. Sato writes that hip-hop served as the foundation for the concept, specifically hip-hop's primary musical tropes, sampling and looping. The sampled object here is a prosaic stool, repeated over and over. Configured in horizontal groupings, it establishes counters, display tables, and of course seating arrangements. Stacked one atop another, the stools serve as shelves and display racks.

Sato/Nendo's designs employ a dramatically "out of bounds" materiality that often jars expectations but reciprocates by inviting the viewer in. Two works of architecture that exemplify this quality are the Book House and restaurant Canvas. The owner of Book House wanted a home, but expressed a desire to share an extensive library with nearby residents. The interior collar of the structure is entirely composed of bookshelves. To protect their precious contents from the elements, panel doors can be manipulated to follow the sun or enclose the house completely. The most satisfying part of the house for the owner, however, is the fiberglass panels that back the shelves. Their translucence mimics conventional

FUKASAWA NAOTO

Above: Fukasawa Naoto; opposite page, top: ±0 8-Inch LCD TV, series 1; bottom, ±0 Humidifier, series 3.

While Yanagi Sori is often cited as the sage of Japanese industrial design, Fukasawa Naoto is widely acknowledged as its dean. It's not only his prodigious success in the marketplace, nor the fact that he's the recipient of upwards of fifty international design awards as of this writing. He is also a prolific author, and his books have become part of the Japanese design canon: *The Ecological Approach to Design*, and *Optimum*, just two of the better known. He is greatly in demand as a lecturer, and holds teaching positions at two universities, one at Tama Art University, his alma mater, and the other at the graduate school of Tokyo University; as well as a faculty position with Musashino Art University, from whence Tei Shuwa among many others emerged (though deposed of its antique trappings, contemporary Japan's adherence to the system of teacher-pupil patronage derives directly from the most ancient East Asian traditions).

Fukasawa attains that rarified distinction among his peers by virtue of the common experience of looking at his designs, which even on first glance prompt a reaction of spontaneous, multiple "a-ha moments". It's the pervasiveness of their thinking, the sense that whoever is behind these designs was present at a point of creation, or at least a propitious junction of the broad streams of modernity and technology. And what makes *that* a contradiction is that Fukasawa himself believes that design's highest ambition is to obliterate every trace of the designer.

Fukasawa's early professional efforts were for IDEO, the San Francisco-founded design think tank that flourished with the rise of the 90's technology explosion (IDEO was responsible for the first production mouse and the Palm Pilot V, among many other technological touchstones). He joined the firm in 1989, and after eight years returned to Japan to establish the company's presence there. While still under the aegis of IDEO, Fukasawa contributed to the success of other budding design companies, notably Mujirushi Ryohin. Although MUJI's designers are anonymous in principle,

when their wall mounted CD player won three major international design awards in 2002, Fukasawa was broadly perceived as wearing the laurels. In 2003 he stepped out on his own and subsequently took his place as Design Director for the epoch-making brand ±0 (PlusMinusZero). In spring of 2007 Fukasawa was named one of the founding directors of 21_21 Design Sight, comprising a research center, workshops, and galleries housed in a building designed by Ando Tadao for the new Tokyo Midtown tower complex.

The ±0 product line manifests Fukasawa's conceptual approach to design at every level. Fukasawa's aesthetics are consciously aligned with the tenets of minimalist art and its notions of spatial structuralization, scale, color, and distribution. At the same time, and somewhat at odds with those rigid ideas, his designs propound a deeply instilled sense of both utility and levity (note that Fukasawa founded ±0 as a joint venture with toy maker Takara). An aura surrounds the work, of two of the most cherished Japanese virtues: gentleness and deference. The dreamy dimpled orb of his ubiquitous humidifier, winner of a 2005 gold "Good Design Award," without any explicit reference, conjures the poetics of liquid. The handset of his cordless phone (a humble servant) is anthropomorphically proportioned, and as it stands ready in its cradle, it bends smartly at the "waist."

Below right: ±0 Umbrella, series 1. "We added a slight depression in the never-changing, easily recognizable shape of the umbrella's handle so that, when [it] is closed and furled, something that many people have tried and failed at becomes possible: hooking their bags on the handle of their umbrella."

Opposite page: ±0 Sole Bag, series 2. "We believe that a great many people are not happy with the idea of putting their bags on the ground. It stands to reason then that they'd go for a bag that they wouldn't be too worried about placing on the ground. So we thought about shoe soles. More precisely, we thought about the rubber-soled shoes that are worn in schools throughout Japan. The color of the familiar rubber part of the shoe forms a focal point."

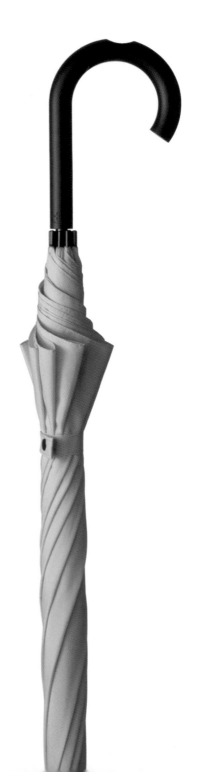

The ±0 philosophy expresses a distinct break with pure stylization, as characterized by, for example, by Streamline Moderne. Streamlining generally concealed existing technology beneath a cowl, which was then given zoomorphic accents to figuratively depict acceleration, efficiency, and other anecdotal properties. Fukasawa begins with the primacy of the form, then seeks the technology that will perform most effectively within that configuration. The ability to work this way is the result of miniaturization and other technological advances that simply weren't available to Fukasawa's design forbears, and he is as keyed-in to advanced electronic technology as anyone working in industrial design today.

Fukasawa is a prolific writer on design, often in a quasi-mystical mode, and his writing displays a pronounced empathy with the user. He calls his work, explicitly, "product art," but the art here is not an effete indulgence. In Fukasawa's design lexicon art is a "reliable product," in that, although our relationship with it changes over time and with experience, the best art continues to stir innumerable feelings and reflections whenever we engage it. A strong promise to make for consumer goods, and Fukasawa, through ±0, adopts it as a commitment.

The other major, and infinitely intriguing, motif of ±0 designs is expressed in the phrase *"arisoude, naimono"* (roughly, "things that seem like they must exist, but don't"). Upon looking at an object, the user should understand that it is so fundamentally practical, so globally appealing to sight and touch, so apt within the setting, that it must have always been there in some form or another. But when intellect and experience try to locate its real world counterpart, the search turns up empty.

Utility and placement are foremost in products like his hot water pot. The Japanese correlative to the western idea of "hearth and home" includes a vessel of boiling water (for guests, for warmth). In the electronic age, the *"poht-to"* (an electric kettle with a pump spout) became a household fixture, but it was always one of those objects, confined to the kitchen, that Fukasawa describes as "never having had design applied to them." Refinement and increased functionality were introduced in haphazard ways, as if the rush to market precluded taking time to re-think the form. The pot was always roughly cylindrical and fabricated to resemble other cylindrical kitchen appliances in size, color and material. The ±0 pot starts by referring to the past. Hot water should be available where guests congregate, where people work, so Fukasawa's pot sits nicely in the living room or den. The material has the satiny "hand" of finished wood but the utility of contemporary, durable, stain-resistant plastic. Its form echoes the shape of books and boxes, shelves and walls. It's no longer a round peg in a square world.

Above: au/KDDI Infobar, Series 1, (l-r) Nishikigoi, Ichimatsu and Building. Opposite page, top: ±0 DVD/MD Stereo Component; bottom: Soccer Mat.

The shapes of ±0 products frequently reflect Fukasawa's homely, playful sensibility; his designs remind people of the contemporary and the familiar. Bread is sold in Japan in loaves shaped like stubby prisms, so the toaster oven is an aggressively cubic chamber. A concept mobile phone for au/KDDI was shaped like a riverbed-polished pebble, because people constantly fondle their cell phones. When it rings, the LED display, glowing and flashing from within, shines warmly through the "rock" surface, that sense of warmth strengthened by reminding people of things contemporary and familiar.

At other times the designs hew more closely to their Minimalist associations. The phone that au/KDDI actually took to market was the audacious Infobar of 2003. The scale of the design puts the conventional wisdom of cellular phone layout in thrall to geometric rigor. The disproportionately large buttons certainly speak to the worldly viewer as successful "product art," but if the aim were merely abstraction, the design would not fulfill Fukasawa's mandate for utility. The Infobar's keypad instead offers the possibility of dialing based solely on binary functions. One needn't read the keys, only note their familiar position and the absence or presence of color at a glance (and there are several color combinations to choose from). For Fukasawa this defines the object's conceptual continuity. Binary functions order the user experience, from dialing to digital data packaging over the air. Not thinking about the markings allows the user to briefly rise above nagging practicality, and as Fukasawa writes, "when peoples' thoughts are within the boundaries of consciousness they are at their farthest from heaven."

This also accounts for Fukasawa's insistence that if the user can sense the presence of a designer, the object is over-designed. To recognize a designer's aesthetic from expressive gestures holds the design, and the viewer/user's feet, to the ground.

Everything that Fukasawa Naoto represents in the design world pirouettes around the significance of the company's name, ±0. The symbol has no specific historical or ideographic reference point, but in the Japanese mind it evokes an idea that has formed the basis of scores of canonical epigrams and axioms. It is the idea that life takes and gives in equal measure, and in the end is in a steady state. One wishes to avoid the hackneyed and often misused "zen," but ±0 is hinting at the condition of equanimity in all matters that practice strives for. Fukasawa seeks to engender this in the viewer/user by producing objects that fill spaces surrounding our humanity, that connote needs and desires, and the presence of which is intuited through absence. The most accomplished design feels as if it was always there. In this way he hopes to circumvent conventional notions about the work of the designer and the relationship of user to object, and to leave in their place a seamless field of fulfillment, a feeling that life is as it should be and that all is right in the world. He's trying to do this one appliance at a time.—*David G. Imber/Yoshida Mika*

Top and bottom: ±0 8 Store, Aoyama (2004). Following spread, clockwise from top left: ±0 Electronic Calculator, series 3; ±0 Notebook, series 1 (with a depression for resting a coffee cup); ±0 A Light with a Dish, series 1; ±0 Cordless Phone, series 2.

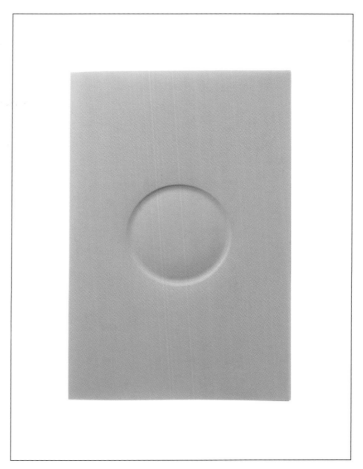

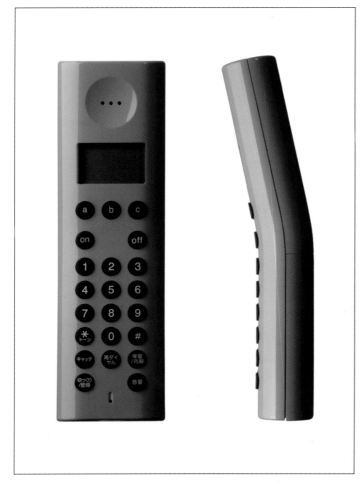

MORITA YASUMICHI
GLAMOROUS

A visitor to Tokyo will learn immediately that the ubiquity of English words on view is immensely out of proportion to the average Japanese person's comprehension of them. In short, most English in use in Japan is decorative. Occasionally an English word or phrase will breech the language barrier, but its meaning will be altered or skewed, and in that state it becomes part of the Japanese lexicon of *wasei-eigo*—"made-in-Japan english."

By any Western measure, Morita Yasumichi could be described as something of a dandy. *Dan-dei* is legitimate *wasei-eigo* as well, but using it to describe Morita to a Japanese person would arouse only a snicker. It's a trendy word from the 80s, and so for Japanese, an archaism. On the other hand, his work is regularly described in the press as *goh-jasu*—gorgeous. East and West would seem to agree on that description, but there would be two distinctly different meanings at play. Just as the word dandy carries a negative hint of foppishness, gorgeous, when used in Japanese, means that a thing's appeal rests largely upon its conspicuous cost.

The internationally recognized, Hong Kong-based designer Alan Chan, who commissioned Morita to design the interiors for a chain of popular restaurants there, echoed a common refrain: "He looked like more of a rock star to me than a designer." The outsized, jewel-spangled glasses, the skinny French jeans, the one-off leather jacket, perhaps a gift from the fashion house—are they a subterfuge, meant to disarm clients from the outset, or is this the soul of Morita Yasumichi? Is the in-demand designer just a "champagne guy" as Chan averred?

Champagne, and all it symbolizes, does play a large part in the designer's life. By his own account he drinks it every day, throughout the day, and has been awarded a medal of Chevalier for his advocacy of the beverage. The raised flute is as close to a manifesto as Morita will ever, in all likelihood, produce.

His breakout as a designer, however, involved lesser potables. As a teenager, Morita was already fascinated by the luxe life. Born in Osaka in 1967, he fell in love early with haute couture. Adoring not only the look, but the life that the House of Versace engendered, he took a job as window dresser to be close to fashion. His windows quickly grabbed the attention of local cognoscenti, and though he was yet too young to drink, his first interior design commission was for the bar "Cool" in Kobe. Trend-conscious entrepreneurs sought him out, and he was soon called on for multiple window display, bar, and café design projects. His reputation for juggling scores of projects at once continues to this day, ostensibly belying his relaxed, party-going image. In early 2007 he was at work on almost 90 full-blown concurrent interior projects on two continents. His designs have earned him numerous international awards, including the Will Ching Design Award of the International Interior Design Association in 2001, and Interior Design Magazine's Hospitality Award in '02 for his debut international project, Hong Kong's Daidaiya. 2003 saw the opening of the first of his two wildly popular Megu restaurants in New York, and in 2006 the W Hotel group tapped him for the top-down design of two new hotels in Kowloon and Shanghai. (Aaron Richter, design director for W Hotels worldwide, has said that, without knowing its creator, he'd long kept a picture of Morita's Hajime Bar in Tokyo on his wall for inspiration. When Megu in New York

Above: Morita Yasumichi; opposite page: Bar "Cabaret" (2002),Ginza, Chuo ward.

opened, he made inquiries, learned it was by the same designer, and contacted him on the spot).

The progress of events over the intervening period between Morita's first local gigs and international renown may have been hastened in part by the Great Hanshin Earthquake of 1995 that devastated his home prefecture of Hyogo. The reputation earned from that early exposure had resulted in his being named chief designer for the Imagine design consultancy, and he might have remained in that position, periodically completing various small, independent projects. He describes the earthquake as an emotionally shattering experience that left him feeling the need to contribute in a public and permanent way, under his own banner. Consequently he opened the Morita Yasumichi Design Office in Osaka in 1996. Soon after, he moved the office to nearby Nishinomiya. By 2000 he'd changed the name of his now successful firm to Glamorous Co., Ltd., and in 2004 the company made its third move to Ashiya, a point about halfway between the Osaka of his birth and the site of his first commercial work in Kobe. It's an upper middle class suburban community and home to a deeply rooted cultural bourgeoisie—quite perfectly suited to his aesthetic agenda. More recently Morita has spun off a graphics and product design firm, Ero Ero, for which he serves as creative director.

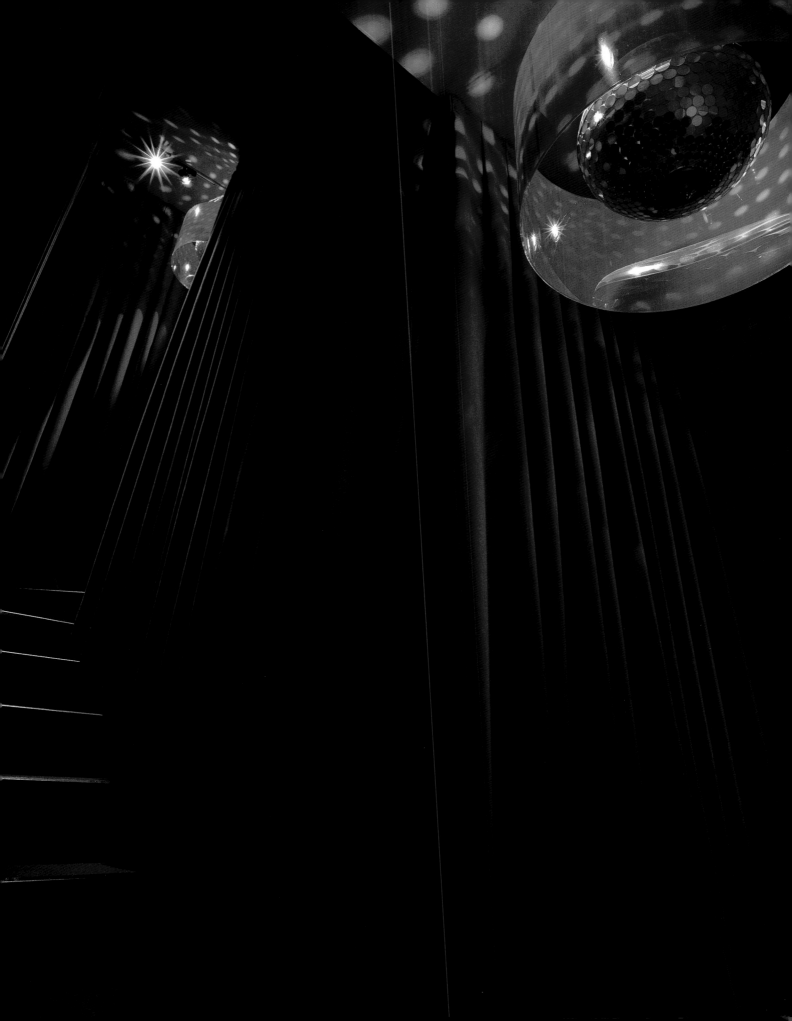

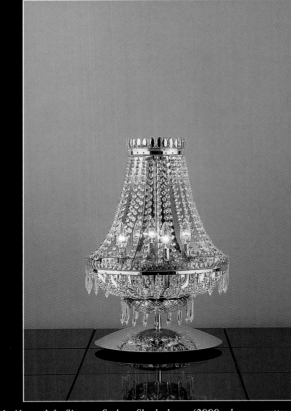

Opposite page:Bar "Cabaret" (2002),Ginza, Chuo ward. Above, left: Sinamo Sudare Shade lamp (2000, chrome, rattan. "Sudare" is rattan, and "sinamo" is a contraction of "simple, natural, modern." Above, right: DST-53819 lamp (2004-05, chrome, acrylic, crystal cut glass). Following spread, clockwise from top left: Bar "Carmenere" (2005), Jingumae, Shibuya Ward; Dean and Deluca Café (2005); Kita-Aoyama, Minato Ward; Château Restaurant Joël Robuchon (2004), Meguro Ward; IDU Co. Office (2004), Ginza, Chuo Ward.

The rise from window dresser to international design presence was truly meteoric, and Morita has openly expressed regret that it left him no time to pursue an academic degree in design (in college he trudged through a business curriculum). His modesty may also be a ruse. Had he followed the scholarly path we might yet be left with little in the way of theory from him; Osakans typically eschew public displays of high-mindedness. A clue to Morita's method is right in his firm's name, "glamour." It is a concept that doesn't translate directly to the classical Japanese style that he clearly adores and constantly refers to. There is intricacy, balance, preciousness, elegance, serenity, tradition. In these things the Japanese classical aesthetic meets and surpasses the West in its rigor. What is missing is that element that requires the gaze of another for completion. That is the element of glamor, and that is what Morita pulls from the West.

Without any body of coherent institutional theory to cling to, and despite an intensely eclectic output, it is nonetheless easy to pick up Morita's trail. Eyes naturally gravitate toward the ecstatic mix of multiple chandeliers, redolent of the *ancien régime*, rows of overbearing abat-jours, mirrors and light boxes, velvet, crystal, and the color red. Though it's equally easy to try to dismiss him as (by his own account) the *"goh-jasu* guy," the "chandelier guy," perhaps he's better thought of as a latter day Cellini (one wonders what a foray into pure sculpture would look like). The air of wicked delight, the excess, the gender elasticity, but most of all Cellini's principle that if a thing is worth doing, it's worth doing in gold (or in Morita's case, faux leopard and Swarovski crystal).

It's pointless to speculate on how much of Morita Yasumichi's glamorous aura radiates from the core of his being. Like his design, it is there to delight in to the extent one wishes, without commitment to a deeper cause. In both his personality and his method he courts that which could most readily betray him. He makes no attempt to suppress a strangely blithe yet earnest nature that begs critics to label him naive, untutored, and ostentatious. At the same time he plays in his design with traditional bromides, kitsch, garishness. But though he courts these things, he never consummates the relationship. Instead, he thwarts expectations with an assiduous work ethic and hypercritical attention to detail. He sidesteps gaudiness and sentimentality by altering the outward presence of worn tropes and readymade symbols such that their essential meaning is winnowed away. Humble bowls, antique sake vessels, temple bells, kimono fabric, rich *urushi* lacquerware—all artifacts of canonical Japanalia become barely recognizable. In the end, the quality that prevails is the courage of his convictions. Morita dares you to look closer with the promise of intrigue, and when he's got you where he wants you all you can see is integrity.—*David G. Imber/Yoshida Mika*

TEI SHUWA
INTENTIONALLIES

Above: Tei Shuwa. Opposite page: JM227 Office Building (2006), Jingumae, Shibuya Ward.

Tei Shuwa would just as soon not design for export outside of Japan, but it's not a question of xenophobia. He just doesn't trust forms to travel on their own. He's concerned, that some will look upon his sleek, stark appliances for Amadana, a high-end brand he developed for Toshiba, and deem them products of a "minimalist" sensibility... or any sensibility. He insists that he adheres to no single methodology but a desire to fit the form to the specific challenge, user, place, and time. It's as if every foray into design is an excursive, *sui generis* statement of intent. Thus he calls his firm Intentionallies. While much of design in the modern era has striven to move beyond historical and cultural context and grasp for a universally interpretable argument, Tei Shuwa's designs proceed so audaciously on those fronts that they arrive at a state at once thoroughly comprehensible and yet peerless in their otherness.

Consider, for example, a designer who believes that if his staff eats food from the local convenience store for lunch, they cannot place themselves in the proper frame of mind to create the kind of work he envisions. So he builds them a restaurant, *Hanamizuki*, where they can dine on food prepared with conviction, in an atmosphere of undisturbed contemplation. Though his work appears to be the essence of simplicity and sparse articulation, its minimalist aspect is not the implementation of theory but the effect of rigorous reduction over time. Still, it is belied by a voluptuary's attention to texture, color, and even aroma. Where glass and steel emphasize precision, and plastics fluidity, Tei's near-mystical affinity with wood connects his design to the most ancient East-Asian traditions while also regenerating them.

He comes from a family of talent. His father is an architect and his older brother is the prodigiously popular musician Tei Towa. Shuwa himself spent time in the DJ booth in the period between graduating from Musashino Art University in the late eighties and starting Intentionallies in 1996. He regarded DJing as a sort of "nighttime curatorship" but soon came to realize that his work vaporized with the morning light, and it was out of the impulse to make something last that he founded his firm. Tei's output has shifted from a protean collection of one-off renditions, ranging from furniture to installation to events, toward a more unified set of radical restatements of existing objects. At the same time, he is probably the contemporary designer whose vision is most steeped in Japanese tradition and its classic notions about the interior life immersed within worldly objects.

The Japanese language contains terms for spatial relationships that are functionally syncretic and not wholly translatable into English, and it is these terms that come up again and again in critical appraisals as well as in Tei's own discussion of his work. They are not merely topological generalities but reflections of *Nihonjinron*, a word signifying the body of thought concerned with Japanese cultural specificity. Western art literature contains frequent references to one of these terms, *ma*, which describes the world as a network of discrete events, separated by intervals of non-event, in palpable, dynamic relationships, entangling chronological, linear, and volumetric perceptions of physical dimension. Tei's work introduces into the discussion lesser-known principles like *shakkei*, the idea that one's physical location includes one's own dimensions plus those of one's subjective field of view. He named his earliest venture into product design Atehaca, an archaic coinage that cannot be neatly contained by rationalist language. The word implies that the degree to which one's essential personality is conveyed through appearance and attitude is the degree of elegance and beauty one can achieve.

Above: Hotel Claska (2003) Meguro Ward; opposite page: Hotel Claska lobby, includes restaurant, bar and lounge.

One can look at the striking simplicity of Tei's work without for a moment referring to its philosophical and psychological underpinnings. This risks, however, overlooking the work altogether. This is especially true of the Craft Design Technology line, which includes a full complement of office notions done in collaboration with former Wallpaper* magazine editor Tyler Brule and calls on the services of several of Japan's classic manufacturers in the field. These objects—scissors, notepads, rulers, desk blotters—recall iconic predecessors like the Moleskine notebook and the Eberhard Faber Mongol pencil. They are precise, hand-modeled, and ultimately functional. Their colors and textures progress toward a sensuousness that acts as a salve to the alienating noise and bustle of the typical office. The craftsmanship is such as cannot be found in most items of the type. Tei's objects possess nearly every tactile and visual quality absent from the commodified office supplies found in office "superstore" inventories.

If any single element stands for Tei's critique of contemporary design practice, it is his inclusion of wood in totally unforeseen applications. Among the most popular single items of his career is his Amadana branded headphone set. The bamboo used in these phones constitutes a rebuke of the modern world and in particular Western attitudes toward the use of resources. The user holds the wood when donning the headphones. It is soft and warm to the touch, not entirely pliable, but not rigid. No two phones are the same. The color and texture will change slowly, subtly over time as the user handles them. They are precious, and are not to be thrown away

easily. They are handcrafted objects of desire, and when one wears them in public they are a statement of distinction in a world dominated by blow-molded and extruded plastic.

Similarly, Tei's 2003 take on the notebook PC for Realfleet, produced in a limited edition of 500, was based on a standard Toshiba Dynabook CX1. The designer lamented the fact that, although the computer has become an essential appurtenance, incremental improvements have been defined solely by the supplier's side, and almost always taken the form of higher processing speeds. As Tei puts it, computer manufacturers "disregard what cannot be digitized." His improvements are subtle. There isn't a putty-beige part to be found. The wrist support is leather—flesh in contact with flesh. The key faces are simplified; Japanese characters are removed as they are superfluous anyway (inputting in Japanese requires knowledge of Romanized phoneticization, which at this point in history has become second nature). Anodized metal surfaces are coated, both for stain protection and to add an element of sensual stimulation, what Tei refers to as an "atmospheric texture."

Whether under the aegis of Atehaca or Amadana, Tei's collaborations with manufacturing giant Toshiba represent a methodological departure from other industrial design firms that produce objects for the larger public. The effort is not to maximize sales, nor is it to create objects of extreme rarity for the privileged few. Tei has expressed his definition of success not as appealing to one person in ten, but as causing one person out of ten to feel deeply moved. What is more, he's enjoyed success; because his commitment to affect is a thorny matter for a manufactory like Toshiba, he also designs the business and distribution models along with the product. Just as he doesn't expect his work to export well, he doesn't entreat a behemoth like Toshiba to know his audience.

Prior to the nineteenth century the very idea of fine art in Japan was confined almost entirely to applied and industrial art, the apogee of that discipline being the creation of useful objects that enrich everyday life on a practical level. Tei has described his ambition in producing consumer electronics as being none higher than to create objects with the interior quality found in the best traditional tableware. Neither simplicity nor minimalism is the point. Tei has said that merely simplified objects lack an inner sense of "romance" (the original *iroke* has a more immediate signification). For

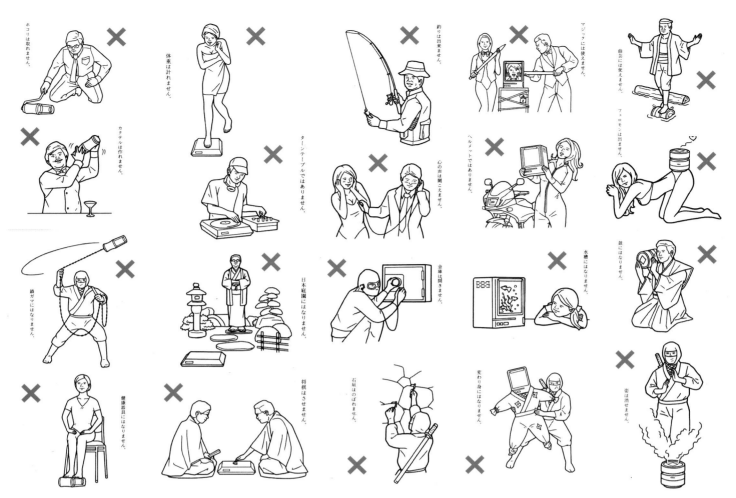

Above: cartoons from the instruction manuals of a variety of Amadana appliances, proscribing their incorrect use. Opposite page. left to right, top row: Citrus Juicer (2006), Earphones (2005); middle row: Electric Oven (2006) & Electric Oven (2006); bottom row: Telephones with Expressive Ringtones, corded and cordless (2005, in walnut, leather, acrylic), Mill & Mixers (2005).

him, a strip of leather upon a block of plexiglass isn't a juxtaposition of forms and colors, it is about the interval in which one runs a finger across the two of them, and feels the subtle quality of friction each separately imparts. All the media he's explored over the course of his career inform his work. So his Amadana telephone has an implanted voice message chip, as do most phones, but he worked with the manufacturer to enhance the audio fidelity, a throwback to his early work in music construction. This, because the impression conveyed to the caller might be the first or the only one, and is therefore of critical consequence.

Of his major contributions to Tokyo's architecture, Hotel Claska stands out. The name is derived from *"Dou kurasuka?,"* meaning "How [best] to live?" In this, one of Tokyo's first boutique hotels, each of the rooms is different. The main floor offers a bar/café/DJ lounge, a bookstore, and a high-end dog salon. The second floor is a variable gallery and performance space. The Meguro area in which the Claska stands is mainly residential and one of the lesser-trod neighborhoods in Tokyo, largely bereft of high-end boutiques and eateries. The building itself was once a dreary business hotel, adding to the legend of its remarkable transformation. Its exterior passes easily for mid-century modernism, though this is solely the effect of architectural augmentations to a plain, thought-free low-rise. The lower floors today host scenes of contemporary Japanese café society. That public transportation passes far from the site means that nighttime revelers must arrive in cars or taxis. This too was part of the intent. The effort made to get there fashions its own reward system. But above the amusements, the hotel rooms are

studies in carefully crafted, wood-enveloped serenity. The top three floors are for long-term temporary residence.

The word quality comes up incessantly in discussions of Tei Shuwa's work. It is the idea of inherent quality—not in the evaluative but the affective sense—that distinguishes both the work and the designer. Few designers attract as impassioned a following. The odd part is that it is a sort of passion that, among design partisans, is usually focused on the outrageous and arrogant, not on one whose presence and products inspire such a sense of quietude.—*David G. Imber/Yoshida Mika*

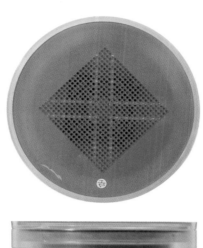

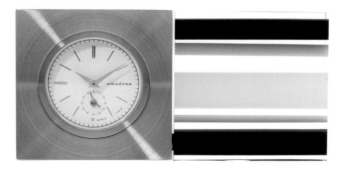

This page, top to bottom, left column: Desktop Humidifier (2004, designed for visibility); middle column: Electronic Handheld Calculator (2004); right column top: Multi-function Remote Control (2003); Super Multi-function Remote Control (2005); right column, middle: IH Cooker (2005, cooks by induction heating); right column, bottom: World Clock (2006, stainless steel, acrylic. Acrylic block pivots to become base.). Opposite page: Amadana Store, Omotesando Hills, Tokyo (2006); following spread: Craft Design Technology Office Products (2005-2007).

MUJI
MUJIRUSHI RYOHIN

Opposite page: Wall-mounted CD player designed by Fukasawa Naoto (2002).

They slunk into consciousness in the wake of the oil shock. Sometime at the end of the 1970s, Americans began to notice that their supermarket shelves were stocked with simple white boxes and cans, labels emblazoned with stark black Helvetica: "Chocolate Pudding Mix," "Conditioning Shampoo," "Beer;" that much and little more. The contents wavered in quality and style, doing their best impression of products consumers grew up with, the taste and texture, color and effectiveness of which had been engraved in memory. Quality also varied from purchase to purchase, and even package to package, because the supermarket would suddenly change its supplier. These were the unselected and the overruns. Canned produce that wasn't good enough for the major label. But they were cheap; the times called for them, and they were accepted.

The scene in Japan could not have been more different. The nation was shimmering in the glow of a flourishing "economic miracle." In the sheer variety of exalted, rarified labels with stratospheric prices, Tokyo's fashionable wards exhibited an embarrassment of riches in every sense.

It was in this atmosphere that Tsutsumi Seiji, chairman of the Saison Corporation, the mammoth diversified conglomerate with interests in retail, food, finance, real estate, and entertainment looked contrarily to the west. There was a potential for the unbranded product concept that, for them, had little to do with cost considerations. Consumers had grown wary of the low and variable quality of store brands sold in Japanese grocery chains. Tsutsumi responded with a hybrid line that focused on the core spirit of the goods, independent of brands or labels. It would offer a value alternative in the manner of America's no-name brand, but setting forth three essential precepts in its development: "selection of materials," "streamlining processes," and "simplification of packaging." Selection of materials meant that standards of quality would be internally consistent, and consistent with the general Japanese public's understanding of what was not merely acceptable, but fundamentally satisfying. In practical terms, streamlining processes was simply the elimination of a number of purely cosmetic steps in the manufacturing process because a consistent and acceptable low-end standard for materials was ensured. Simplification of packaging is the most interesting precept in the establishment of a "no-brand brand." For one thing, minimal packaging allowed the company to avow a philosophy of environmental friendliness. Like American no-brand packages, these bore only the barest description of the

product and a price. But the uniformity and transparency of the packaging allowed the consumer to focus on the quality of the product inside, immediately boosting confidence in the purchase. They called their brand Mujirushi Ryohin, a suitably basic name meaning "unbranded quality goods," MUJI for the overseas market.

In addition to the three precepts, MUJI addressed another quintessentially Japanese preoccupation. Though the products would carry no designer identification, that would not preclude their having design principles applied to them. Unlike their American counterparts, MUJI products would have a characteristic look and feel that would extend to everything that bore the name. Their style would transcend trends and class signifiers rather than flirting with or imitating them. It would aim directly for an expression of utter utility, leavened with an air of *yasashisa*, gentleness—in color and cut, conveying a non-aggressive urbanity and native intelligence. What consumers did not know was that over time MUJI had quietly begun commissioning some of the best minds in contemporary design to ensure that look and feel, and to apply the refinements necessary to achieve it. Although never admitted, it is conventionally believed that when consumers buy MUJI products they are buying the work of people like Enzo Mari, Jasper Morrison, Konstantin Grcic, and Fukasawa Naoto. (In recent years the contributions of these designers have been made explicit by the designers themselves.) The designers understood that their mandate was not to interpret the MUJI concept according to their sensibility, but to apply their talent and ingenuity in the creation of products that conformed to the platonic MUJI ideal.

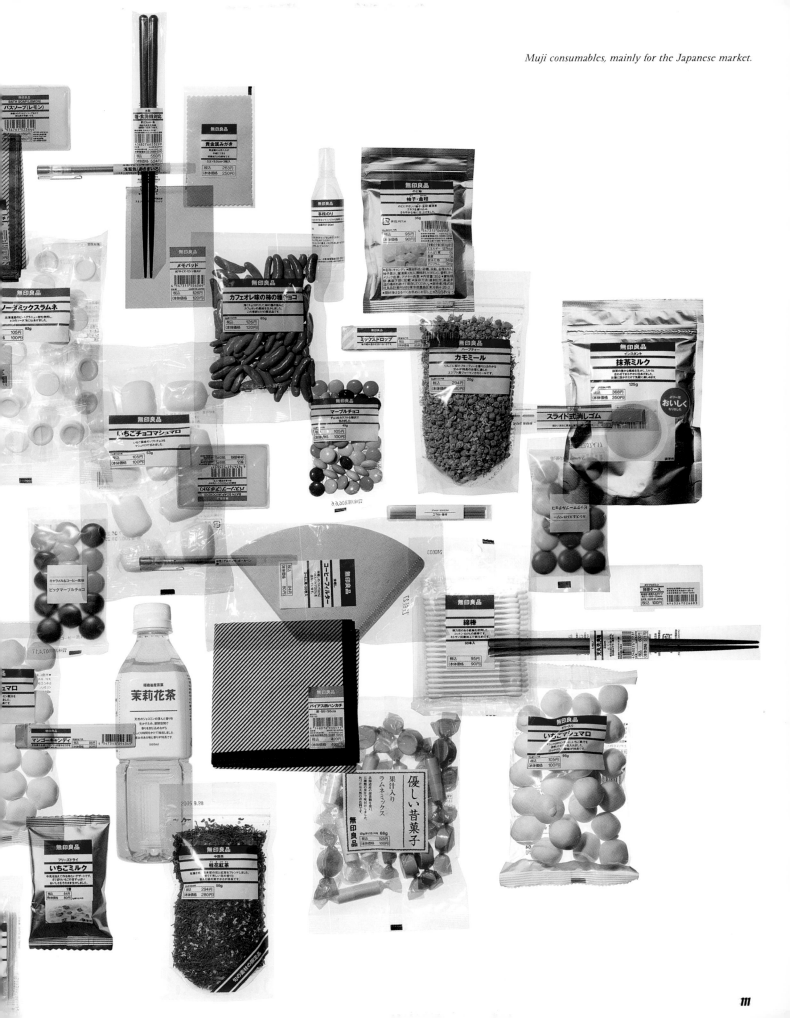

Above: childrenswear, from Fall/Winter 2005-06; opposite page and following spread: interior view of prefabricated Muji house, 2006.

MUJI's initial 1980 line included a mere nine household products and thirty-one foods. Basic clothing, mostly underwear, was added the next year. By the start of the 21st century, virtually every extant consumable had a MUJI version. Today one could literally live entirely in a MUJI world, from food, to appliances, to clothing, and ultimately to one's very dwelling. Indeed, there is a MUJI "no-brand" house, as well as three campgrounds. MUJI stores, which began as a Seiyu subsidiary brand, were soon standing free, and replicating in every city in Japan under the stewardship of holding company Ryohin Keikaku. From there it was on to London and other U.K. cities, and a host of capitals across Europe and Asia, with a New York flagship opening in 2007.

One of the brand's cherished products is illustrative of its approach to every item in its ever growing, ever changing catalogue: dried shiitake mushroom bits. In a discount store, picking up a package of broken and partial shiitake would remind one that they are buying an inferior product. The assumed "compromised" quality of the contents would be hidden, their state not remarked upon. When MUJI packaged broken mushrooms (one of its 31 original food items) it put them in a crystal clear packet with a simple, one-line assertion of their quality provenance. The message rang loud and clear to the consumer: "These mushroom parts are every bit as good and tasty as the wholes they broke off from. They're cheaper than whole shiitake, but we're declaring the reason for that up front, so you can confidently purchase them, understanding the means by which you've benefited from our efficiency."

The key to MUJI's success is the feeling that you're not buying cheap, but buying smart. With its restrained color palette, consistent quality, attention to detail, simplified design and packaging, and "no-waste" profile, there's no question that MUJI today is perceived as a brand in itself. But by remaining obstinately true to its original principles, its products still serve as a balm in an over-branded world. —*David G. Imber/Yoshida Mika*

FLOWER ROBOTICS

Opposite page: Posy, the flower girl robot.

Matsui Tatsuya set himself upon a short, straight path toward a life in design at a tender age. In the late seventies, when he was about ten, his parents decided to renovate their home. The carpenter, typically expecting either a blank look or hyperbolic fantasy, asked the boy what he wanted his bedroom to look like. He ran off, pored over magazines and measured corners, and the next day gave the carpenter specific plans, measurements, and furnishing selections, down to the hardware. So impressed was the carpenter that he made the realization of the boy's design a mission, and so impressed was Matsui at getting precisely what he'd pictured that he knew at that moment what would be his life's calling.

How that path carried Matsui to become Japan's foremost designer of robots is far more complex, and provides insight into both the designer's personality and a central feature of the Japanese national character. Like most Japanese children in the 60s and 70s, Matsui grew up surrounded by the influence of the so-called "God of Manga," beloved artist Tezuka Osamu. Tezuka established the look that would come to be associated with most all later comics and anime: the physical features of the characters, their surroundings, and the framing and elisions that form the narrative structure. He also created a lexicon of onomatopoeic phrases denoting actions that has since become part of the regular vocabulary, as well as four content standards that he believed artists had a responsibility to articulate: Reverence for the environment, valuing the preciousness of life, harmony among individuals and with nature, and the depiction of progress and technology as a positive expression of the human capacity for reason.

One of Tezuka's most cherished creations is Tetsuwan Atomu ("Mighty Atom," aka "Astro Boy"). It's a story—suffused with equal parts heroism and melancholy—of a scientist who, anguished over his son's death, vows to create a new boy from the "power of the atom." The robot he creates resembles a boy, but possesses superhuman powers and skills. He pledges to use his powers to help and protect humanity, but privately he suffers because the treasure of true humanity can never be his. Compare this tale to the Western depiction of another animated, manufactured, humanoid entity that acquires self-awareness, the "monster" of Mary Shelley's "Frankenstein," who is depicted as an object of fear and revulsion, an unpredictable harbinger of chaos and destruction. That malignant image of technology turning against its creator persists today in stories of communities that, though they desire greater protection, reject the use of the most cost- and otherwise effective technologies, such as robotic surveillance cameras and biometric identification programs, as inherently malevolent incursions upon privacy and civil liberty.

This social conundrum—the hope and fear engendered by technology—is a subject that the stylish, surface-cool Matsui waxes uncharacteristically emotional about. Advancing Tezuka's dicta, particularly the fourth, it is his belief that designers must take responsibility for impressing on society the notion that our technology can only reflect the motives we design into it, making conscientious design more than simply a search for greater efficiency and more harmonious forms. It is also his belief that Japan, specifically contemporary urban Japanese culture, is in a unique position to usher the world toward this understanding. And he believes this movement is critical, because we are now on the verge of creating an array of automated, data-gathering entities that can assist us in every aspect of our lives, physically and otherwise. All that remains is for society to come to intellectual and emotional terms with these automated assistants.

Posy, the flower girl, is one facet of Matsui's response. Posy is the size of a small child. Matsui asserts that when people bend at the waist to speak to a child there's a reflexive change in facial expression that conveys a passive smile from below. The individual's body, he believes, is awash in benign feelings as a result of feedback from muscle memory. Posy is a robot, but unlike the inhumanoid robots that build cars and clean floors, her only job is to bring flowers, which she does with an unerring grace and absence of inessential movement that can only be achieved by employing the highest level of mechanical and program engineering. Call Posy an ambassador from the future if you will (Matsui has undertaken a serious effort to make Posy a UNICEF ambassador).

Matsui's own background is straightforward enough. Born 1969, he attended Nihon Daigaku Geijutsugakubu, a liberal arts college with conservatory leanings that boasts celebrated graduates like novelist Yoshimoto Banana and dramatist Kudo Kankuro. It was while working for architect Tange Kenzo that he became interested in applying fundamental structural principles in architecture to movement. He needed to understand the mechanisms that control movement, and so he pursued a graduate degree in computer systems interface design at the École Nationale Supérieure de Création Industrielle in Paris, and subsequently began working for IBM's Lotus division there. He returned to Tokyo in 1997 to spend three years studying robotics alongside engineers and scientists at the Kitano Symbiotic Systems Project. In 2001 he started Flower Robotics, a studio where each day one member cooks for all the others, because Matsui believes that as busy designers defect from the travails of everyday life, their capacity to design for human needs is diminished.

Left to right: Posy in All Nippon Airways (ANA) "Visit Japan" campaign (2004).

The obsession with flowers comes from an occasion in New York, where he witnessed Steve Jobs introducing a new OS with typical bombast, against a bank of dozens of black monitors that suddenly flickered on. It was an epiphanic moment wherein he recognized that the bloom of creation could be effected digitally. Flowers and monitors and little android girls all elicit the same gasp of awe when they burst "alive."

Though fashion houses like Mori Hanae and Louis Vuitton have used the graceful, shapely Flower Robotics girls to model apparel, it is with his crowning creation, Palette, that Matsui and Flower Robotics hope to change the human-machine dynamic forever. Palette's agenda is rather more ambitious than her little sister Posy's. She's a fashion model, a marketing pro and a security guard, but what she really wants to do is change the entire nature of the relationship between humans and machines, to enable us to live with the their burgeoning intelligence. Palette's movements use motion-capture technology to match those of top fashion models, and like a live model, she plays to the crowd. Approach her, and she senses your presence. Her posture will change with your position, and while she's looking at you, her recognition programming will be gathering data about you—your sex and age— and about the movement of shoppers in the background, and transmitting it to the company for demographic and marketing analyses. She can also be programmed to prevent you from walking away with unpaid merchandise, but with far more charm and allure than your typical bulldog at the door. She doesn't have a face because Matsui, ever-aware of the human reaction to humanoid presences, believes that would be a cloying distraction from the goods. Also, without a face there's little possibility of identification, and absent that, a low risk of alienation.

Matsui's attitude toward his robots' putative humanity was first explored with Pino, this time a little boy who Matsui claims, without irony, is ancestrally linked to Pinocchio. Of course the largest part of Flower Robotics' research is devoted to bringing humanity into an environment where assistance by machines is literally second nature, and of course this pursuit is aided by increasing the anthropomorphic qualities of robots. But as opposed to the traditional approach of making the image of the robot stronger, bigger, more enduring, Matsui seeks to imbue his humanoid robots with human-like vulnerabilities. Part of the way we come to accept our connection with others is by recognizing common human frailties. We recall that in the fable of Pinocchio, the puppet-boy was never quite completed; he was (mirroring our condition, and like that of Tetsuwan Atomu) in constant pursuit of his own humanity. Accordingly Pino's programming software and specifications were made open-source, so that they could be distributed free. Anyone can build a new Pino, who has the physical dimensions of a child at age one or two, just learning to walk, and shares a human child's unsteadiness of gait. Matsui left it to the global village to complete Pino's coming into being, an aspect of the constant dialogue with society that surrounds his mission. He saw a lifetime dream come true when in 2001 Pino became the first robot exhibited at New York's Museum of Modern Art, though he was shocked and dismayed to see the robot in a glass vitrine, which to him looked exactly the same as a casket. To Matsui Tatsuya a robot is only meaningful when interacting with humans; it only lives through that relationship.

When he shows his robots in the West he notes that he's always asked when robots will be capable of fighting wars. But he's determined never to design a robot for that purpose, and says that any robot he designs would be a liability in combat. He's also scrupulously avoided the show-robot craze exemplified by those developed by Sony and Honda. He compares those efforts to supermarket chocolate, and his own shop to the sort that's been making hand-made candies in Kyoto for centuries. It's a low-yield enterprise, but he's not without larger ambitions. In 2002, on the centennial of the Wright brothers' first flight, the new southern Japanese airline StarFlyer announced that Matsui would be developing its entire marketing scheme from the ground up, working with SGI, the company Matsui has collaborated with in his robot fabrications. Bucking conventional wisdom, he made the planes a deep solid black, in order to evoke an image of the limitless universe. He had fabricators study traditional *urushi* lacquer ware, the finishes on grand pianos, the style of original Chanel interiors in Paris. He designed the uniforms and the waiting rooms. He made all the seats leather to suggest a feeling related to what in Japanese is called "skinship" for travelers in every class, and he made the seats into "service units," with various sorts of plug-in functions that he envisions as "mothering" the passenger in a very literal evocation of umbilici.

Matsui wants to demolish the *otaku* image associated with robot development. In his research he draws upon the assistance of dancers, fashion designers, musicians, and creators from other disciplines, and he frequently portrays himself as a conductor more than a designer or engineer. His ultimate dream, one that he hopes to realize by 2030, is to put Posy on the stage of the Paris opera, dancing alongside a human ballerina. Part of what draws us to classical ballet is the dancer's shedding everything that is weak, inefficient, unbalanced, subject to gravity, in order to be more than human. That level of flawlessness, Matsui says, is where robots begin, and it is his aim to move them in the other direction, toward what will put them more in touch with our experience. To see these parallel aspirations embodied in dual interacting figures, one human, the other human-made, is Matsui Tatsuya's halcyon vision of the future.—*David G. Imber/Yoshida Mika*

Statement by the designer, written expressly for this volume. Translated by Yoshida and Imber.

What I See Beyond Design

What robot design hopes to achieve is an artificial intelligence that appears as the affect of Modernism in an information society.

The era of industrialization propelled the evolution of modern architecture tremendously. As the invention of the automobile necessitated the development of precise, solid structures, the invention of the Internet has had a similar effect on the meta-conscious level. Design has always been intertwined with society, economy, technology, industry, and the environment, and has in turn reified the Zeitgeist by imposing structures and systems back onto society, using the means of philosophy and aesthetics.

From early industrial society's use of iron, glass, and concrete, via an era of mass production employing highly advanced ceramic technology, modernists of the contemporary period are formulating concrete relationships with the universe of information. Robot design in the 21st century is offering an unprecedented view of the possible to an information society that has propagated around it, due to the fact that it is a new principal discipline –one demanding extensive knowledge of traditional architecture, industrial design, and information architecture.

Artificial Intelligence, which has begun to appear in commercial application, encompasses various approaches and methodologies, but overall it is simply a means of deriving an optimal solution from available experience data and feeding it back to the user: An Internet search engine culls words from a network and displays them in an organized way. Amidst the complexity of a city, a car navigation system offers precise directions to take us to our destination. In urban life, recognition and distinguishing data affect critical differences in judgement and performance.

The next generation autonomic robot is a complete departure from that which came before, forming its own judgements in interactions with us. "Human" robots, cleaning robots, rescue robots, industrial robots and the like, all have systems that allow them to make decisions based upon internal experience data. Eventually these systems will migrate to cars, cell phones, televisions, etc., and our own consciousness will cohabit with them in a way that will govern this robotic intelligence. The way this dynamic is instantiated in design will manifest its effects on society and industry, and may lead the way toward the next phase of the information society.

The systems designers construct will impact society enormously, and that is why I believe that the contemporary trend is toward a new realization of the principles of Modernism, through putting forward methodologies for design in the robot era.

I'd like to design new values within this framework of a robotic society. I believe it's the work of a designer to create structures that put people in contact with a more enriching sensitivity, in order to better experience the joy inherent in the wonder of living in this moment.

A robot that captures the present Zeitgeist should be one that possesses a universal, sensitive beauty, like so many of the great works in history. Today I'm envisioning my robot, walking around on its own, in the Villa Savoye.

This page: StarFlyer, Inc. aircraft (Airbus A320-200).In addition to the aircraft, Matsui designed uniforms, environments, tickets, and all amenities. Views of StarFlyer Lounge at New Kitakyushu Airport, Kitakyushu. Opposite page: P-Noir, the interactive dance robot.

YOSHIOKA TOKUJIN

The egotism of creative individuals is the stuff of legend and epic literature, but it's impossible to lay a finger on Yoshioka Tokujin in that regard. One cannot touch a cloud, which is the object Mr. Yoshioka has said he best identifies with. Like a great cloud, Yoshioka Tokujin's influence on the contemporary Japanese design scene crowds the firmament, and appears massive in the vista. But like the physicality his work comprises, clouds are evanescent and largely insubstantial.

He has said that he'd like the next step in his creative evolution to be toward "pure," which is to say non-functional, art. To Japanese critics, even his most functional objects and interiors primarily meet that description already, although the designer is reasonably skeptical that this quality translates well to Western thinking.

Vestiges of that creative evolution emerge clearly in the present work, though Yoshioka has traveled lightly along the path, bringing only that which is necessary to continue to propel him forward. Born in Saga in 1967, he graduated from Kuwasawa Design School in 1987 and immediately made his way to the studio of Kuramata Shiro, whom he celebrates as his first mentor. Kuramata, who died in 1991, was a giant of postwar Japanese design whose work appears in every major museum collection and whose influence transcended cultural and artistic boundaries, extending beyond a generation of younger Japanese designers to reach, for example, a budding English architect named John Pawson. The minimalist architect observed the master in his studio for months before setting out on his own career and corresponded with him until his death. Kuramata's designs tinkered with notions of mass and substance through the use of materials like clear acrylic and objects that appear willowy but strategically support their own weight. Yoshioka takes some of these concerns from Kuramata, as well as a willingness to turn away from traditional Japanese materials and embrace all manner of new and unaccustomed technologies.

From his second mentor he takes an experimental methodology. Kuramata had formed a working relationship with fashion designer Miyake Issey that Yoshioka solidified, signing on as his designer of interiors and accessories in 1988. He has described the design and development of Miyake's "Making Things," an interactive environment that, from 1998 to 2000 served to illuminate the designer's methods and materials in an interactive way for audiences in Paris, New York, and Tokyo, as the most satisfying working experience of his life. Once again, the materiality of Yoshioka's later work was informed by observation of a master's methods, in particular, Miyake's use of folded, pleated fabrics to combine structure and surface in a single gesture. Years later Yoshioka proved an apt pupil with his TO (tee-oh) watch for the Issey Miyake brand. Every discrete element associated with watch crafting has been eradicated to leave a timekeeping device that appears to have been carved from a single disk of metal—a highly precise machine that appears more parsimonious in its structural details than a sundial.

The Yoshioka Design Office set out taking on the types of interior projects for which the designer had been superbly seasoned, along the way garnering accolades and awards, including the Award of Excellence from the I.D.

Above: Yoshioka Tokujin; opposite page: 2001 Robot Meme installation for the International Robot Design Association, National Museum of Emerging Science and Innovation, Tokyo.

appear in museum collections throughout the world, including the Museum of Modern Art in New York, Centre Pompidou in Paris, the Vitra Design Museum in Berlin and the Victoria & Albert Museum in London.

Ever the light traveler, the weight of a well-burnished reputation has failed to hold Yoshioka to a narrow set of strategies and materials. Through his installations over the years, no matter the sponsor, Yoshioka has shown a facility for engaging spectators through movement. In some cases it is the movement of surfaces to suggest anecdotal passage through an abstract landscape. In the 2004 presentation for Peugeot's new model 307CC convertible, held at the Spiral Garden in Omotesando, a 49-meter undulating black resin scrim crossed the space, studded with 100,000 LEDs in red, white, and blue. The challenge was to evoke freedom, openness, and most of all speed using an economy of means. Yoshioka has repeatedly emphasized that there is no substitute for the visceral experience of actually moving within his constructed environments, and therefore it is virtually impossible to describe the spectators' visual interplay with the LED projections. Using color, movement, and computer generated imagery, such as the Peugeot logo, cityscapes, open skies, and fields, Yoshioka altered spectators'

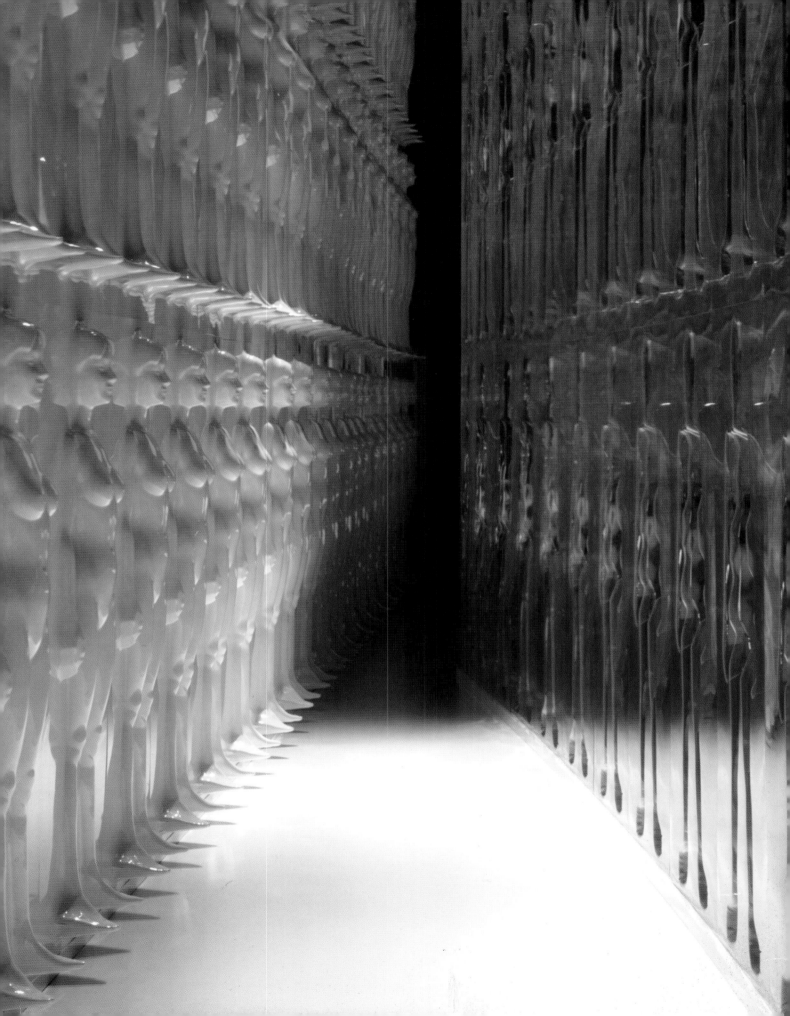

Opposite page: Honey-Pop Chair, detail (2001). Above, left to right: "constructing" the Honey-Pop Chair

way that could never be achieved in a static showroom environment.

In other cases the design actually instigates movement through a path. This was the case with the 2001 Robot Meme installation on behalf of the International Robot Design Association, held at the National Museum of Emerging Science and Innovation in Tokyo. Humanoid robots are a significant area of inquiry in Japan, where the general public has shown itself highly receptive. Yoshioka's own take on them is that while they represent benign "visitors from the future," society must accept that it is currently giving birth to robotic infants, and that in their eventual movement toward perfection they will have, if not the appearance, then the complexity of the human form, which he regards as an ultimate design package. He thus erected high, meandering walls formed of 700 perfectly proportioned human bodies in clear, blown polycarbonate. The aim was to propagate the meme of humanoid creation, again using immersion, but here through a static agglomeration of forms. The exhibition hosted over 53,000 visitors during its two-month run.

The design that came to be most emblematic of Yoshioka's conceptual framework, at least until his most recent work in hand-wrought fiber optics, is the Honey-Pop chair, on display in MoMA's permanent design collection. Yoshioka sums up the least evident aspect of his design methodology, saying that he never envisions the final form, but focuses only on the material and its potential to let form emerge naturally. Using this approach he began toying with the paper packaging material found in a box of chocolates. Its utility derives from being able to hold a rigid shape by means of pressure, achieved by adhering multiple layers or leaves at various points across the surface. Pulling the outer surfaces apart reveals a honeycomb configuration, which, when taut, is considerably stronger than the weight of the leaves would suggest. Yoshioka had samples of this material manufactured to human scale, incorporating 120 layers of paper. The dye-cut chair arrives flat, looking like a large, oddly shaped drawing pad. As the outer layers are spread, the shape of a chair takes form. But this is where the functional object assumes a philosophical dimension. The accordion-like paper form remains the suggestion of a chair until the first time a person sits in it. At that moment the chair changes from a primitively mass-produced commodity object to the ultimate in personalized design.

In fact it is fair to say that the pervasive thesis of Yoshioka Tokujin's work is that the aim of design is to proceed from the first point of human contact. This is shown vividly in his Media Skin phone, which houses a panoply of communication devices within the most minimal, yet functional packaging possible. Thus it has a texture complementary to human flesh, is extremely thin, and hides all but the function being utilized at any given moment. It is meant to be the thinnest membrane between technological hardware and human "wetware," literally "media" contained by nothing more than a "skin."

As his career has progressed, Yoshioka Tokujin has systematically shed complexity in design production in favor of deploying the fewest possible elements to the greatest effect. His most recent environments point toward a state where volume and substance are instantiated by the refraction of light alone.

Despite this disavowal of material substance, Yoshioka has done something that cannot go unmentioned in discussing his production output. It is a statement unlike any other he has made, and indeed seems to have issued from a unique, rather non-Japanese perspective. For most contemporary Japanese, tearing down and building anew is the norm. For his own studio Yoshioka dismantled an old rice storehouse and had it transported, piece by piece, to Tokyo's most fashionable Daikanyama district, where he reconstructed it and uses it as his base of operation to this day. This act flouts conventional thinking on multiple levels. Old structures of a sacred cast are often rigorously preserved in Japan, but even an antique rice storehouse is considered only as sacred as a grocery store shopping bag. Whether it was an overt display of humility, or an act of defiance against fashion and modernity, this single act of reverence for the most modest of materials, and for that which is fundamentally Japanese, has ended up only adding to the sheen of Yoshioka Tokujin's creative aura. —*David G. Imber/Yoshida Mika*

KATAYAMA MASAMICHI
WONDERWALL

Opposite page and following spread: Bapexclusive (1999, 2006), Minami-Aoyama, Minato Ward.

Perched up a steep hill from Ebisu Station, the offices of Katayama Masamichi's Wonderwall sheds precious insight into a design philosophy that "effectively negotiates between commerce and play."[1] Ever a hive of activity, the common and private zones of his atelier are strewn with the memorabilia of an *otaku*—whose tastes have matured a great deal—but is still an unabashed and obsessive collector. Rare Kubrick and Bearbrick toys by MediCom, Emeco aluminum Navy Chairs, a radioactive pink piggybank by Areaware, a vintage Brionvega TV, and plush Warhola on an Eames chaise vie for attention with shelves groaning with recent, large-format architectural tomes, their variegated spines forming an adaptive, mnemonic wall. Books and toys are the material sources of Katayama's own vocational philosophy— "I work 24 hours a day, in other words, I play 24 hours a day"—and the knowledge and pleasure he clearly derives from them are at the core of his designs.

Born in Okayama prefecture and the veteran of at least one partnership before incorporating Wonderwall in 2000, the designer's present global rep as a purveyor of Tokyo cool, recently bolstered by the sleek New York flagship for the apparel label Uniqlo, was decisively established by his work for Nigo and *A Bathing Ape®. Dating back to 1998, their partnership began with a Bape Busy Work Shop in one of the basements of Ura-Harajuku, but has since migrated to over a dozen cities in Japan, as well as outposts in London, New York, Taipei, Los Angeles and a mini department store for all things Bape in Hong Kong. Typified by the icy, Miesian *gestalt* of the three-story Bapy (now APEE) Aoyama boutique from 2002, Katayama's modernism, for all its apparent levity, is designed and programmed with an exacting rigor and technical ability. The home of Bapy, Nigo's "Busy Working Lady" line, the spare retail program of the store reifies the bathing metaphor as it describes a glass dollhouse where every room is a bathroom, a comic effect amplified by having the artifacts of this most intimate of spaces revealed to the street below. Other projects closely associated with Nigo, such as the Pharrell William's Billionaire Boys Club (BBC) Ice Cream Store in Harajuku (2006), and the OriginalFake store in Aoyama (2006) for the Brooklyn-based artist KAWS supply Katayama's *ouvre* with more mischief. Diluting the irony of the sophisticated joke in the Bapy/APEE store nearby, the OriginalFake store even engages in some literal toilet humor in the iconography of the white, custom relief tiles lining the walls of the shop—to say nothing of the oversized, action-figure whose vivisected bulk ghoulishly presides over the small shop.

Pranks aside, Katayama is emphatic about the stand-alone projects he's designed outside of the Planet of the Apes. These "side projects" do in fact constitute the overwhelming majority of his freestanding buildings and interiors, and while this parallel portfolio is still dominated by retail, it nonetheless substantiates a much larger scope of typologies. The Katayama "look" and it attendant conceits have matured particularly in the last five years, and is now recognizable well beyond a tight circle of fashionistas and design journalists. The Aoyama offices for Wonderwall subcontractor D. Brain Co., Ltd., (2005)—the manufacturers of the industrial-grade shoe conveyors in Bape stores—give proof of a studied mid-century cool, unified by

rich brown floors and paneling. Chunky wood again becomes a major plot element in the 100% Chocolate Café (2004) in Kyobashi for the confectionery giant Meiji, and this time it assumes the form of a coffered ceiling that looks awfully like a huge suspended slab of dark chocolate.

Alluded to in the stores for Bape, the application of domestic metaphors in non-residential interiors is one of Wonderwall's organizing principles. In ample evidence at Inhabitant Aoyama (2004), the Q Ebisu-Nishi select shop in Daikanyama (2003) and the Pinceau boutique in Omotesando Hills (2006), the treatment gets royally pimped-out in the boutiques for Iwaya Toshikazu's baroque fashion label Dresscamp, and the Aoyama home of the Harajuku label Hysteric Glamour (2006) next door. A rock star decadence suffuses the two-story shop for Hysteric designer Kitamura Nobuhiko, and the ostentatious fragments of an imaginary celebrity's life are on display, replete with a VIP room plastered with original Bettie Page photos, and a black, super-sized Chesterfield sofa on the second level.

Wonderwall's latest—and largest—retail contribution to date is not in Tokyo but in New York. A collaborative effort with the creative director Sato Kashiwa (formerly of the vaunted Hakuhodo ad agency), the new Broadway superstore comports itself like a SoHo native as it flashes a knowing Aoyama pedigree. Hidden behind a white mask of vernacular cast-iron and twice the size of Uniqlo's Ginza flagship by Klein Dytham (2005), the retailing footprint of the 3,344 m² shop is distributed over three ample floors. Spatially and conceptually, it shares none of the anonymous appeal of Uniqlo's other permanent digs in suburban Japan (or indeed in New Jersey). Deployed with Katayama's palette of clear glass, stainless steel, blond wood, and matte white, and demonstrating his requisite mania for reflective surfaces and misdirection, the design is linked explicitly to local typologies on both the exterior and interior. Details like ersatz pressed-tin ceiling panels and the conservation of ornamented steel columns frame the new space, without detracting from a client mandate to create an "ultra-rational" feel. Gestural touches include an existing brick

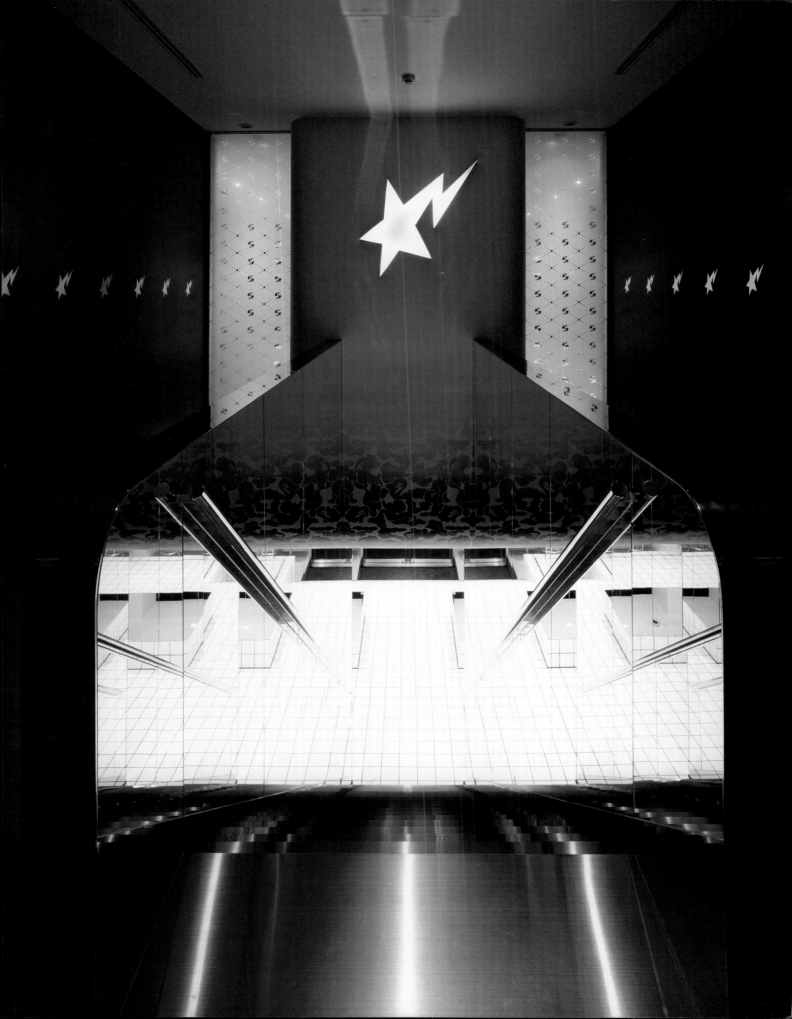

Above and opposite page: Hysteric Glamour Aoyama (2006), Minami-Aoyama, Minato Ward.

wall encased in glass, and a double-floor-height grand staircase to the back of the store—from the landing of which the chef Morimoto Masaharu filleted a massive slab of tuna on opening night. These scenographic touches owe less to the overt theatricality of Prada's subterranean wave on Prince Street by OMA (2001) or the titanium swirls of Miyake Issey Tribeca by Gordon Kipping and Frank O. Gehry (2002) but to the subtler wiles of the old Helmut Lang on Greene Street by Richard Gluckman (1997), and Mori Toshiko's Pleats Please for Miyake Issey (1998).

And carpetbagging all the way from Tokyo is never *ever* shunned in Manhattan. The store is, after all, a stone's throw away from Katayama's own Bape Busy Work Shop in New York (2005), the venerable Yamamoto Yohji flagship on Grand Street, and shares spiritual proximity to the long-gone Comme des Garçons boutiques on Wooster Street and West Broadway—two shops that left indelible marks on the neighborhood's retailing profile. The profligacy of Tokyo fashion in New York, the enduring appeal of its standard-bearers, and the willingness of consumers to embrace its latest exports attest a local affection for Japan's prodigious gifts that is as deep as it is wide. Ever invested in the commodities of surprise and delight, the store and the culture that spawned it embody the twinned sensibilities of Katayama's beloved Tokyo and New York—megalopolises, that like the designer, are much too invested in the dynamism of the new to ever rest on past glories.—*Ian Luna*

Following spread, clockwise from top left: D. Office, Aoyama, Minato Ward (2005); Not Found appointment-only boutique, Azabu-Juban, Minato Ward (2007); 100%Chocolate Cafe, Kyobashi, Chuo Ward (2004); D. Office, Aoyama, Minato Ward (2005). Pages 138-139: KAWS/OriginalFake shop, Aoyama, Minato Ward (2006).

Notes

[1] Luna, Ian. *Retail: Architecture and Shopping.* New York: Rizzoli, 2005, p. 49-50.

FASHION IN POSTMODERN TIMES
ESSAY BY KAWAMURA YUNIYA

Opposite page: campaign image from United Bamboo's Spring/Summer 2007 collection.

There are signs of cultural turmoil everywhere. The broad social and cultural shifts precipitated by the transition from modernity to postmodernity have not only transformed western societies but also non-western societies. The concept of the "postmodern" captures at least certain aspects of this change. Postmodernity is difficult to characterize because of its preoccupation with ambiguity and contradiction. It has no fixed meanings or has countless meanings that are unstable, contradictory and flexible, but the social content of the postmodernist work is not that of opposition to the dominant culture.

In the spheres of fashion, design and art, we can point to the emergence of postmodern styles, that is the collapse of hierarchical distinction between high art/culture and popular art/culture, an eclectic mixing of aesthetic codes, a combination of past traditions and novelty, hedonistic attitudes instead of moral certainties. While modernity presumes the existence of clear distinctions between different types and genres of aesthetic endeavors, postmodernity no longer recognizes them as legitimate. Postmodernity does not view high culture as aesthetically superior to popular culture and/or dominant culture. Fashion emphasizes images and incessant change, and this constitutes the epitome of a postmodernist cultural form.

Therefore, we are making a postmodern turn, and one of the major themes of this postmodern turn is the de-centering of the subject and the social world. Postmodernity suggests multiple minds, subjects and knowledge reflecting different social locations and histories. A process of de-centering is evident in every social structure. There is no center, no unifying ground of order, coherence and purpose. For much of the 19th and 20th ashion information used to originate from one source, Paris. Consumers throughout the world who were fashion conscious emulated the French style, which epitomized and legitimated the most aesthetic appearance. Today's postmodern consumers look elsewhere for fashion, or they create their own styles and become designers themselves. At the same time, they redefine what fashion is.

These transitions are the consequences of social, political and cultural changes that have altered the relationships between different social groups as well as categories.

Consumption vs Production

An object is manufactured before it is purchased, and we therefore have a tendency to see consumption activities as the result of or as a process that is secondary to the development of manufacturing and other forms of production. However, in postmodern culture, the boundary between consumption and production is starting to collapse. As Howard Becker in his *Art Worlds* explains, there is no distinction between production and consumption in art worlds.[1] The audiences are undistinguished from the artists. Everyone participates in producing and distributing his/her work. Becker discusses the socially constructed nature of art, and how it is valued. He demystifies art. Becker starts with the assumption that, as in all social fields, it is in the regularized interactions among creators and their supporting personnel that social meanings arise. All become participants in the creative process, and production and reception merge.

The same phenomenon is found in fashion. Punk fashion exemplifies the disappearance of the boundary between production and consumption.

It first manifested itself among groups of students and the unemployed in London in the mid-1970s. Punk culture developed as a reaction to the depressed economy and the general pessimism of youth. It was an anarchic, nihilistic style which was deliberately and consciously menacing. Punk clothes were often hand-made or bought from secondhand thrift shops, and worn dirty or torn. The punks violated the conventions and norms that society forced upon people, and their challenging message attracted a large audience. It gave a sense of belonging to those who were in search of an identity. More recently, it is the Japanese teenagers wandering around the fashionable districts in Tokyo, such as Harajuku and Shibuya, who are the tastemakers and the producers of fashion. They are fashion fanatics but also conscious innovators.

In postmodern culture, consumption is conceptualized as a form of role playing, as consumers seek to project conceptions of identity that are continually evolving. Social class is less evident and important in one's self-image and identity in contemporary society than before. Style differentiation no longer distinguishes social classes because there is a great deal of interclass and intra-class mobility. Social identity that used to be based on the economic and political spheres is now based on something else. Diana Crane, in *Fashion and Social Agenda*, remarks that the consumption of cultural goods, such as fashionable clothing, performs an increasingly important role in the construction of personal identity while the satisfaction of material needs and the emulation of superior classes are secondary. One's style of dress conveys initial, and continuing, impression-making images. The variety of lifestyles available in contemporary society liberates the individual from tradition and enables him/her to make choices that create a meaningful self-identity. Crane writes:

Clothing itself is less important than the frames that are used to sell it, which can be used in turn to sell licensed products. Consumers are no longer perceived as "cultural dopes" or "fashion victims" who imitate fashion leaders but as people selecting styles on the basis of their perceptions of their own identities and lifestyles. Fashion is presented as a choice rather than a mandate. The consumer is expected to "construct" an individualized appearance from a variety of options. An amalgam of materials drawn from many different sources, clothing styles have different meanings for different social groups.[2]

It becomes easier to construct an identity by belonging to a subculture that shows a way of handling the experience of ambiguity and contradictions and the questions of identity. Each subculture provides its members with style, an imaginary coherence, a solid identity which coalesces around certain selected clothes which in turn stand for a new set of values, norms, beliefs and attitudes.

As consumers become increasingly fashionable and creative in postmodern societies, they themselves become the producers. Fashion had been historically defined as dressing up, but the concept of dressing down began to emerge as class boundaries became less rigid and more flexible. Street fashion first began as anti-fashion, but it was later acknowledged as fashion. The contemporary Japanese designers in this book are the best examples in understanding fashion in postmodern times when categories and classifications no longer exist or have become increasingly blurry and are less significant.

Japanese Designers in Postmodern Times

Directly or indirectly, many designers had been influenced by Kawakubo Rei of Comme des Garçons. When Kawakubo joined Miyake Issey in Paris in 1981 along with Yamamoto Yohji, they set the stage for many other postmodern designers to follow their footsteps. Kawakubo, Miyake and Yamamoto reinterpreted Western sartorial conventions by suggesting different ways of wearing clothes; there can be two neck holes instead of one, or three sleeves instead of two and leave it up to a wearer to decide which hole or sleeve she wants to wear. They also redefined the nature of Western clothing itself and suggested what clothes can look like. Western female clothes had always been fitted to expose the contours of the body, but the Japanese deconstructionists introduced loose-fitting clothes, such as jackets with no traditional construction; their clothes often have a straight, simple shape, and their large coats with oversized proportions can be worn by both men and women. Their designs were known for being gender-neutral or unisex.[3] After these three Japanese designers, the younger Japanese designers flocked to Paris one after another, and many of them could be traced back, personally or professionally, to this pioneering trio.[4] For instance, Tayama Atsuro used to work for Yamamoto's office in Paris, Watanabe Junya is Kawakubo's disciple, and Tsumori Chisato has had Miyake's financial backing to start her own label in Japan.

The younger generation of Japanese designers grew up in postmodern times, and their perception of fashion is different from the previous generations. Designers are no longer simply those who design clothes. Many of them consider themselves artists who can engage in any creative activity even without any formal training in the field. Their goal is not to become world famous but remain underground or even anonymous, and by using their marginality as a status, they attract a small group of cult followers who worship their labels. However, it is ironical that their popularity that often emerges out of teenagers in street subcultures makes some of the labels mainstream and commercially very successful.

Takahashi Jun of Undercover, reportedly supported by Kawakubo, emerged out of the backstreets of Harajuku—known as Ura-hara—where groups of artists and designers collaborated together to establish the informal creative community through personal social networks. Takahashi tied up with now-famous Nigo and launched a brand called Nowhere. He then started his own label Undercover, and by 2002, he was taking part in the Paris collections. N. Hoolywood by Obana Daisuke is a menswear brand, which also originated from Ura-Hara. Like Undercover, it began as a "street fashion" label but is now distinguished from other street brands because of its exclusivity and limited editions—which used to be the marketing strategy for high fashion and not street fashion. The distinction between popular and high culture is often debated in the studies of culture and the arts, and this may extend to the classification of high fashion and popular fashion. However, as Crane argues, the high and popular distinction is becoming arbitrary, and thus we have to investigate how it is disseminated rather than its actual content.[5]

Furthermore, occupational categories are blurry in postmodern times. While some designers, such as Fukuzono Hidetaka of Whereabouts who graduated from Antwerp Royal Academy of Fine Arts and Katsui Hokuto of MintDesigns from Parsons School of Design and Central St. Martin's

School of Design, have been formally trained in fashion, others have never received any professional training. The professionalization of designers as an occupation is disappearing. Those who have a good taste and an eye for fashion can become designers. Mihara Yasuhiro started designing shoes in 1994 while he was a student at art college, Tama University, and set up his own brand Miharayasuhiro three years later. In 2000, he made a debut as a womenswear designer whose trademark is leather, and in 2001, he was hired by the major German footwear manufacturer Puma to design a sneaker line. By 2004, he was showing at the Milan collections.

Creative boundaries and genres are also less rigid. Artistic collaborations are now the norm and are used as a way to expand their creative horizons. United Bamboo, a design duo by Aoki Miho and Thuy Pham based in New York and Tokyo, work with artists, musicians and other creators involved in artistic activities. Similarly, Yagi Nao, Takeyama Yusuke and Katsui Hokuto of MintDesigns go beyond the genre of fashion and design and are committed to creating a fashionable lifestyle for people. Iwaya Toshikazu of Dress Camp collaborated with Champs, an American sportswear manufacturer, and organized a fashion show in Tokyo in 2004. He also put up a show in 2007 called the "Art Couture," designing dresses printed with classical Japanese paintings using couture techniques. Many Japanese designers today or in the past pride themselves in creating fabrics that are one of a kind and hard to manufacture. Minagawa Akira of Minä Perhonen and Tsumori Chisato are not only fashion designers but are also textile designers. Tsumori started working for Miyake Issey in 1977, who is famous for his original fabrics, and has been influenced by him ever since.

Japanese designers today are postmodern in every sense. They break every rule in the clothing system, not even realizing what the rules are, and denying every existing genre and categorical classification. It makes us wonder what fashion is. And one thing we know for sure is that it is becoming increasingly difficult to define.

Notes

[1] Becker, Howard. *Art Worlds.* Berkeley: University of California Press, 1982, np.

[2] Crane, Diana. *Fashion and Its Social Agenda: Class, Gender, and Identity in Clothing.* Chicago: The University of Chicago Press, 2000, p. 15

[3] Cocks, Jay. "A Change of Clothes: Designer Issey Miyake Shapes New Forms into Fashion for Tomorrow," *Time,* January 27, 1986, pp. 46-52; Duka, John. "Yohji Yamamoto Defines His Fashion Philosophy," *The New York Times,* October 23, 1983; Sudjic, Deyan. *Rei Kawakubo and Comme des Garçons,* New York: Rizzoli, 1990

[4] Kawamura, Yuniya. *The Japanese Revolution in Paris Fashion.* Oxford, UK: Berg, 2004

[5] Crane, Diana. *Fashion and Its Social Agenda: Class, Gender, and Identity in Clothing.* Chicago: The University of Chicago Press, 2000, np.

*A BATHING APE®

Opposite page: Nigo.

Variously identified in the Japanese press as celebrity DJ, indie record producer, magazine editor, action-figure designer, and wrestling promoter at least once in the last dozen years, the protean figure known simply as Nigo achieved true and lasting notoriety for launching a pop-culture phenomenon almost straight out of fashion school. Blessed with an abiding nostalgia for the New York B-boy scene of the early 1980s, he drew iconic inspiration from a personal trove of Planet of the Apes ephemera—one of the largest in the world—and founded Japan's most influential streetwear franchise in 1993. Spun around the simian mythology of the classic sci-fi romp, *A Bathing Ape®—or simply Bape—redefined the height of urban cool for a new generation of Tokyo hipsters.[1]

Incorporated under the holding company Nowhere Co., Ltd., the label specialized in tricked-up, one-of-a-kind hip-hop clothing, set apart from its mass-produced competitors by superior manufacture and detailing. Nigo's aspirations to the commanding heights of Tokyo fashion led him away from the mass market to cultivate a guerrilla sensibility. With relatively small seasonal collections, and initially with very little advertising, Bape depended on the word-of-mouth appeal of limited-edition T-shirts, messenger bags, and hooded sweats to keep the kids coming. This fanatical commitment to the new, and a dizzying capacity for reinvention ensured the brand's underground credentials—even with well-publicized tie-ins with Pepsi, Sony and MAC Cosmetics that came later.

And the Bape master plan for terrestrial domination is still very much on track. Through 2008, the most recent lines of attack have had the Ape General hanging out with Kaiser Karl Largerfeld in New York, hooking up Pharrell Williams with his very own apparel and accessories line in 2004, the artist KAWS with pretty much the same in 2006, and dressing up most everyone else in hip-hop worth knowing in the interim. This interminable drum-and-bass of activity coincided with the opening of more than a dozen fresh stores from Sapporo to Los Angeles in the last five years. The newly-minted Bape mini department store in Hong Kong—appointed as ever by court designer Katayama Masamichi—is proving to be the most profitable of the franchise, and even the $5 Bape knockoffs from the nearby sweatshops of Shenzhen and Zhuhai has had no real effect on receipts. In a fit of virtuoso salesmanship, Nigo has even taken a page from the bootleggers, marking up those ubiquitous *Scarface* t-shirts in ghetto-licious Bape editions worthy of Pacino's Tony Montana, the fully-licensed makes stuffed in a plastic case in the form of a champagne bottle and wrapped in gold foil.

*A Bathing Ape® begins and ends with Tokyo however, and the success of his overseas campaigns has had Nigo toying with the idea of a Harajuku superstore to keep things real at home. And lest anyone get too distracted by all the added value, the front office is always about retailing clothes. Spring 2006 saw the launch of a proper Bape Kids line with its own shop, and the women's collections —practically invisible outside of Japan—were split formally into two distinct lines. APEE, patterned after the beefier men's lines now coexists with the relatively understated Busy Working Lady—Bapy—collection which debuted in 2001. Bapy is the sophisticated foil to Bape's more recognizable swagger, infusing a wry elegance to the proceedings and an unlikely source of many sartorial surprises. Using rich wool gabardine, lush knits and the occasional swish of lace and taffeta, Bapy keeps its select patrons engaged with an arch-cool that is never above a little parody: a staple of the collection is a fitted jacket and skirt ensemble that graciously nods to the classic Chanel suit—as it flashes a toothy smirk here and there.—*Ian Luna*

[1] Luna, Ian. *Retail: Architecture and Shopping.* New York: Rizzoli, 2005, p. 49.

This page: Bape Spring/Summer 2005—Spring/Summer 2007.
Opposite page: Bape Kids Harajuku, Shibuya Ward (top); Bapexclusive Aoyama,
Minato Ward, both by Katayama Masamichi/Wonderwall

UNDERCOVER

The presumptive heir to the heavy mantle of Japanese deconstruction, Takahashi Jun's fashion is not borne out of an excessively intellectualized agenda. While not quite populist, his generative influences are instead romantic—even gothic. Already a fixture of the Paris collections for over five years—plus seventeen uninterrupted seasons in Tokyo prior to that—Takahashi has yet to tire of the outrageous ride, and the steady progress of his life's work confirms a maturation from self-conscious artifice and rebel pastiche to a steely, withering elegance all his own.

Hailing from Gunma Prefecture like his friend Nigo of *A Bathing Ape®, Takahashi Jun's long association with the undisputed king of Ura-Harajuku, and their joint founding of the seminal Nowhere Co., Ltd., in the early 1990s is now the stuff of local fashion lore. But Takahashi would blaze an entirely different path to legend and notoriety. Beginning with a brief stint fronting a punk band called the Tokyo Sex Pistols—a history that the designer now petulantly heaps scorn on—he nevertheless acknowledges the experience as a formative influence on Undercover, which he started in 1988 while in Bunka Fashion College. The violent rending and hasty reassembly that characterized his early work, its calculated imperfections and sutured seams, have given way to collections that he himself now admits as being "sexy and feminine." But a malevolence still roils under the most polished of surfaces. Holding court from a menacing steel "laboratory" looming over the outskirts of Harajuku—and his annoyance at mild pejoratives like "the reigning prince of darkness" notwithstanding—the designer will forever be taking bits from life's sinister underbelly.

His portentous worldview is fully-formed, evangelistic, all-encompassing and brave, obtaining a definition of beauty that is insistently transgressive as it is surely aestheticized. As if to underscore his disdain for a prettified fashion that resists crossing over to the dark side, he went on to call two of his collections from Fall/Winter 2004-05 through 2006 "But Beautiful..." referencing a baleful torch song composed by Johnny Burke in 1947 and later performed by a number of popular recording artists. But regret and unrequited desire, sung in mournful tones by Nina Simone, will inevitably elicit a different set of responses when crooned by Nat King Cole. Beauty is in the eye and the ear of the beholder, but Takahashi does not trifle with ambiguity. Nina suits him just fine, and his choices have earned the praise of no less a figure than Kawakubo Rei, who allegedly declared that Takahashi is "the only one with courage" among his peers.

In time though, this plaudit has become something of a curse. The designer is stung by the frequent suggestion of sponsorship and other intercessory patronage from Kawakubo, and admits only to some strategic guidance from Adrian Joffe, her husband and managing partner. The true nature of his association with Comme des Garçons might never be a matter of public record, and may well be immaterial. Takahashi is now fully the sorcerer and no longer the apprentice.—*Ian Luna*

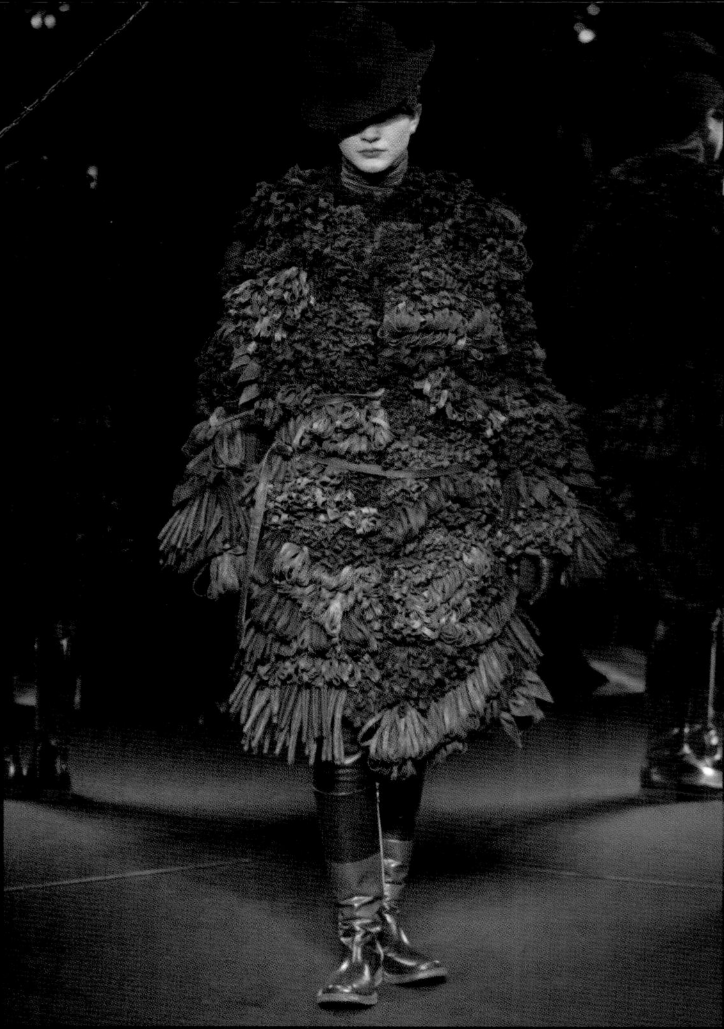
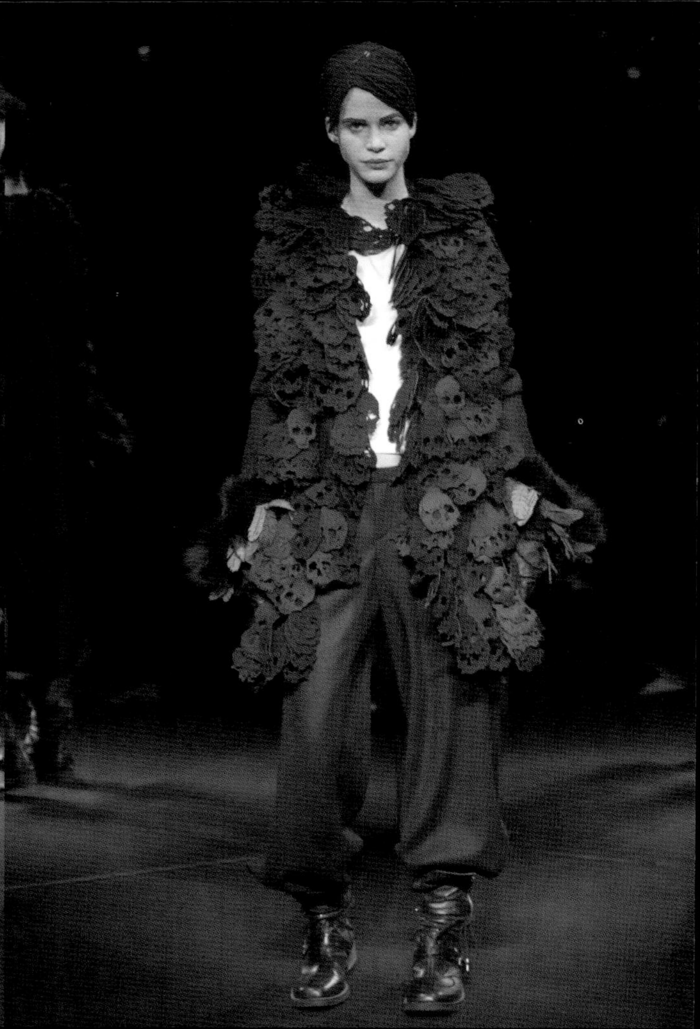
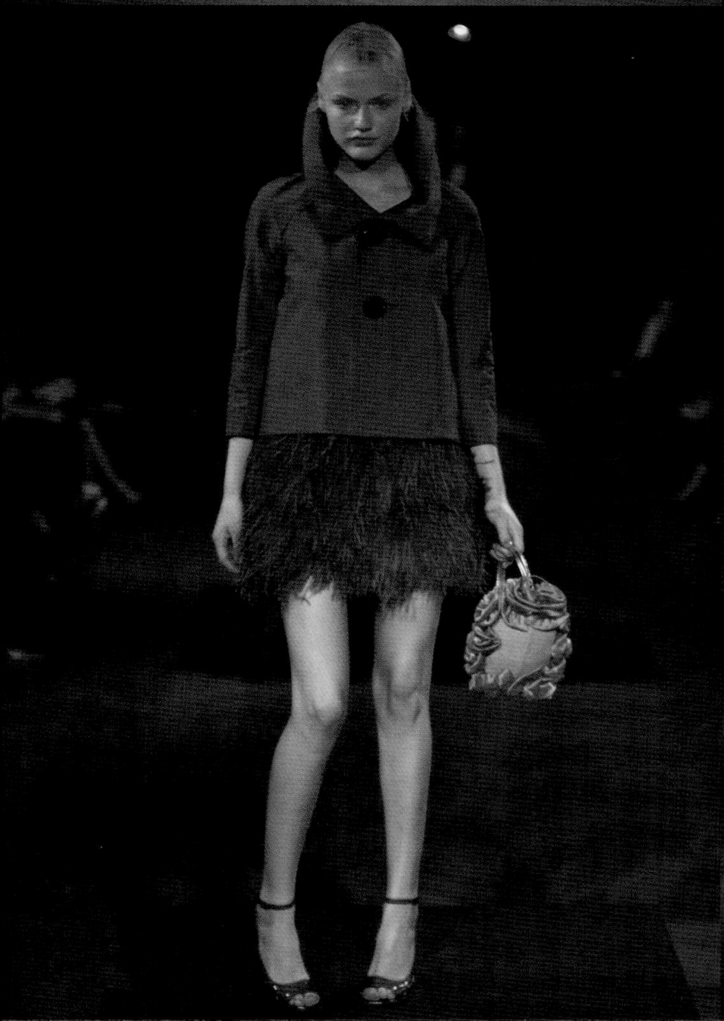
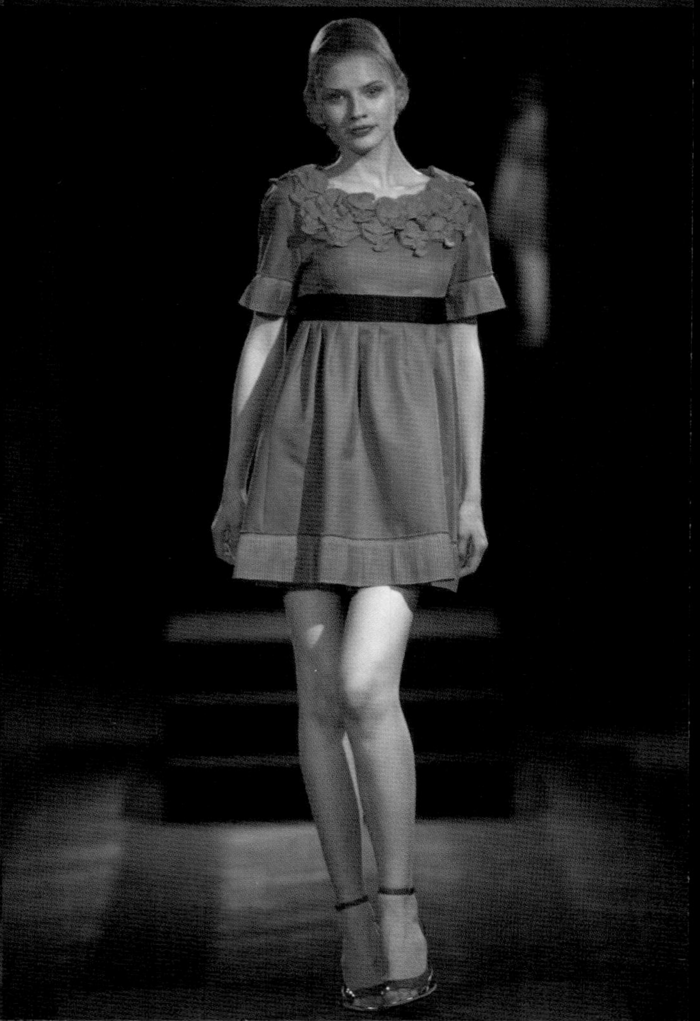

Fall/Winter 2005-2006 (top row); Spring/Summer 2007 (bottom row).

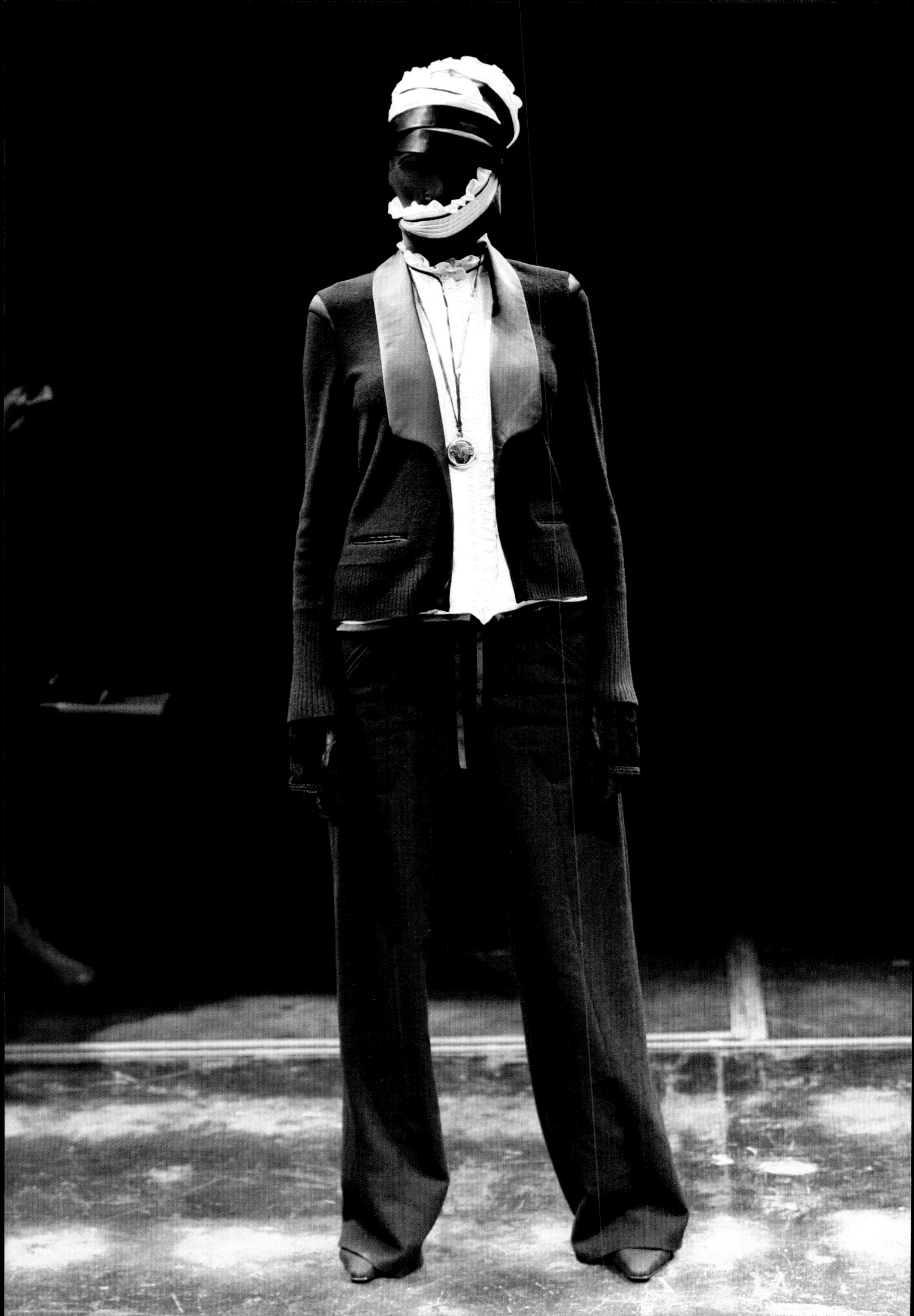

Fall/Winter 2006-2007. Following spread: Spring/Summer 2004.

TSUMORI CHISATO

Opposite page: Fall/Winter 2005-2006 campaign.

Tsumori Chisato ascended to the commanding heights of Japanese and international fashion in the 1990s with color as the critical virtue. And with the label firmly on its second decade, the conceptual and thematic ambition of its creator's recent output best illustrates the knowing resolve with which a lush, singular palette is applied and broadened. The absolute values present in Tsumori's inaugural collections—bold, dappled prints, lively knitting and embroidery, dense patternmaking and ever-novel approaches to sheathing the human form—still gird the meticulous structure of her dreaming world. Reacting to the somber minimalism that is even now conjured by any mention of "serious" Japanese fashion in the West, this new world is blithe and playfully ironic, self-possessed in its delicacy, unabashedly romantic in its femininity—and as ever, awash in vivid color.

The brand's consistent presence in the Paris collections (since 2003), its Paris flagship (1999), the half-dozen or so other freestanding boutiques, and its cult following in Japan, as well as in Hong Kong and Taiwan are undisputed markers of longevity in notoriously fickle Tokyo. This global reach, which of course translates to a broad measure of respect for her at home, speaks not only of Tsumori's prodigious and inexhaustible gifts (she was awarded the Mainichi Fashion Grand Prix for Best New Designer in 1985 and Best Designer in 2002); but also of her ability to attract, foster and retain the talents of others. No creative enterprise can exist without the proper roots, and hers twist deep into a rich earth of emotional and professional support. Hailing from Saitama Prefecture, Chisato revealed her design chops at a young age by crafting inventive garments for her dolls. With encouragement from her mother, this incipient skill flourished, ultimately leading to a degree in 1976 from the elite Bunka Fukusogakuin (Bunka Fashion College), where venerated alumni Yamamoto Yohji and Kenzo Takada still [cast] long shadows.

[Tsumor]i's storied apprenticeship with Miyake Issey began within a year of her graduation when she started designing for the former Issey Sport Line. She looks back on these years with great affection having found more than a mentor in Miyake whom she reveres both as father and master. This close working relationship empowered the protégée with the necessary discipline and confidence to become her own designer, as she benefited immensely from his stern tutelage, and the security and prestige supplied by his atelier. Indeed, long after she flew the coop to establish I.S Chisato Tsumori Design in 1983, the present iteration of her studio is managed by A-Net, a holding company closely associated with Miyake that is also responsible for the upkeep of a number of prominent labels, including Kuwahara Sunao, Zucca/Cabane de Zucca and Utsugi Eri's Mercibeaucoup.

By turns streetwise and homespun, Tsumori's last few collections convey most eloquently the maturation of a style: one that derives much of its power from the telling of stories. The inner life and aspirations of the designer are revealed to near excess by her ensembles. At once the products of and an escape from endless hours of toil, each look is a one-way ticket to destinations that exist only in her mind. In Chisato's cosmos, the fantastical affects the everyday and memories are made tangible, wearable constituents of the present. With a stylistic and thematic repertoire that has drawn upon Nordic, nautical, and the 1970s, these collections occupy an interstice between fantasy and reality. Formally represented as a fine balance between function and gesture, Tsumori Chisato makes a strong case for this psychic and visual median as the most logical plane for fashion to reside.—*Lauren A. Gould/Ian Luna*

Fall/Winter 2005-2006. Opposite page: Fall/Winter 2005-2006 campaign.

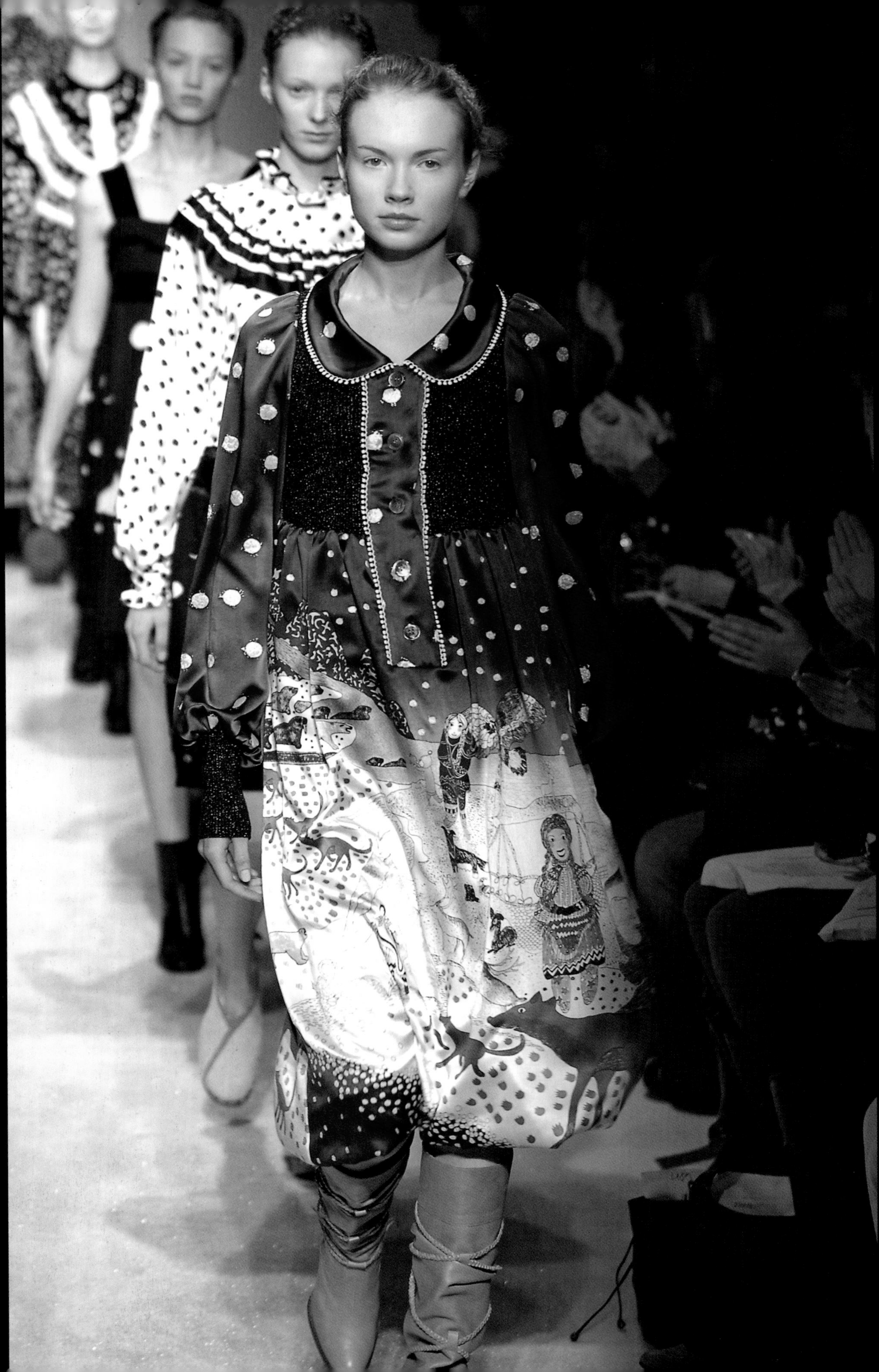

Fall/Winter 2006–2007.

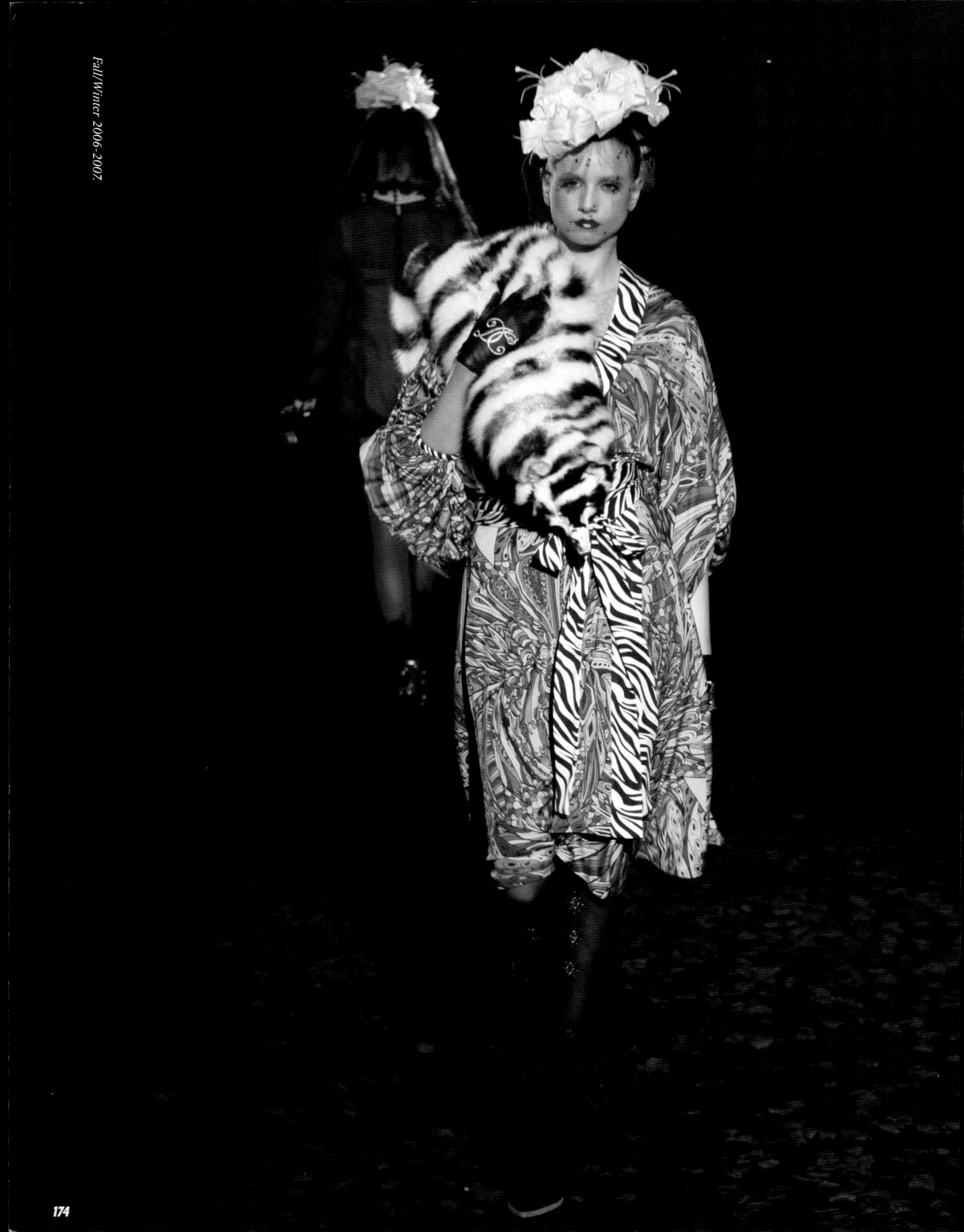

Fall/Winter 2006–2007.

Following spread: interior of Aoyama store, Minato Ward, by Katayama Masamichi/Wonderwall (2005).

175

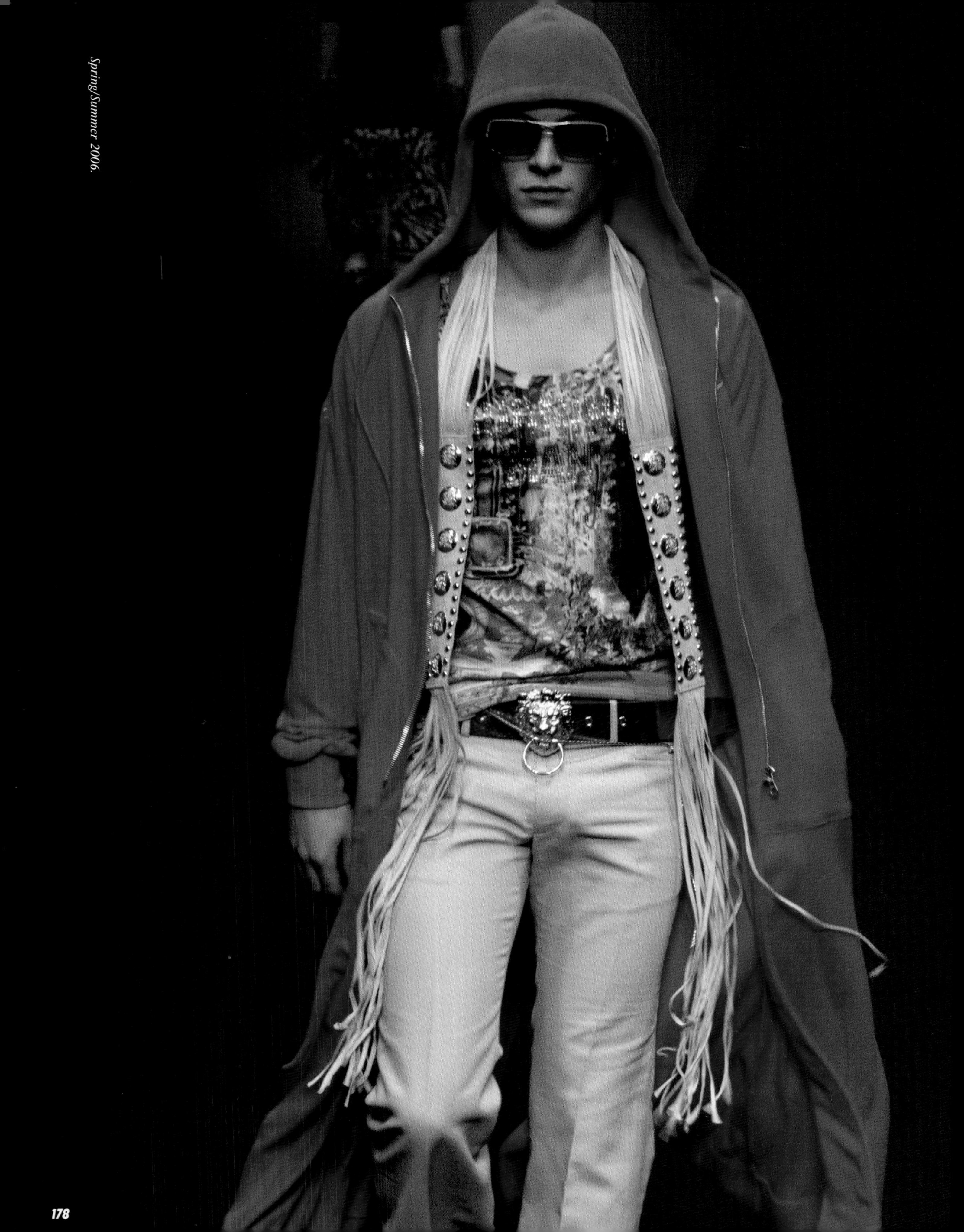

Spring/Summer 2006.

MINÄ PERHONEN

Above, left to right: Swan chairs with patterns "Tambourine" and "The Egg Angel." Opposite page: Fall/Winter 2006-2007.

The affective use of all things Scandinavian provides an inimitable undercurrent to Minä Perhonen, one of the most profoundly Japanese of the women's lines in the Tokyo collections. Drawing its name from Finnish—"perhonen" translates to butterfly; "mina" means "I" and is also a pun on the first two characters of the designer's family name—the principal themes of delicacy and flight, and a tenacious individuality have made the label a favorite among the young women of the Ebisu-Daikanyama-Nakameguro orbit. Dovetailing with a pervasive trend for LOHAS (lifestyles of health and sustainability) and its many derivative subcultures (slow food, building green), Minä Perhonen is as much an interdependent world view as it is a brand thriving on a quiet subjectivity and a love for handmade goods that singles it out from much of Tokyo's fast fashion.

Despite its referential debt to northern Europe, the vaguely Scandinavian forms belie a deep reverence for the simple, elegant forms that saturate traditional Japanese arts and crafts. Minagawa Akira—who founded the brand in 1995—was trained as a textile designer, and he exploits an impossibly large range of fabrics and colors in every collection. Diaphanous fabrics combine with heavy wools, with the seeming absence of Lurex and newer synthetic textiles creating an impression that the palette is composed entirely of organic materials. This comprehensive and self-conscious approach to materiality lends much to the label's appeal, providing an infinite number of visual and textural variations and a level of exclusivity that young patrons crave. And the idolatry has moved well beyond clothes. In 2006, the Danish textile manufacturer Kvadrat forged concrete links between Minagawa and Scandinavia by commissioning him to design fabrics that now grace Arne Jacobsen's Swan armchairs, sending the designer into the headlong pursuit of a total lifestyle brand.

Obtaining sure inspiration from simple geometric forms and, most explicitly, modernist graphic and textile designs, the Minä Perhonen attitude to form and pattern-making is rich as it is witty, with details and incidental graphic motifs uniting divergent looks and seasons. Apples, bees, electricity pylons, birds, and vegetal forms are rendered either through weaving, embroidery, appliqué, or intarsia. Sometimes these are applied over abstracted geometric patterns to suggest several layers of meaning, creating visual compositions common to the world of woodblock prints and the design of the kimono and its summer variant, the *yukata*. When affixed to modern A-line shift dresses, billowing skirts, and asymmetrical peacoats, these delicate gestures contribute a weightlessness to the clothing that is further reinforced by a near-complete dismissal of black from the working palette. In its stead are rich earthy hues and washes of soft pastel, with bright accessories in cunning, unexpected shapes, which provide lively exclamations to Minagawa's gently persuasive statements.—*Ian Luna/Lauren A. Gould.*

Following spread, top row, from left to right: "Triangle" from Fall/Winter 2002;"Sakuranbo" from Fall/Winter 2002; "Ringo" from Spring/Summer 2001; "Flower Box" from Spring/Summer 2001; Bottom row, from left to right: "Nanahoshi" from Fall/Winter 2004; "Yuki-no-hi" from Fall/Winter 2000; "Roof" from Fall/Winter 2002; "Match" from Spring/Summer 2001.

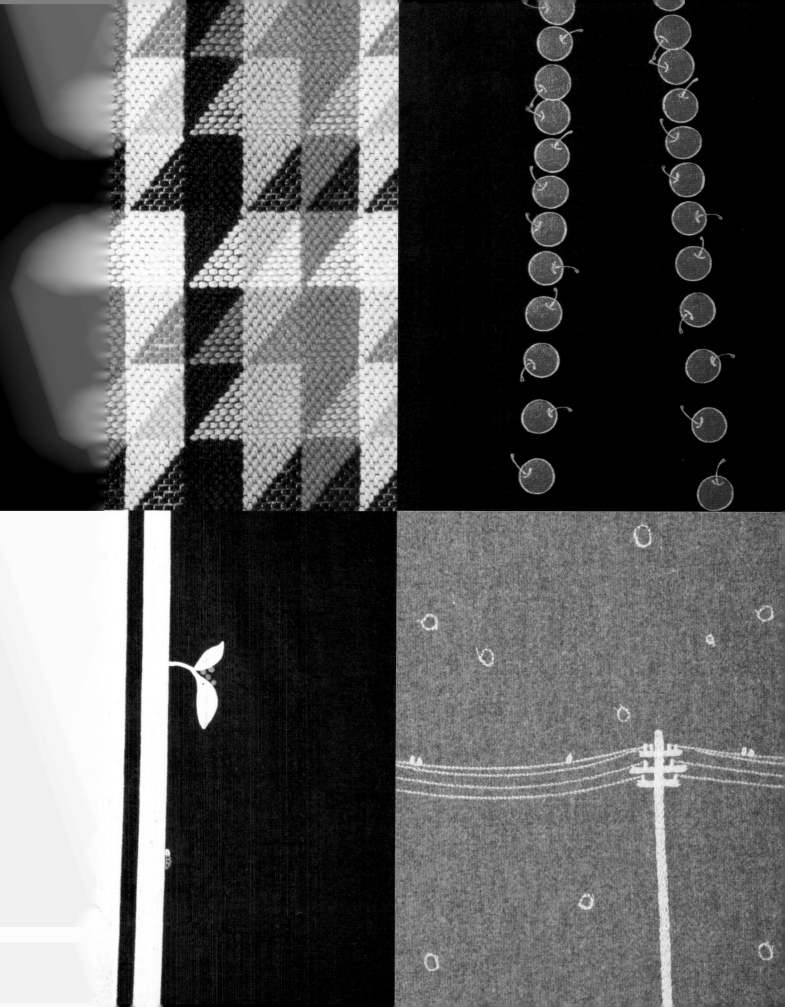

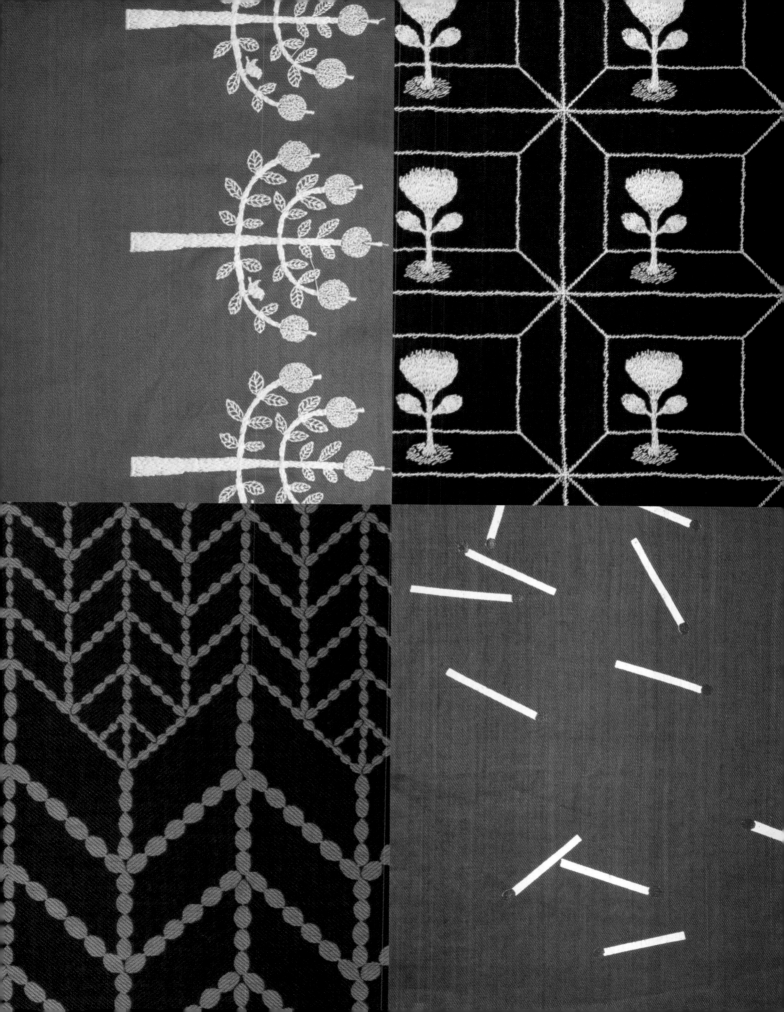

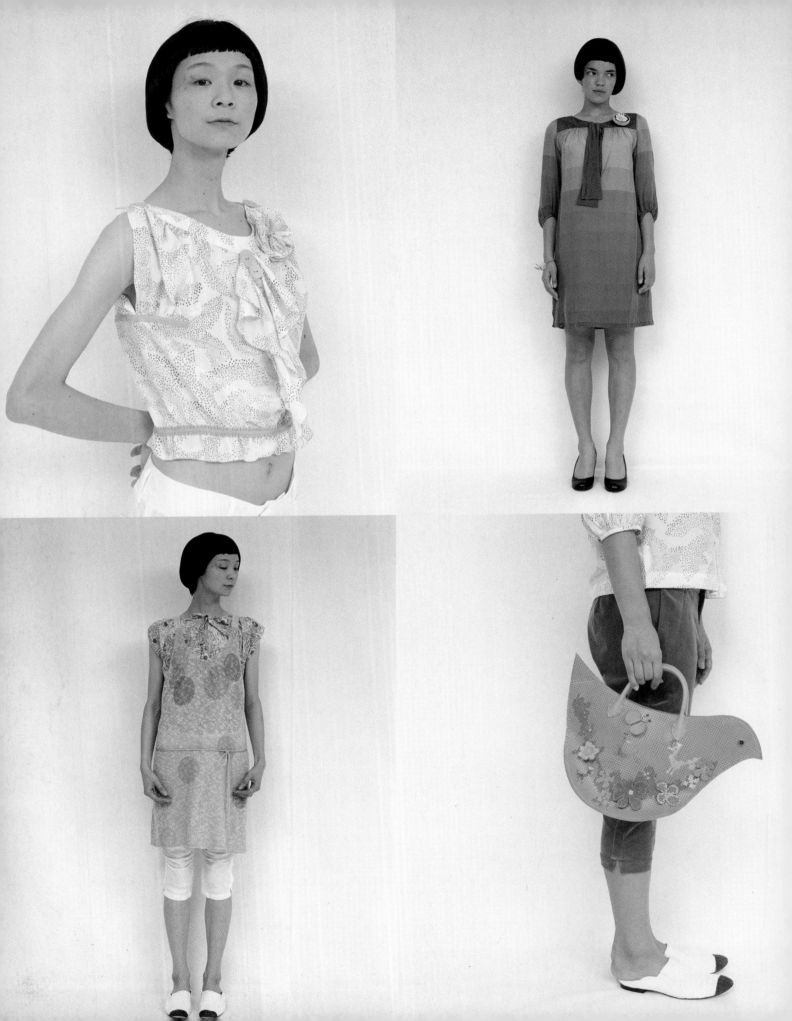

Above: Obana Daisuke; opposite page: Spring/Summer 2004.

Its name an amalgam of N. Hollywood and hooligan, the menswear line N. Hoolywood owes much of its narrative to the transpacific ambitions of its young principal designer, Obana Daisuke. Dubbed Mister Hollywood by his American friends, Obana ran his erstwhile career as a buyer for the vintage clothing trade from an office in Los Angeles. Now firmly a member of Tokyo's young guard, he mainly directs the scope of his activities from the upper floors of a small apartment block in a secluded residential corner of Shibuya. Cluttered with small, elegant collectibles, the wood-framed vitrines lining the reception spaces of the studio reflect some of the calculated eclecticism the designer employs in his collections—and the earnest, almost childlike curiosity that Obana freely admits is what propels his work and aspirations forward.

The lived-in character of vintage clothing and the culture that surrounds it portend in the conception of the brand. As a teen, Obana kept up with the trend for *Amekaji* (American casual) with his Calvin Klein and Ralph Lauren-toting buddies by hitting the humble predecessors of modern consignment and "recycled" clothing stores that now mostly specialize in gently-used designer makes. The experience introduced the budding designer to the certain allure of vintage clothing—something he'd always associated with the simplicity and ease of American fashion. And the versatility afforded by his shrewd shopping choices, apart from helping him cope within a fashion-crazed milieu, imparted an advanced facility for ensemble.

Combining mod, expert tailoring with the rakish charms of American streetwear, the N. Hoolywood look is an extended ode to a recombinant West Coast sensibility, typified by a recent homage to uppity school uniforms that have more to do with elite West Los Angeles academies than they do with any English precedent. The spare forms and hushed palette of previous collections mine and reconfigure American markers, with rep ties and letterman jackets infecting a collection of sharp suits and mildly subverted

shirts. Alternately expressive and doggedly minimal, Obana's creations—accented by a mania for details and finely rendered in maroons, tans, blues, greys and creams—propound a thorough understanding of color and materiality in men's fashion. With the seasonal collections often a conscious attempt to replicate the different genres of mid-to-late 20th century cinematic elegance, the decision to offset traditional forms with quotations from more modern, utilitarian garments—windbreakers, military fatigues, drawstring pants, medical garb—inject a level of whimsy into an aesthetic of performance.—*Ian Luna*

Fall/Winter 2003-2004; opposite page: Spring/Summer 2005.

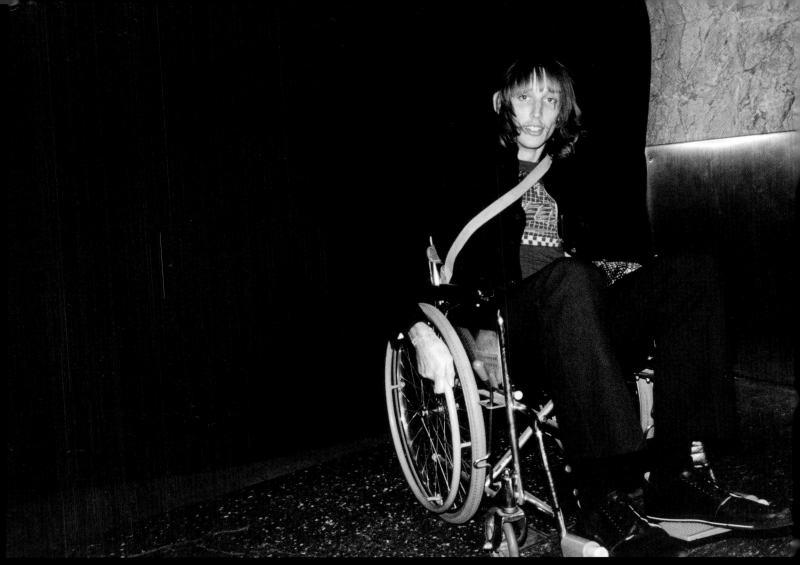

Above: Spring/Summer 2003; opposite page: Fall/Winter 2005-2006.

TRIPTYCH

Above: Fukuda Harumi; opposite page: Spring/Summer 2006.

An enigmatic femininity abounds in Triptych's flowing silhouettes and layers of material and meaning, a romanticism abstracted largely from binary juxtapositions of black and white, the everyday and the ceremonial. A Sapporo native, designer Fukuda Harumi studied art for over two years before immersing herself in the world of graphic design at Tokyo National University of Fine Arts and Music. Now creative director of the brand she founded in early 2003, Fukuda imbues Triptych with an artistic sensibility leavened by a wealth of cultural and semiotic references, alluding to an education focused on the analysis of form.

The name "triptych" finds easy resonances in the history of art, with a hinged, tripartite devotional painting common to medieval Europe as the most straightforward referent—or, more aptly, the secular, gilded *byobu*, or traditional Japanese folding screen. When asked about the label's etymology, however, Fukuda brings up the image of a three-part mirror, whose reflective panels create distorted shapes that overlap infinitely. Fukuda declares that it is this moment—when the multiple layers of the self are at least superficially revealed—that gives our true identities occasion to stand out. Such expositional purpose grants Triptych its material mission: to create works of art whose multifaceted designs and adaptability allow individuals to project their personalities. Triptych achieves its object primarily through a combination of loose and fitted garments, separates and meticulously ordered ensembles, textured accents and origami-esque strata of natural and synthetic fabrics.

It is also possible to view Fukuda's Triptych as an extension of the designer's commercial activities, since she first engaged Tokyo fashion on the retailing side as the founder of the Aoyama-based select shop WR. Founded in 1998, WR is a shopping mecca for the depth and edge of the labels that stock its two-story height. Embodying the synergy between art, commerce, and fashion, rousing music and Fukuda's susceptibility to hosting art exhibitions

and creating alliances with up-and-coming designers and stylists keep the store vibrant and offbeat. Founded on this tried-and-tested equation of Aoyama cool, Triptych is certainly an expression of practical lessons learned and a testament to an irrepressible desire to give shape to ideas that had always been deeply felt and held.—*Ian Luna/Lauren A. Gould/*

Spring/Summer 2005; opposite page: Spring/Summer 2006.

198

MIHARA YASUHIRO

Opposite page: Spring/Summer 2004.

Even a cursory scan of Mihara Yasuhiro's relatively long career in fashion, from his early days as an entrepreneurial shoe designer at university to his recent debut at the Paris Fall 2007 collections, suggests something of the significance of family origins in the cultivation of talent. The son of a modern painter and a scientist, Mihara grew up in a home that nurtured creativity, and a tendency to abstraction and obsession is very much apparent in the detailing of his eponymous men's and women's lines. Hand-in-hand with his artistic education is a worldview informed by a deep-seated environmental and social consciousness, and a philantrophic bent—he habitually donates to Greenpeace—and while these sympathies are not explicitly propounded in his work, he nonetheless attributes some of the generative process to these philosophical underpinnings.

Mihara claims to have resisted a headlong descent into fashion, but the arc of his early experiences made his opposition all but academic. Hailing from Fukuoka, Mihara majored in textile design at Tama Art University, but was soon crafting his own footwear line Archi Doom with corporate support from a shoe company. Soon after graduating in 1997, Archi Doom morphed into Miharayasuhiro, and an Aoyama store popped up in short order. Dubbed Sosu, which can be translated as prime number or infinity, the store also shared the name of Mihara's holding company. The designer's big break came a few years later when a German footwear giant reeled him in to create his own line. Launched in 2001, Puma by Miharayasuhiro became an international success. And Mihara is not at all defensive about the role the contract with Puma played in building a global reputation, a relationship that he regards as a an "overseas pipeline" crucial to all of Sosu's activities.

But shoes are clearly only part of the story. An evolving critical experiment, Miharayasuhiro has pulled off many dazzling turns, displaying a thorough-going grasp of fashion's crosscurrents as it as sustains an acclaimed capacity for invention and commercial appeal. The end result is often a hybrid look that melds sharp tailoring and hand-made refinements with a finely tuned deconstructive slant. The strong retail presence in Tokyo and his inclusion in the Milan and Paris collections validate what can often be a fickle conceptual methodology. Mihara has himself alluded to the unpredictability of his brand, having quipped before, "I'm always trying to produce the un-producible." Those in the know find a certain comfort in the ever-changing nature of his designs—which of late incorporate militaria or futuristic inspirations—and appreciate his skill at incorporating the unexpected.—*Lauren A. Gould/Ian Luna*

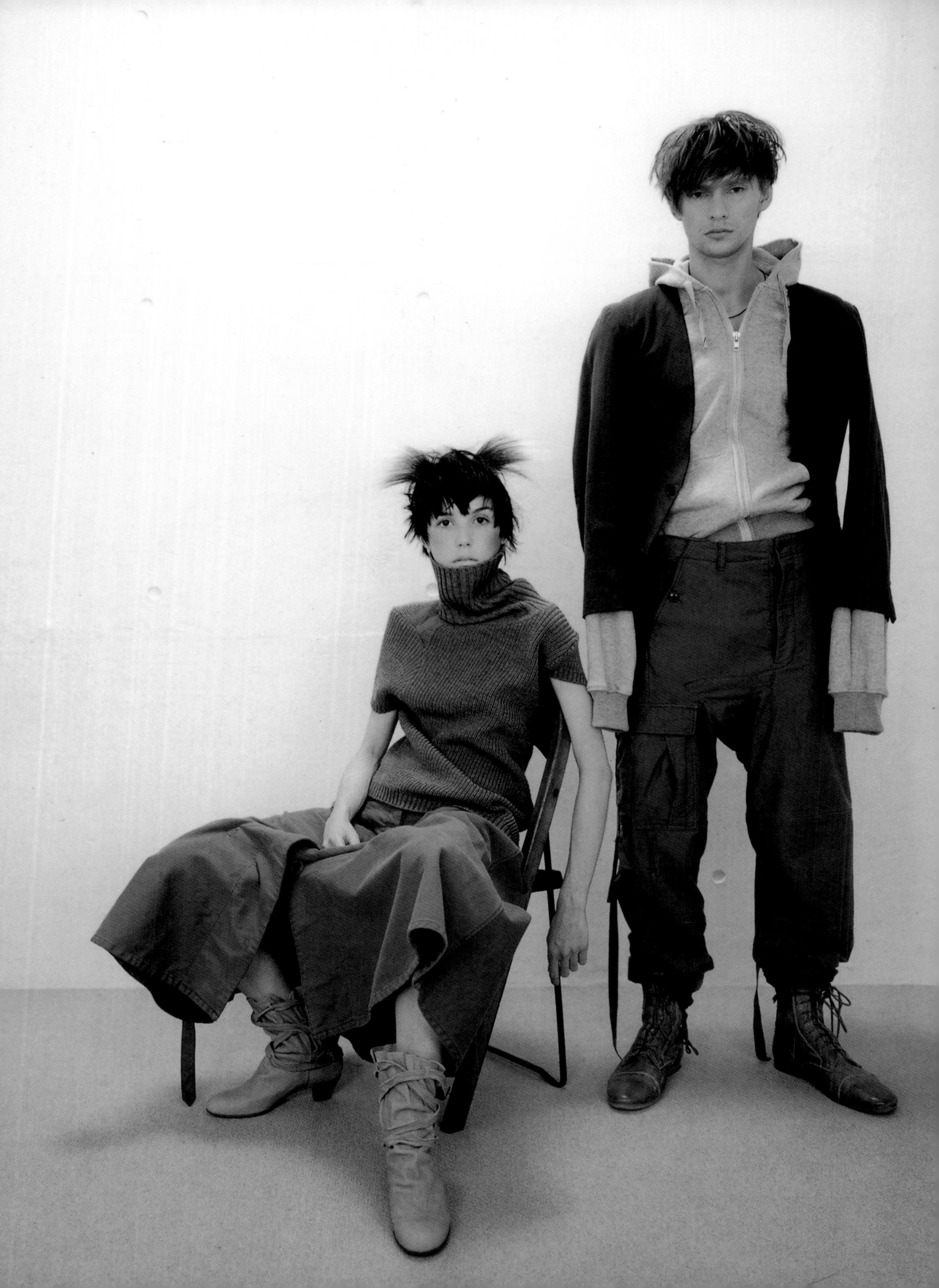

Spring/Summer 2004.

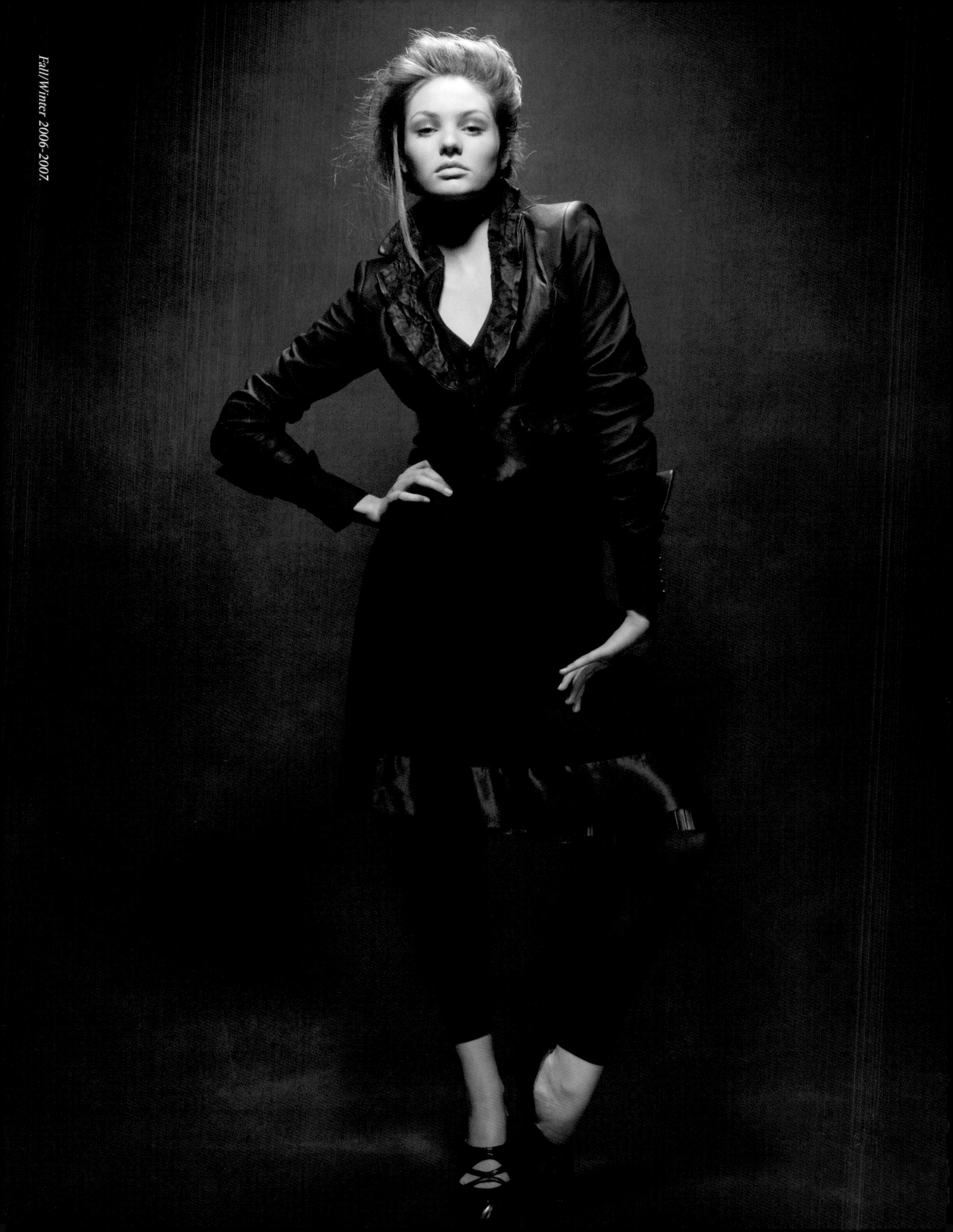

Fall/Winter 2006–2007.

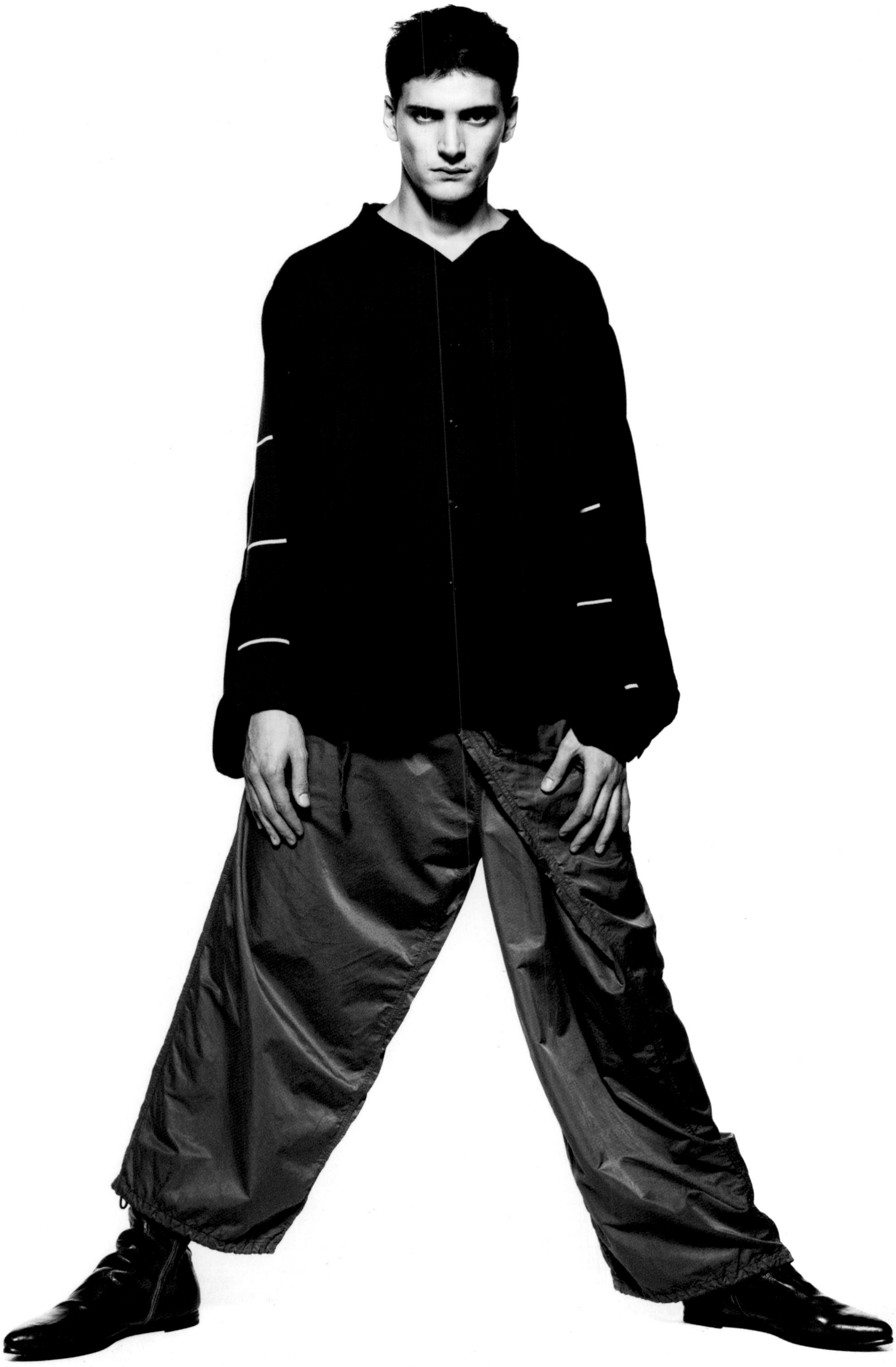

Spring/Summer 2004.

Above: Fall/Winter 2005-2006; opposite page: Spring/Summer 2005.

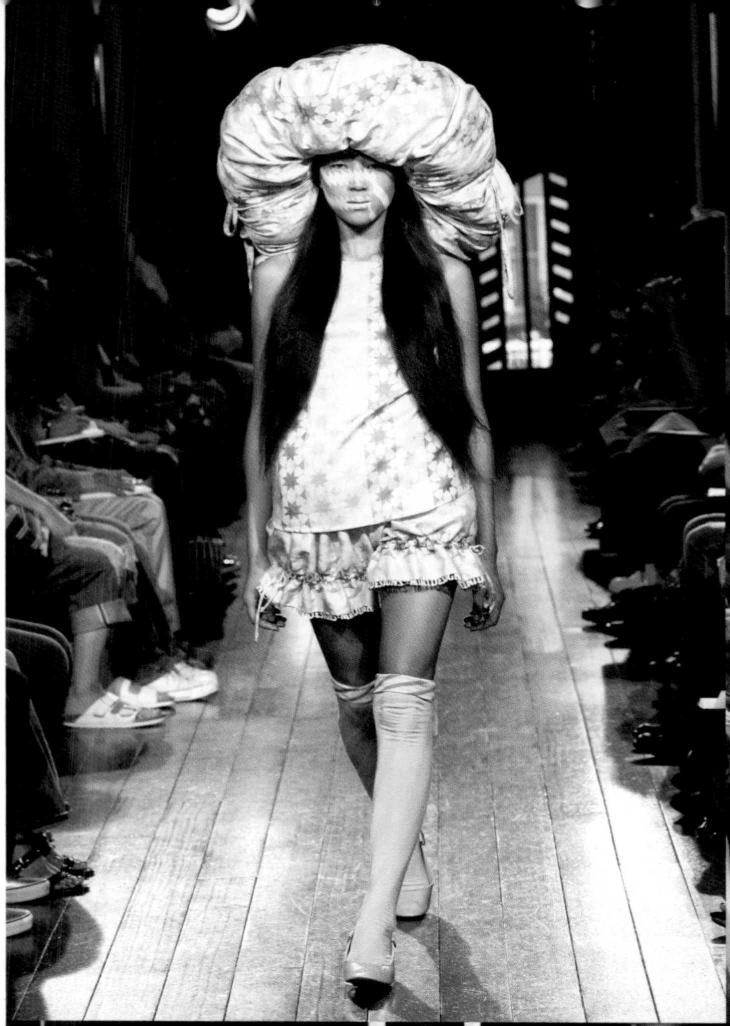

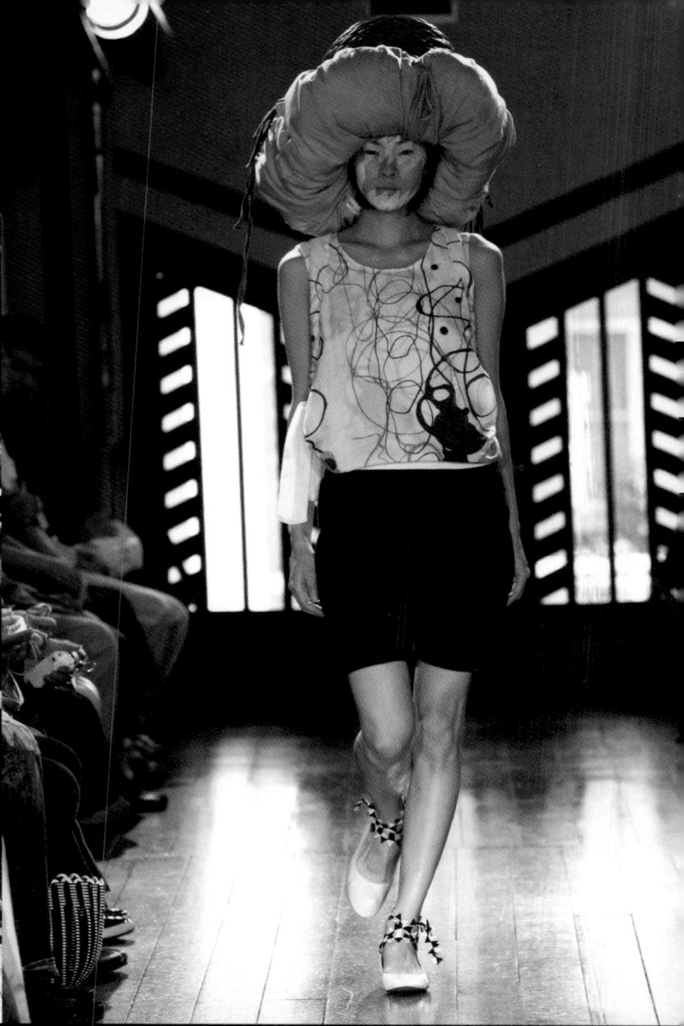

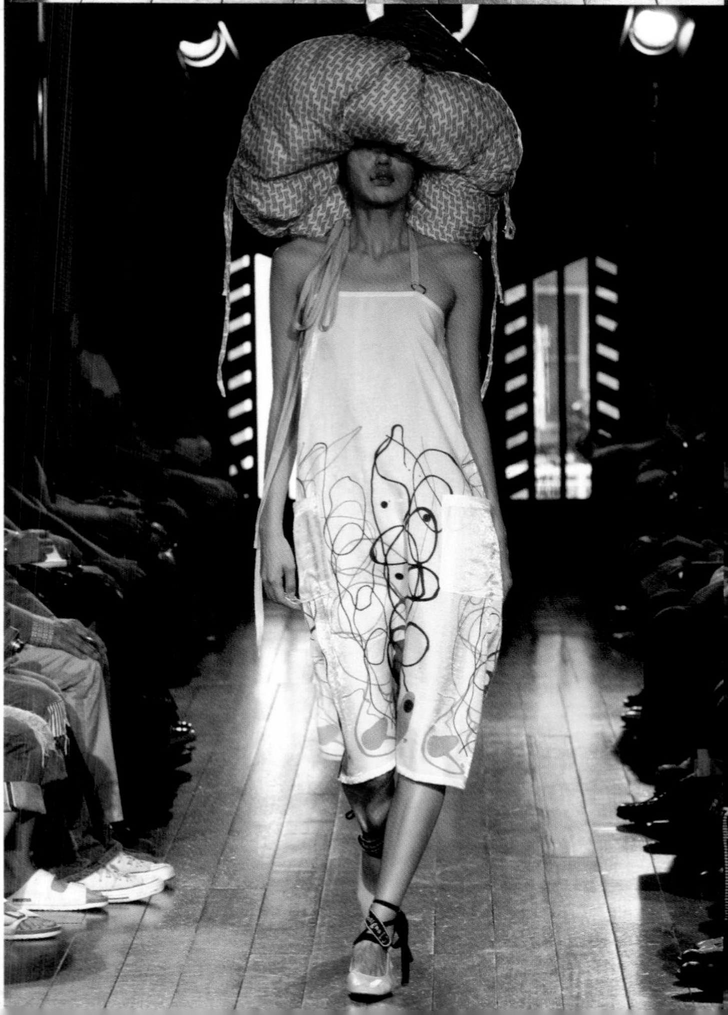

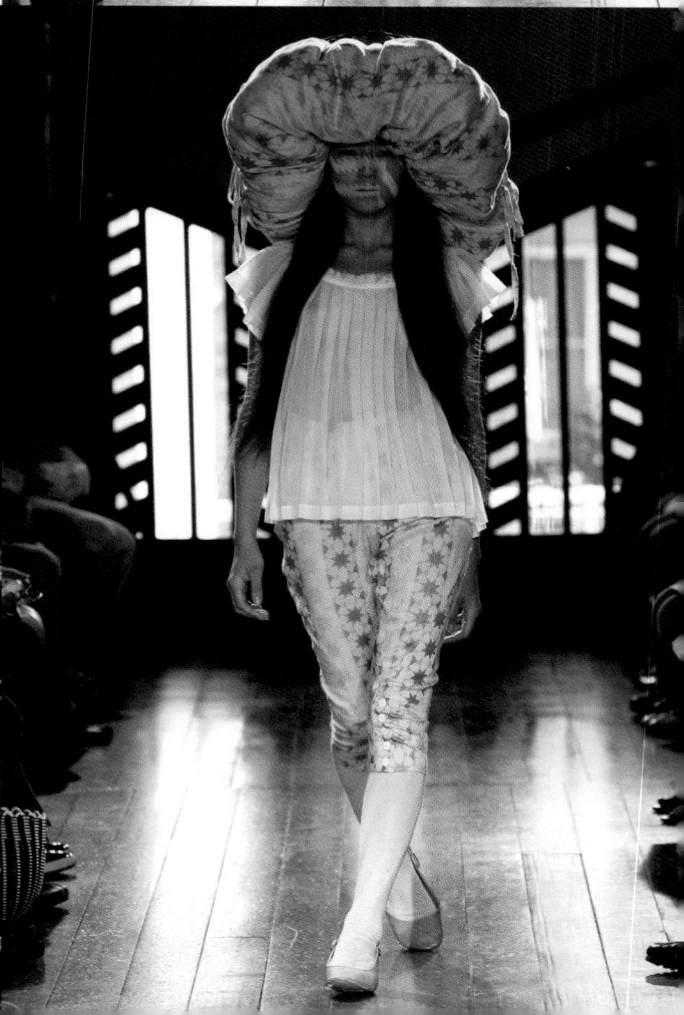

UTSUGI ERI
MERCIBEAUCOUP,

Above, left to right: Utsugi Eri; flyer for Spring/Summer 2007 show. Opposite page: flyer for Fall/Winter 2006-2007 show.

The 2006 launch of Mercibeaucoup signaled the triumphant return to the catwalk—from an admittedly brief creative pause—of one of Tokyo's fashion's darlings. Fun rules in Utsugi Eri's latest adventure. For her inaugural line, she banished the usual dour-faced models, and flooded the runway with kooky face paint, Cheshire cat-grins, animal-shaped 'fros, pun-laden t-shirts, flashy prints and bright, peek-a-boo color. Set against a clever *mise-en-scène* and fuelled by pop-culture trivia, the designer's provisional approach to restraint is stitched into every seam. But there is clearly much more to this mischief beyond the layering of scenographic effects. Draped over models sweeping confetti off the floor with oversized brooms is a women's and men's collection that reveals a maturing aesthetic, conceived with a unity of design that reveres both Japanese and Western forms, and is assured in its creative direction. Declaring that a fashion designer has "an original look" says very little, and stands for even less in a universe where every upstart is the "hot young thing." But Utsugi is the real deal, and in Mercibeaucoup, she finds that happy medium between high fashion and street savvy, a juncture much sought after in Japanese fashion.

Having first received critical acclaim for designing the A-Net label Frapbois a few years back, Utsugi has chosen to embark on an appreciably divergent path with Mercibeaucoup, though many of her inspirations remain the same. She continues to mine the richness of everyday encounters—from her travels (a trip to Hawaii injected her Spring/Summer 2007 collection with eclectic fruit prints), to the pages of comic books (which hinted at the heavy-metal face paint that appeared in the same show) to afternoons spent playing with her son (to which she imputes the origin of her collection's carefree vibe). In fact, Utsugi's tendency to draw from her nearest and dearest

contributed significantly to her success as a designer. Born in Tokyo the daughter of a dressmaker, it was only a matter of time before she took on the family business, using scraps of fabric to create her own work with instruction from her mother. Honing her skills at a catalog of institutions, including the Joshibi Junior College of Art and Design, Esmod Japon—the Tokyo outpost of the l'Ecole Supérieure des Arts et Techniques de la Mode—and Paris' Studio Berçot, Utsugi ultimately rose above her peers to a coveted place in a teeming Tokyo marketplace.

Having previously described her vocation to the Japanese press as a means to articulate "the idea that conventional wisdom isn't the only correct way of looking at things," Utsugi modestly suggests that her label has satisfied the primary criteria for designing in Tokyo—inventiveness—and has responded to her good fortune with gratitude. Her proven ability to accommodate—and sometimes work around—the capricious temperament of Japanese fashion owes much to an irrepressible, eternal adolescent, and one Mercibeaucoup will do well to nurture.—*Lauren A. Gould/Ian Luna*

メルシーボークー、
mercibeaucoup,

8/10 青山店　　8/24 銀座店　　8/25 新宿ミロード店　　9/1 渋谷パルコ店　　9/15 京都店 藤井大丸　　10/1 原宿店　　8/中 A-net Web Store

OPEN

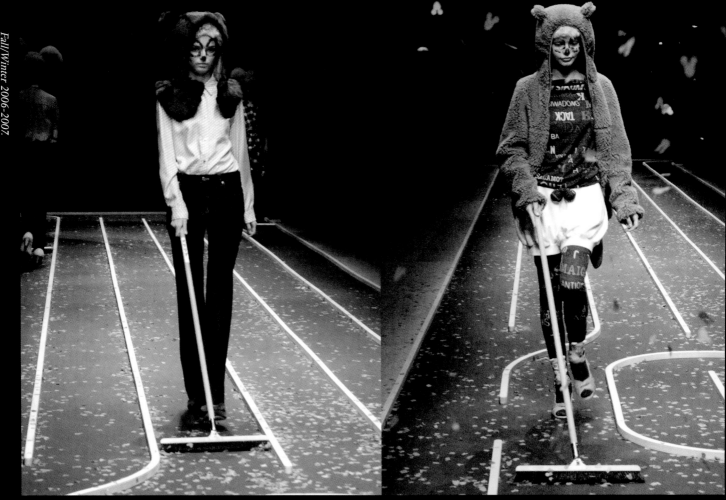

Following spread, clockwise from top left: exterior, Aoyama shop, Minato Ward; interior, Shibuya shop, Shibuya Ward; exterior, Ginza shop, Chuo Ward; interior, Aoyama shop.

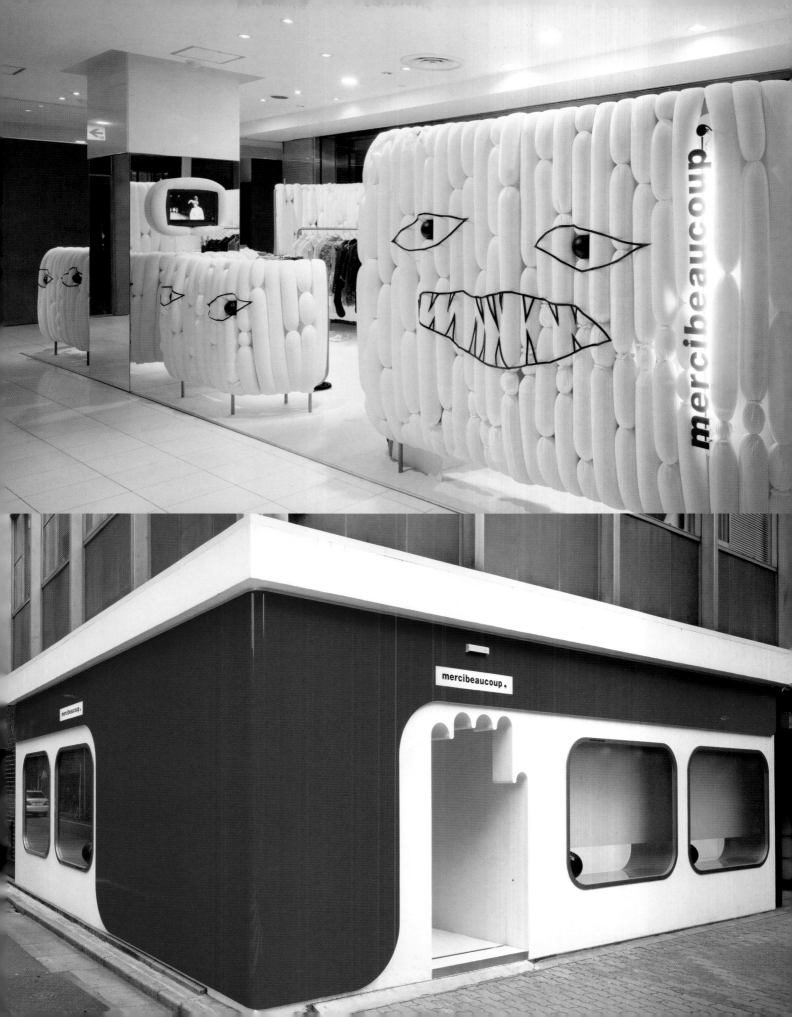

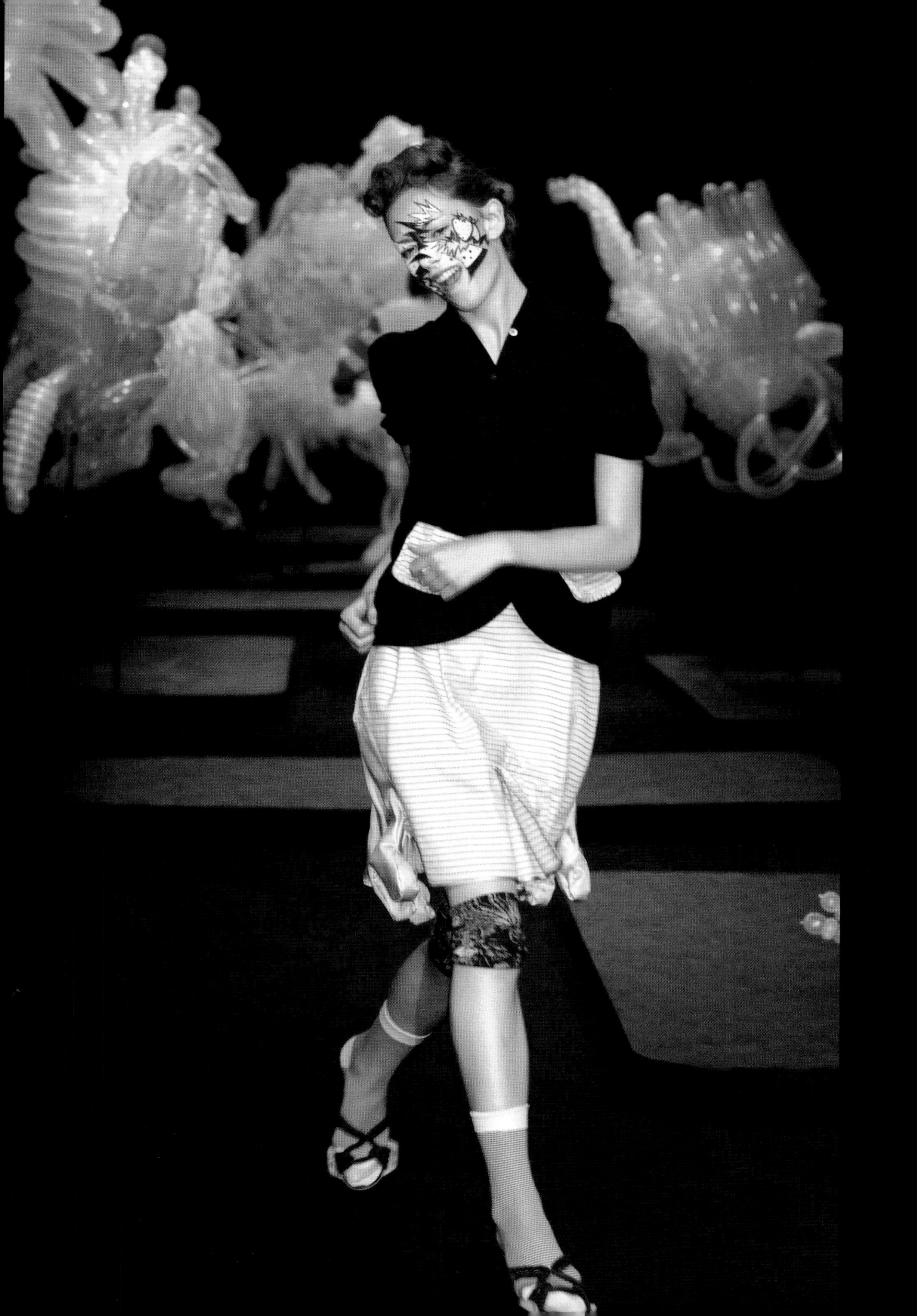

UNITED BAMBOO

Above: Thuy Pham and Aoki Miho; opposite page: Fall/Winter 2006-2007 campaign.

A scrappy New York- and Tokyo-based label with a more pronounced retailing profile in Japan—as the stand-alone flagship shops in Daikanyama and Omotesando attest—United Bamboo's presence in both cities evidence some of the flexibility indie transpacific business models have achieved in the last decade. More tellingly, it demonstrates the capacity of its creative authors to transplant and then sustain a strong local following to what is essentially a hybrid East Coast worldview, one that combines a lean, American look pared down with a firm grasp of Tokyo cool. Associations with Tokyo trends like *Amekaji* (America casual)—that in earlier waves, capitalized on a preppy-fied, thrown-together swagger—certainly helped, and the evolution of Bamboo's signature look has lately come full circle. The Fall/Winter 2007-2008 collection is noteworthy for a number of expressive, and distinctly Japanese markers, like the application of interlocking fabric strips that evoke origami or indeed the patterns on the decorative *yuzen* or *chiyogami* papers used to make them.

The duo behind United Bamboo, Aoki Miho and Thuy Pham, have been working together for the better part of the decade. Aoki, a graduate of New York's Fashion Institute of Technology, and Pham, a former student of architecture at Cooper Union, met at the Manhattan art collective Bernadette Corp., where Pham was both designer and founding member. Yet it was Aoki, a native Japanese, who launched the label in 1998, with Pham soon joining the following year. The pair emerged out of the New York fashion scene with a gush of critical acclaim, with Pham providing the direction and organization Aoki says the enterprise then lacked. Several legends have grown up around christening the brand United Bamboo, including an antiseptic one about Asian unity based on a Chinese proverb, although it is also likely that the name was taken from a notorious Triad syndicate operating out of Taipei.

With their first formal outing announcing the Fall 2004 line, United Bamboo sauntered down the runway as the functional incarnation of two distinct mindsets, with a self-described aesthetic of "disheveled glamour." Initially a send-up of the preppy look, the pair's all-American creations now run the gamut from sporty to evening glam, deconstructing safari jackets, seersucker pants and Chanel suits in collections that are by turns reductive and elaborate.

Aoki and Pham's twinned point of view is eloquently phrased, fusing hints of the manor-born—a touch of tweed and argyle here, a ruffled collar there—with the patterns and pleats that evoke the intellectual rigor of Japanese high fashion. In passages, their creations magically transform the human silhouette into studied architectural forms. But an enterprising undercurrent of pop and mischief pervade the work as well. Both designers have sourced their motivations well beyond the rarified world of fashion, and this is borne out by a raft of side-projects. These have of late included branding strategies, that are not incidentally, quite familiar to savvy Japanese consumers: "curated" t-shirt collaborations with on-the-rise artists and musicians; tie-ins with European sportswear labels like the Florentine brand Sergio Tacchini; as well as their own music label UUAR, that produces eclectic compilations of experimental, mainly New York-based artists. With United Bamboo's seasonal design influences derived from movies and literary classics, to modern architects and media images of working women, this marriage of sophistication and street-wise cool—a "downtown chic going to an uptown party"—propel the work ever-forward.
—*Ian Luna/Lauren A. Gould*

Above: Spring/Summer 2004.

This page: Fall/Winter 2002-2003 campaign; opposite page: Spring/Summer 2002.

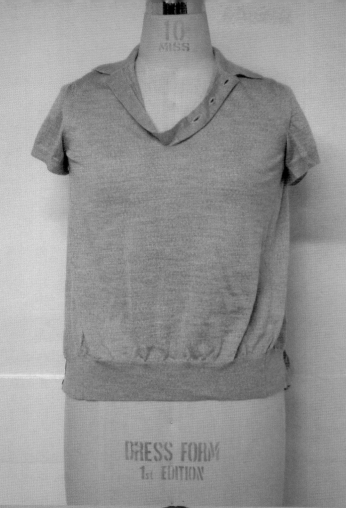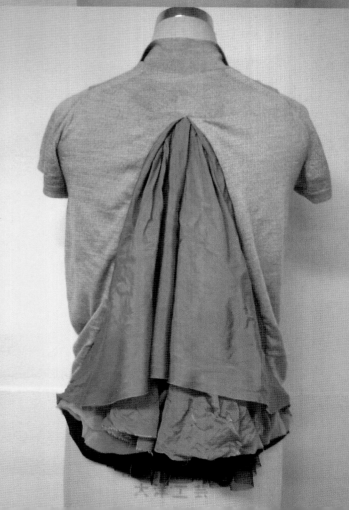

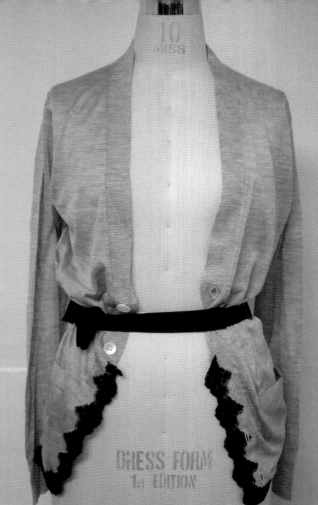

GREEN

Above Ode Yukiko and Yoshihara Hideaki. Opposite page: the Green shop in Daikanyama, Shibuya Ward (2002).

In 2002, designers Ode Yukiko and Yoshihara Hideaki opened the doors of Green in Ebisu, revealing a split-level shop/studio partial to the trappings of old offices and libraries. The clean lines of their current collection now stand alongside traces of the pair's first venture—an upmarket vintage clothes shop called Bowles—that they shuttered in 1999 after two years of business with hopes of creating of their own clothing line. And focus they did. The perfect home for the enigmatic Green, the gallery-like expanse is prim but sharp, its walls lined by a clever mix of artifacts from early- to mid-century interiors and antique dress forms.

Amid stacked filing cabinets, card catalogues, wood-framed vitrines and mechanical typewriters, Ode and Yoshihara's fashion settles comfortably into its literal and metaphoric confines, between the fast clip of an over-worked metropolis and languid pleasures of a quiet retreat. Since its first entry in the Tokyo collections with its Fall/Winter 2003-2004 line, Green stood out with an uncomplicated, monochromatic look softened by a gentle romanticism. The persistent use of brown, black, white and gray betray none of the severity of analytical Japanese minimalism. Tailoring is the touch-stone of Green, its slim silhouettes generating a look of casual elegance that is at once militaristic, nautical, corporate and preppy, and is, above all, func-tional. Smart pantsuits, delicate dresses, and sleek, structured daywear are at the core of a collection informed by a precise historicism. Edwardian capes, multiple variations on the Chesterfield coat, and retro nods to the Teddyboy movement of late 1950s Britain are rounded off in the warmer months by a nostalgia for classic 1980s *Amekaji* (a Japanese take on American casual) and a relaxed, naval look straight out of the French or Italian rivieras.
—*Lauren A. Gould/Ian Luna*

green

open 12:00–20:00
close monday

WHEREABOUTS

Above: Fukuzono Hidetaka; opposite page: Fall/Winter 2005-2006.

Born in Kumamoto Prefecture, Fukuzono Hidetaka's road to the Tokyo collections diverges slightly from the dog-eared script followed by his peers. Leaving home for that all-important move to Tokyo, he later followed it up with obligatory studies in Paris. He felt restless once in France, however, and dropped out of school. He soon found himself in neighboring Belgium, lured no doubt by the more ambiguous charms of the "Antwerp Group." Like Dries van Noten, Martin Margiela and Ann Demeulemeester, Dirk Bikkembergs and Marina Yee before him, Fukuzono matriculated at the Royal Academy of Fine Arts, graduated in 2002, and returned to Japan.

The lessons learned along the way were myriad and vital, and the most consequential was a decision to abandon women's fashion for menswear. The second most important was a healthy disrespect for orthodoxy, and with the reticent sensibility of the low countries still in his system, the young designer made his debut with Whereabouts at Tokyo Fashion Week in early 2004. His lingering nostalgia for northern Europe is evident in his inaugural collection for Fall/Winter 2004-2005. There, a fixation with 18th-century style, and the dignified portraits of working-class Germans from legendary photographer August Sander's *Face of Our Time* (1929) supplied the inspiration for a subdued yet expressive line of impeccably tailored clothes. This exacting sartorial point of view expresses itself in a thorough understanding of men's formal wear, and the elegant details of this rarified world pop up in even the most unlikely ensembles.

Humor has some part to play in Whereabouts' elevated sense of irony as well, with the Fall/Winter 2005-2006 collection dedicated to a species of player that "fully knows how to handle women but fails at the last moment." As expressed, this frustrated lothario look takes the form of a tailored jacket with a bold floral print, or a black suit with a subtle checkerboard pattern created by contrasting textural effects. "Happiness and relaxation" is another ongoing concern, with an idealized 1970s, and the culture of contemporary outdoor music festivals the theme for Spring/Summer 2007. Holding the show on a strip of fake lawn grass, security armbands, rainbow-colored hairbands and all-access passes complete a premise that combines a muted, organic palette with vaguely ethnographic quotations and ponchos. But the cut is still key, and in a sequence of standard- and full-length summer jackets and suits, this uncompromising attitude to craft hasn't wavered since that very first show.– *Ian Luna*

This page: Theatre Products & Kingly Theatre Products, Spring/Summer 2005.

COMME DES GARÇONS

The full scope of Comme des Garçons's activities in the last ten years has seen the material and spiritual borders of the house expand to regal proportions. Not merely an empire but now fully a "universe," the multiplicity of independent collections, collaborative projects and their attendant lines of accessories—scarcely recognizable from its origins nearly four decades ago—would now need an illustrated organizational chart to be completely apprehended. But in no way does this growing complexity even imply that the brand has swapped an erudite, revolutionary identity for a more commodified and anonymous charm. With its nucleus still very much the enigmatic and resolute Kawakubo Rei, Comme des Garçons has lost nothing of the rock-solid appeal and respect it commands in the shifting tumult of Tokyo—or for that matter in Paris or New York.

And it helps to have very capable lieutenants. In concert with the vital Comme des Garçons and Comme des Garçons SHIRT collections, the Comme des Garçons Homme and Homme Plus lines, which trace their origins nearly three decades ago have found further expression in the masterful stylings of Watanabe Junya. The knitwear Tricot line set up in 1981 is now under the charge of Kurihara Tao, who has been with the firm for nearly a decade, and like Junya, now has her own collection, tao Comme des Garçons. Rei's diversifying interests have even given birth to a number of unpredictable collaborations. Workaday streetbrands like Nike, North Face, Speedo and Fred Perry are recast with startling luster. As ever, these side projects are overseen by Kawakubo with little sentiment, but as with everything else that comes into her range of vision, all are animated with a deft, brooding and all-knowing magic.

Kawakubo's advocacy of intelligent forms eminently translates into furniture design and architecture; modalities that, like fashion, depend entirely on physical structure. The minimal and objective clarity of her environmental design is wholly conceived and comprehensive., and is typified by Kawakubo's own Chair No. 1, a steel composition with a mesh seat and an angled frame that the critic Deyan Sudjic "describes as elegant but unyielding," As applied, and always in combination with an interdependent graphics, this philosophy is arguably one of the most consistent strategies of space planning in high-fashion retailing.

Largely responsible for making a retail destination of Minami-Aoyama with the inaugural of the first Comme des Garçons store there in 1976, her regular collaborations with architect Kawasaki Takao are examples of a remarkable, intuitive synergy, and this continuing partnership found sure expression in the early 1980s through the present day.

Conducted under the Rei-sutra—"I never repeat anything"—the Comme des Garçons building program now utilizes a bevy of global consultants and has expanded the world over, with key shops by Ab Rogers and Shona Kitchen in Paris and Jan Kaplicky and Amanda Levete's Futuresystems in New York and Tokyo. But in contrast to these manicured spaces, the "guerrilla store" concept of temporary boutiques—which Comme des Garçons famously set up in places where it did not have a significant sales footprint—like Ljubljana, Stockholm or Warsaw—have preoccupied Kawakubo of late. But even these anti-boutiques have been formalized into more permanent guises in some of the label's major markets. The first of these was the Dover Street Market in London, and its un-designed design was ultimately transported back to the Aoyama store closest to Kawakubo's own offices, and was first enshrined within a plywood and fiberboard shell by the Belgian conceptual artist Jan de Cock in 2006.—*Ian Luna*

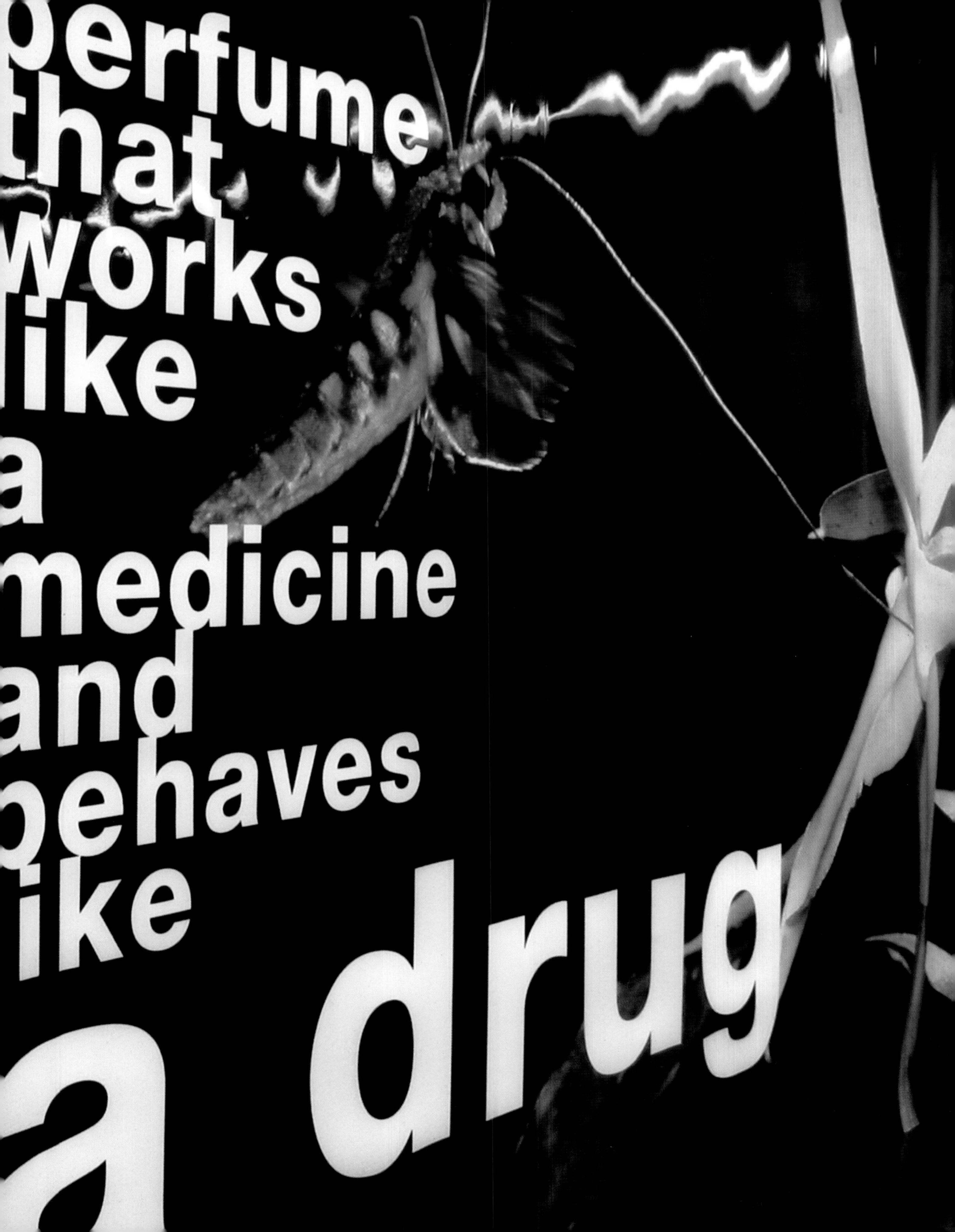

perfume
that
works
like
a
medicine
and
behaves
like
a drug

Six

Number 8 / 1991

Number4 1989

Six

コム デ ギャルソン
秋冬コレクションより ダーツツエック
のベスト ¥67,000,
 フスカート ¥79,000

Transformed Glamour
COMME des GARÇONS
*

COMME des GARÇONS

2·1
COMME des GARÇONS is Here

tricot
COMME des GARÇ

power
of
fashion

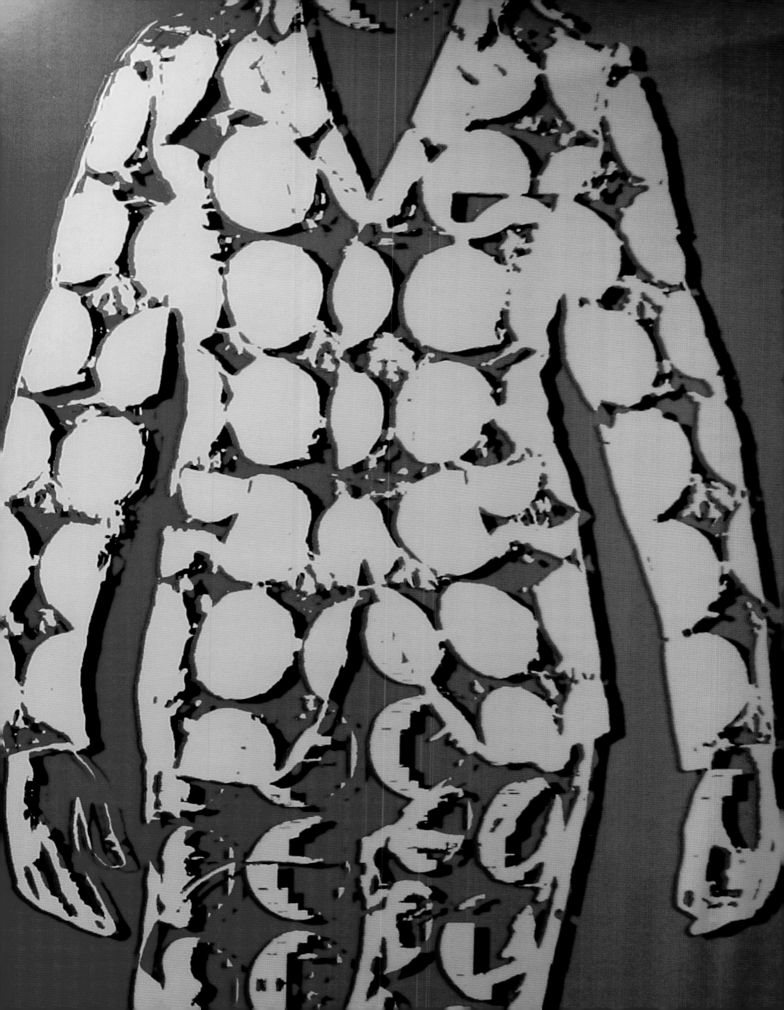

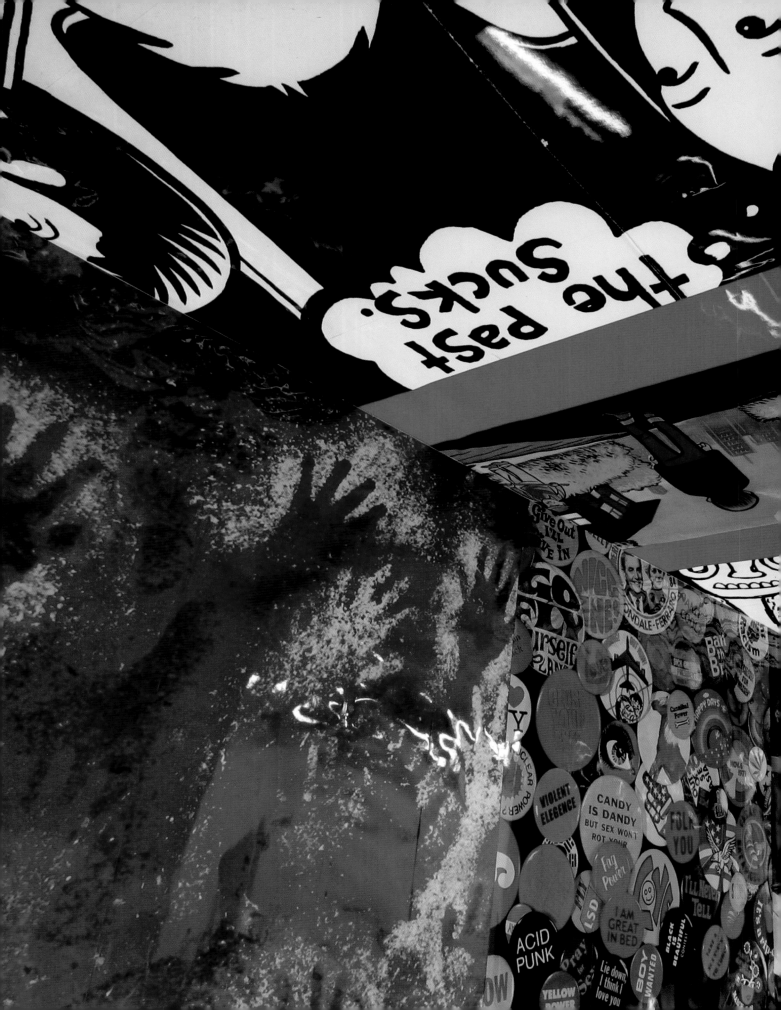

CENTER STAGE CITY
TOKYO IN THE MOVIES
ESSAY BY TOM MES

The city of Tokyo is the unrivaled setting for contemporary Japanese cinema. There are obvious reasons for this—a capital city's place in the cultural fabric is nearly always a predominant one, and in this sense Tokyo has always been a fixture of the Japanese film. However, its present, dual role as the center of film production and principal cinematic landscape had not always been so undisputed.

There are three major reasons behind Tokyo's ascendance, which are all socio-economic rather than artistic in origin. Firstly, there is the gradual process of foreclosure of film studios in other parts of the country. During World War II, the Japanese film industry was gathered and centralized into three major poles, with smaller and independent production companies forcibly merged or absorbed into larger outfits. Between 1941 and 1946, the Toho, Shochiku and Daiei corporations formed the entirety of the Japanese film industry. As the war ended and the Allied Occupation found in cinema a major tool for its policy of the democratization of Japanese society, this structure was kept largely intact. Allied politics allowed many of the same faces to remain in the same positions, including those initially categorized as war criminals to be "permanently removed" from their posts, like studio heads Hori Kyusaku at Nikkatsu, Osawa Yoshio at Toho, and Nagata Masaichi at Daiei.[1]

In the direct postwar years, this hegemony was secure enough to allow three newcomers to enter the market, leading to the six-studio model that formed the Japanese film industry during what is usually referred to as its "Golden Age" in the 1950s. Nikkatsu had been one of the pylons on which Daiei rested, but after the war it shrugged off its shackles and resumed its activities, though it had to start out with only a distribution network, its production facilities having remained part of Daiei. Shintoho (literally 'New Toho') was formed after one of a series of strikes at its mother company made part of its talent base decide to try their hands at self-management. Toei, finally, was a newly founded outfit that began by making period action films at a studio complex in Kyoto in the early 1950s.

These six majors effectively formed the entirety of the Japanese film industry, employing actors, directors and crew under contract and running large-scale studio complexes that churned out several films a week, programmed in double bills at studio-owned film theaters around the country. This situation endured into the 1960s, when it received its first of a series of blows. Largely due to the introduction of television, audience numbers in the nation's cinemas began to swiftly erode, dropping from over 1 billion in 1960 to a quarter of that number in the space of a decade[2]. Shintoho was the first to go down in flames, filing for bankruptcy in 1962, followed less than a decade later by Daiei. The others had to take drastic measures to avoid the same fate, and often this meant jettisoning the costly management of large studio complexes. Shochiku, for example, abandoned its set-up in Ofuna,

famous for producing the contemporary family dramas of Ozu Yasujiro. The company held on to its Kyoto compound, as did Toei. With the abundance of age-old locations surrounding the old capital, the Kyoto studios were traditionally devoted to the production of period films. But, as Mark Schilling puts it: "period dramas (jidaigeki) featuring sword-wielding samurai moved en masse to the small screen in the 1960s"[3] and were almost entirely absent from the theatrical line-up by the mid-70s. The television market became the main client for the Kyoto studios. As a result of all this, the majors centralized their activities in and directly around Tokyo, leading to a decrease in the number of film productions in other parts of the country. The city consequently and almost naturally became a more prominent backdrop.

What remains of filmmaking outside the capital today firmly belongs in the category of regional filmmaking. Most of this is due to individual initiatives: international film festival favorite Kawase Naomi, director of Suzaku (Moe no Suzaku, 1997), Hotaru (2000), and Shara (Sharasoju, 2003) remains loyal to her hometown of Nara, where all her films set; Kobayashi Masahiro has a penchant for the snowy wastes on the island of Hokkaido. Osaka developed into a hub of indie filmmaking activity in the mid-1990s, thanks to a group of film students at the local Osaka Geijutsu Daigaku arts university. However, alumni such as Kumakiri Kazuyoshi, whose graduation film Kichiku (Kichiku Dai Enkai, 1997) was selected for the Berlin Film Festival, and Yamashita Nobuhiro, director of slacker comedies Hazy Life (Donten Seikatsu, 1999) and No One's Ark (Baka no Hakobune, 2002), have since left the Kansai and found their way to Tokyo, where the work is. In recent years regional governments have offered incentives to film productions, but usually with the idea of using the resulting films as extended tourist board promos. The results so far have been scant, with veteran directors like Konuma Masaru and Higashi Yoichi heading into the provinces to make what amounts to little more than inconsequential travelogues.

The second reason for Tokyo's dominant position among the backdrops of choice is the lack of financial means, which the film industry has been coping with since the collapse of the major studio system in the 1970s. The film studios that survived the years of crisis largely diminished or even abandoned film production during that decade, laying off the filmmaking personnel under contract and retreating into more secure positions as distributor-exhibitors, leaving the risk of actual filmmaking to smaller, independent outfits. Budgets naturally had to dwindle: fewer people showed up to buy film tickets, returns on investment were lower and none of the small-time production companies had access to the kind of means and facilities the studios had had at their disposal during their heyday.

This situation has remained largely unchanged to this day, although the number of production units mushroomed during the early 90s, thanks to an influx of investments from outside the film world. This period, the height of Japan's bubble economy, saw many a new millionaire seeking attractive tax shelters and opportunities to launder money, and finding it in low-budget filmmaking. The video market was living a boom after Toei had discovered the medium's commercial potential quite by accident, when it released Okawa Shundo's *Crime Hunter* (*Kuraimu Hanta: Hikari no Jodan*, 1989)—a film that had utterly failed to set the theatrical box office alight—with enormous success on home formats. With that, V-cinema or Original Video (OV) was born: the straight-to-video industry which made genre movies on two-week schedules and US$ 300,000 budgets, which bypassed the cinema screens entirely and were released directly on videotape. Minimum investment, minimum risk, maximum returns.

Around the same time, amateur filmmaking was making serious inroads into the commercial distribution networks thanks to a number of high-profile titles. Self-financed productions like Tsukamoto Shinya's *Tetsuo: The Iron Man* (*Tetsuo*, 1989) and Hashiguchi Ryosuke's *A Touch of Fever* (*Hatachi no Binetsu*, 1993) did remarkably well on their theatrical releases and received acclaim at overseas festivals. This hardly formed an incentive for any of the established film companies to raise budgets. As Hashiguchi remarked: "People in the industry were quite shocked by this, because they found out that a successful film could even be made on a small budget. So they suddenly started making films at much lower budgets, resulting in a whole series of awful, cheap studio films."[4] Low-budget filmmaking flourished in the 1990s, allowing, at least in the independent sector, for the rise and the maturing of several generations of young filmmakers.

These budgets, however, did not allow for the construction of elaborate sets or the rental of studio facilities. Subsequently, location shooting and contemporary settings became the norm and the capital, where nearly all production companies were based, automatically developed into the location of choice; the Tokyo cityscape has become indissociable from contemporary Japanese cinema.

The third reason, finally, lies with proliferation of high-quality digital video equipment and its increasing acceptance as a legitimate filmmaking medium. Professionals and amateurs alike have been using DV to shoot everything from brief stylistic exercises to entire features, but the binding characteristic, thanks to the medium's ease of use and the perceived 'realness' of DV footage, has been a form of moviemaking that is more directly aware of immediate surroundings.

All of this is not to say that Japan's filmmakers employ the city like any other interchangeable backdrop. Production circumstances may demand a great deal of pragmatism of directors, but this has never been a hindrance to their creativity. The upside of the sparse means afforded to filmmakers is that they receive a lot of creative leeway in return. The low risk of investment removes the need for producers to curb directors' wilder instincts. As long as they remain within budget and on schedule, Japanese filmmakers are free to do as they please: modify scripts, shoot new scenes, or change locations.[5] The notion of "final cut," so elusive to their Hollywood brethren, is a given for directors in Japan. Even though many filmmakers work within recognizable genres—yakuza gangster films, *pinku* erotic films, horror, comedy, romance, and so on—the best of them move so freely within the framework that their films have only the scantest resemblance to genre works.

One such filmmaker is Miike Takashi, who began his career in the early 90s during the V-cinema boom. He epitomizes today's creative pragmatists, positively relishing the energetic, off-the-cuff production methods and moving from one project to the next with an ease and speed that knows no equal in world cinema. The majority of the sixty-plus features Miike has churned out in his 16-year career are in the gangster genre. Tokyo's Shinjuku ward features heavily in these films, in particular two landmarks on either side of labyrinthine Shinjuku station: to the West the twin-towered Tokyo Metropolitan Government building and to the East the enclave of Kabukicho. The reason for their predominance is self-explanatory: the former is the seat of police, the latter the city's red light district and a traditional hub of underworld activity.

Miike certainly isn't the only filmmaker to have aimed his lens at that gleaming structure or taken his camera into those streets lined with strip joints and *soapland* massage parlors, but he has shown an astute and distinctive way of regarding them. Toward the Metropolitan Government building he remains distant, nearly always filming it from the air to emphasize its isolation from the mostly low structures in its vicinity. It comes across as aloof, cold, monolithic. In his 1995 film *Shinjuku Triad Society* (*Shinjuku Kuroshakai*), about a cop of mixed heritage caught in the middle of a struggle between Taiwanese and Japanese gangs for control of Kabukicho's streets and spoils, the scenes set within the walls of the government high-rise are virtually drained of color, a flat, clinical blue dominating the image.

Miike films Kabukicho as its polar opposite: a flurry of garish neon, a huddle of people, street punks running criss-cross through the crowd. It's a place of frenzied, vibrant energy, an ordered chaos whose protagonists still act on instinct rather than by rules. Emblematic is the opening scene of 1999's *Dead or Alive* (*DOA Deddo oa Araibu: Hanzaisha*), a frantic, seven-minute montage of strippers at work, cops on the beat, drug deals gone sour and murders most foul. The excess and exaggeration lift it above the everyday reality of the place, making Miike's Kabukicho almost mythical. Yet—unlike for example Lee Chi Ngai's *Sleepless Town* (*Fuyajo*, 1998), an underworld romance whose Kabukicho was entirely reconstructed on a studio backlot—the director relies entirely on location shooting. He enlarges reality, but cannot do so without firmly grounding his films in that very same reality. Judging it too inflexible and cumbersome, Miike habitually refuses to coordinate his film shoots with the police and local authorities, preferring to set up his camera and adapt himself and his films to the environment as it presents itself. There are no blocked-off streets to avoid curious onlookers or passers-by stumbling into the frame. Those passers-by form part of the film. Even if there are actors within the frame, around them daily life goes on.

That Miike thrives on this is borne out by his occasional use of hidden cameras. Both *Ley Lines* (*Nihon Kuroshakai: Ley Lines*, 1999) and *Graveyard of Honor* (*Shin Jingi no Hakaba*, 2002) contain scenes shot in this way, in which one of the actors is made to stumble, covered in fake bruises and blood, among the street crowds. Capturing the spontaneous reactions of the onlookers, Miike captures the vibe of a town, sometimes even a sign of the times, as when the blood-soaked lead actor of *Graveyard of Honor* is steadfastly ignored by everyone he passes.

Miike uses the city environment to his advantage, making fiction and reality part of the same realm, paradoxically creating myths that are inextricably linked to reality. This is not only limited to the films set in Kabukicho or Shinjuku. His three-part television series *Tennen Shojo Mann* (1999) ventures down into Shibuya youth culture. Filming with a small, consumer-market video camera, Miike weaves his way through the throngs in the shopping streets, once again foregoing crowd control. Expressing the nimble vitality of Tokyo teens, the camera never stands still, looks at things at lopsided angles and takes on the points-of-view of its schoolgirl characters and their favorite objects alike.

Other directors have shown themselves similarly adept at not simply filming but capturing an essence of Tokyo and its vibes. Ishii Sogo's hypnotic *Angel Dust* (*Enjeru Dasuto*, 1994), with its story of serial murders by poisonous syringe in the city's subway network, was positively prophetic, pre-dating by just a few months the sarin gas attacks on that same subway system by followers of the Aum Shinrikyo cult. Miike's style on *Tennen Shojo Mann* is greatly indebted to Anno Hideaki's *Love & Pop* (1998), which is likewise set among the youth of Shibuya and employs light, handheld video cameras to shoot the goings-on from every imaginable angle. Based on Murakami Ryu's novel of the same name, which made the social phenomenon of *enjo kosai* or 'paid companionship' a headline issue, *Love & Pop* juxtaposed the energy of its youthful subjects with the excesses of the consumer culture that surrounded them, making the boutique-lined and advertising-crammed streets of Shibuya as much a player in the narrative as its 17-year-old protagonist.

Anno's film spawned a host of movies about youth gone wild in urban Tokyo. The very same year *Pornostar*, set among the *chinpira* or wannabe gangsters of Shibuya, marked the arrival of director Toyoda Toshiaki, one of the most promising newcomers to emerge in Japan the past few years. Toyoda's relationship with Tokyo is ambiguous, at once accepting its presence and expressing a fervent desire to transform it into something different, although like his young protagonists he is often at a loss to come up with the alternative. In *Pornostar* the arrival of a mute, knife-wielding kid in an anorak among the street punks helps the film take on the allures of a spaghetti western, with Shibuya's footbridges, alleyways, and steep slopes standing in for Sergio Leone's dusty town roads and windswept desert corridas. More commonly, Toyoda will take a plunge into surrealist dream sequences, the most remarkable being the one that opens his *9 Souls* (2003): in a panoramic shot we glide over Tokyo and watch as the city gradually turns to ashes, with only Tokyo Tower left standing at its center. In *Hanging Garden* (*Kuchu Teien*, 2005), a torrential rain of blood engulfs the brand new, ultra-geometric Machida suburb of a seemingly perfect family, just when their skeletons begin to come out of the closet. A wish to transform the city, without having a good notion of a healthy alternative, also marks 2001's *Blue Spring* (*Aoi Haru*) in which pupils take control over their suburban school building, but have little inkling of what to do next beyond covering the walls in messy black graffiti and playing games of dare to decide their internal hierarchy.

In a similar vein were Yamamoto Masashi's *Junk Food* and Tsukamoto Shinya's *Bullet Ballet* (both 1998), which dealt with another aberrant strain of Tokyo youth culture, *chiima* or Teamers—teenagers from well-to-do backgrounds forming groups and beating up the hapless salarymen that personify the generation of their own fathers. They are kids in open revolt against the dominant lifestyle in postwar urban Japan, devoted to company instead of family, though again without much of an idea of how to replace it. Tsukamoto in particular made the urban environment an intrinsic feature of his film. Cut together from scenes shot in Shibuya, Ikebukuro and Shinjuku, *Bullet Ballet* turns Tokyo into a maze of alleyways, backstreets and construction sites, the high-contrast black-and-white photography only contributing to the impression of an endless uniformity of landscape.

Takenaka Naoto in Ley Lines *(1999), Miike Takashi.*

This image of concrete Tokyo as cramped, oppressive, and threatening is a staple of Tsukamoto Shinya's entire body of work. No other Japanese film director of the past 25 years has been so obsessed with the effects of the urban environment on the human body and psyche. A Tokyo native, Tsukamoto spent his childhood in Shibuya at the height of the city's post-war reconstruction. Spurred on by the 1964 Tokyo Olympics, fenced-off lots and office blocks quickly encroached upon and replaced the diminutive, rickety emergency housing erected in the wake of the war, among which Tsukamoto played as a child.[6]

This experience marks nearly all his later films. Tsukamoto's protagonists are city folk, living lives of drudgery among the concrete; office drones who offer no resistance to the packed commuter trains, the long working hours or the sweltering summer heat. The sterility of their existence and the total detachment from nature have numbed their senses. His 1989 breakthrough *Tetsuo: The Iron Man* contained the germ of all this, but, being entirely homemade, was set mostly in suburban and residential locations. From its more affluent sequel *Tetsuo II: The Body Hammer* onward, though, the world of Tsukamoto's films would be composed of slabs of concrete and glistening steel. His Tokyo is a sterilized, inhuman environment, where all signs of decay are eradicated and the only emotion felt by the inhabitants is a continuous but vague, subconscious sense of frustration.

In the two *Tetsuo* films, this lingering irritation literally turns the protagonists into biomechanical monsters, rampaging through the city with an appetite for destruction, something repeated later, though in a different form, in the films of Toyoda Toshiaki. From 1995's *Tokyo Fist* onward, however, Tsukamoto would begin to offer alternatives, a new life that awaits beyond the destruction. Not coincidentally, *Tokyo Fist* is also the clearest expression of the filmmaker's favorite motifs. Tsukamoto himself plays an insurance salesman selling policies door-to-door in the stifling summer heat. The city is seen to actively promote desensitization: the decaying body of a dead cat he spots in an alley has been removed when he passes by the same place only hours later; his father is terminally ill in the hospital, but surrounded by busybody nurses in a profusely white room, he looks almost angelic. The salesman arrives too late to see him die—the bed has already been cleaned and remade for the next patient when he comes stumbling in. The main intrigue kicks into gear when an old school friend, now a boxer, pops up again and starts making advances at the salesman's wife. Seeing his better half's fascination for the fighter's tight, muscular body, the suit-and-tie man is painfully reminded of the physical inadequacies that have resulted from his own complacent lifestyle. When he begins a training regimen and confronts his nemesis, *Tokyo Fist* transforms into a symphony of burst eyebrows and spurting blood. Embracing the sensation of pain is revealed as the way to deliverance from the city's oppression.

In his more recent films, Tsukamoto has moved away somewhat from these themes, acknowledging that the situation in reality isn't quite as black and white as his films have portrayed it. Both *A Snake of June* (*Rokugatsu no Hebi*, 2003) and *Vital* (2004) show isolated pockets of nature and vitality existing within the city, particularly during the early-summer rainy season when plant life springs up from the cracks in the concrete. In the 50-minute *Haze* (2005), the director plays around freely with his old obsession: its otherworldly story of a man who finds himself imprisoned in a maze of narrow concrete passages is nothing if not a playful, symbolic reprise of his former main motif.

Another filmmaker who makes the urban environment an intrinsic component of his cinema is Kurosawa Kiyoshi, a man whose career has interwoven with all the major streams and developments in Japanese film since the late 1970s (8mm experimentalism, assistant directing on the last gasps of the studio system, low budget pink films, V-cinema and the festival-lauded 'new new wave' of the late 1990s). Where Tsukamoto fully identifies with the claustrophobic urban turmoil of his protagonists, Kurosawa takes the position of the detached observer. The spatial composition of Kurosawa's films are marked by a modernist's predilection for geometrical shapes. Whether shooting in Tokyo or its immediate environs (from which he rarely strays), the director renders space as thoroughly man-made. Even when a film takes place in a forest, like in 1999's *Charisma* (*Karisuma*), everything is shapes—trees vertical, ground horizontal, hills diagonal—and one can't go far without bumping into human activity or its traces. *Charisma*'s burn-out case police sergeant (played by Kurosawa's alter ego of choice, Yakusho Koji) decides to sever all ties with his urban lifestyle and wanders into what at first seem rather desolate woods. Before long, he is caught up in the struggle between a crazed biologist, a battalion of park rangers and a young man nursing a wilting tree, each of whom come with assorted hangers-on.

In Kurosawa's films, mankind is everywhere, constantly re-shaping the environment to suit its needs, even when it is not aware of exactly what those needs are. In the end, though, it is that very same process that ends up trapping his characters. Ironically, the spaces mankind creates for itself all too often end up feeling inhuman. Thanks to the director's ability to render any environment as a

films is a cold, barren place. Kurosawa's penchant for literally trapping his characters inside frames within the frame (doorways, windows, tunnels, etc.) only accentuates this impression. In *Pulse* (*Kairo*, 2002), a group of youths tends to a glasshouse on the roof of an apartment block, but despite the ample greenery, the sunlight and the kids' short sleeves, the atmosphere is chilly and the skeletal structure of the conservatory cage-like.

Similar to Tsukamoto's films, the only respite and escape for Kurosawa's protagonists lies in decay. Crumbling warehouses, dilapidated buildings and rundown cellars form a refuge, a portal to experiences beyond the unfeeling (and indeed numb) geometry of daily life. They are places where unseen things dwell, which appeal to instincts buried deep inside us. In the director's masterpiece *Cure* (*Kyua*, 1997), serial killings are committed by proxy by normal, everyday folk who have been hypnotised by an enigmatic drifter, a young man whose experiments with Franz Mesmer's theories of animal magnetism have blanked out his mind. Investigations lead a police detective (Yakusho again) to the hypnotist's former hideout, a weathered wooden storage facility that stands forlorn in a windswept no man's land just outside town. In *Pulse*, the lonely ghosts of the dead haunt dank basements and rusting, deserted factories, sealed inside by bright red duct tape over doors and windows – which form a geometric pattern that ironically attracts mortals rather than warning them away.

Kurosawa's inclusion of decaying spaces give his films a time capsule-like quality. The director has stated that one of the reasons he enjoys filming existing rundown buildings is the knowledge that, what with Japan's lack of inhabitable soil and the resulting land prices, such structures will inevitably be torn down and replaced with something new. Kurosawa's cinema chronicles the country's urge to constantly renew and urbanize itself, by filming both the decaying past and the cold, angular structures that replace it and that bury the mystique under concrete—our roots and sensations disappearing with it.

Not all Japanese filmmakers regard Tokyo with a look of doom and gloom, though. There are many that celebrate the town's atmosphere and energy or the distinct ambiance of a particular ward or neighborhood. Shinozaki Makoto, a former assistant of Kurosawa's, has more than once pointed his camera at the *shitamachi* to capture the fading glories of the old entertainment districts Asakusa and Ueno, whose lure has long since been lost to the postwar bustle of Shinjuku, Shibuya and Ikebukuro. Himself an Asakusa native, Shinozaki set a large part of his superb old-meets-young drama *Not Forgotten* (*Wasurerarenu Hitobito*, 2001) in the tree-lined lanes of old Tokyo. He particularly honed in on the remnants of the district's pleasure quarters with the made-for-TV adaptation of Kitano Takeshi's autobiography *Asakusa Kid*. The story covers Kitano's teenage years as an apprentice comedian at the Furansu-za ('France Theater'), a small-scale Asakusa strip club. In addition to a vivid portrayal of backstage ennui, Shinozaki's *Asakusa Kid* was a loving tribute to the area, using numerous street scenes filled with peddlers, amusement arcades, and an endearingly old-fashioned sex industry that is leagues away from the neon flash of Kabukicho. Opting to set the story in the modern day may have been forced upon Shinozaki by budget restrictions, but the choice has the pleasant side-effect of evoking how little has changed in Asakusa since Kitano's humble, pre-Beat days sweeping floors and practicing his dance steps in the late 60s.

Similar paeans to the washed-up denizens of the *shitamachi* can be found in Mochizuki Rokuro's three-part *Wicked Reporter* series (*Gokudo Kisha*, 1993-95). Mochizuki, who would later become better known for his exceptional location shooting in Tokyo's Kansai cousin Osaka, lovingly portrays the lives of those that skulk around the race tracks, betting their meager earnings away on horses and hounds and drowning their misfortune in nearby bars. Though less concerned with architecture than with human behavior, Mochizuki's trilogy captures a side of life in the capital that is rarely seen by foreign eyes, and all but forgotten by the suburban population that spend half their lives commuting to and from work.

A similarly affectionate look is aimed at Kamata in Hiroki Ryuichi's *It's Only Talk* (*Yawarakai Seikatsu*, 2005). Once the site of a Shochiku studio complex, today it possesses "not an ounce of chic" according to protagonist Yuko, but is no less fascinating for it. Unemployed, Yuko traverses the area with her camera, in search of hidden corners whose snapshots she publishes on the website that documents her daily life. Suffering from manic depression, Yuko is the victim of violent mood swings that tie her to her bed for days on end, guzzling medication and mineral water. The forced isolation only serves to accentuate the importance of the street scenes, which candidly capture Kamata's vibe and the vivacity that exists in this seemingly nondescript area of Tokyo.

By far the most intimate portraits of the bonds between Tokyo and its residents can be found in the work of the young, amateur filmmakers currently beavering away with little digital cameras, making both fictional and documentary films in which their own lives and surroundings take center stage. Compared to these grassroots *jishu eiga* (literally 'independent films'), all the filmmakers mentioned above seem like mere distant observers. The immediacy found in Ono Satoshi's *Homemade Sake* (*Danchizake*, 2001) is symptomatic. It is the chronicle of the then 24-year-old director's own family life, or what is left of it. His parents inhabit separate apartments in the same tenement building, a prefab concrete monstrosity typical of the cheap housing erected during the 1960s to accommodate the massive influx of people from rural areas. These white slabs stand in rows like

guishable from one another but for the giant numbers painted in black on their façades. In Ono's film, the father is out of work and alcoholic, rarely venturing outside his apartment. He spends his time painting and, due to a permanent lack of money, brewing his own sake using rice and household items bought at a nearby convenience store. Back in 1976, Fukasaku Kinji opted to have the wild dog cop protagonist of Korean descent of his film *Yakuza Graveyard* (*Yakuza no Hakaba: Kuchinashi no Hana*) live in one of these districts to underline the character's outcast status. Already then, when the buildings were still relatively new, Fukasaku made the place seem like an inhuman ghetto, shooting the area in a decidedly grubby panoramic shot that emphasized the structures' interchangeable nature.

A similar intimacy, albeit of a more cheerful sort, marks the work of Murakami Kenji, who became known in the late 1990s for mini features like *Tel-Club* (*Natsu ni Umareru*, 1999), all of which he shot on digital video, then still something of a rare format. Armed with a DV camera wherever he goes like the bastard son of Shohei Imamura and Woody Allen, Murakami makes films that blur the lines between fiction and documentary in a playful, self-deprecating way. Despite seeming lightweight, his works skillfully challenge viewers' preconceptions about reality and fiction in cinema. Though he has since moved on to a professional filmmaking career (he has several more conventional V-cinema genre films to his name) and also teaches filmmaking at a university, Murakami has continued turning out homemade video productions on the side. One of the most interesting and downright entertaining of these is *How I Survive in Kawaguchi City* (*Kawaguchi de Ikiro yo!*, 2003), in which he culls together footage of his marriage and subsequent relocation for financial reasons to the titular suburb. Taking his camera on strolls through his new habitat, he discovers, much like Yuko in *It's Only Talk*, the peculiar little details of an otherwise charmless residential quarter: an iron foundry tucked away in a side street, a field of reeds on the edge of town. After participating in the communal marathon, he proclaims his everlasting devotion to Kawaguchi.

The deftness displayed in Murakami's works can also be found in the fruits of other indie videomakers. Particularly noteworthy in this context is *The Gaze* (*Shisen*, 2004) by Yamamoto Yosuke, a student at Kawasaki's Japan Academy of Visual Arts. Part of a collaborative program between the school and Germany's Nippon Connection film festival, *The Gaze* plunges camera-first into the chaotic rush of Tokyo's subway system. Yamamoto mimics the behavior of a stalker, choosing people from the dense crowd and following them for a while to see where they go and what they are up to. The effect is reminiscent of Edgar Allan Poe's *The Man of the Crowd*, whose premise was the thought that many of us have had while walking through a busy city street: "Who are these people, where are they going and for what purpose?" By fixing his gaze on a single person among many, Yamamoto pulls his subject out of anonymity. Most of his picks become visibly aware of his presence, showing signs of discomfort at being followed by someone with a camera. What is normally an unwanted side effect for a documentary filmmaker—i.e. the presence of the camera influencing what is being recorded—in Yamamoto's film actually underscores the success of his approach. The result of his method is that the subject is no longer simply a component of the surroundings or a cog in the big-city mechanism, but an individual

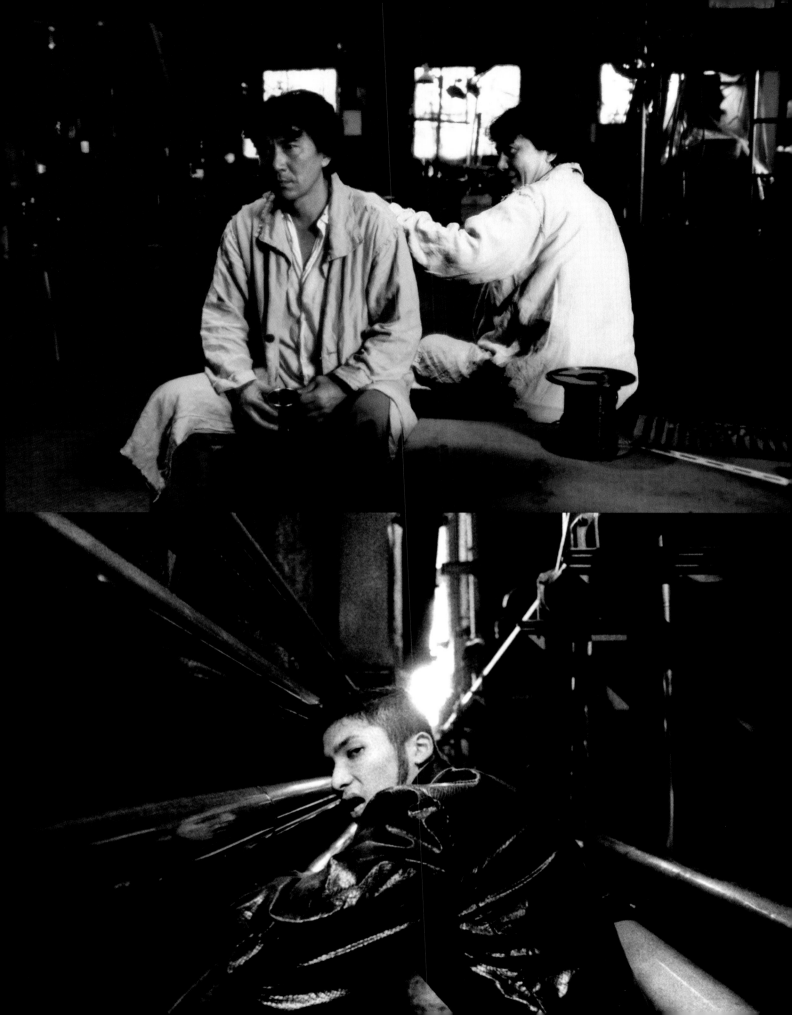

Above and opposite page: Terashima Shinobu and Toyokawa Etsushi in It's Only Talk *(2005), Hiroki Ryuchi.*

Working without money, without studios and with equipment that is perfectly suited to shooting in any imaginable location, the *jishu eiga* filmmakers are the logical culmination of the three factors that have put Tokyo in the center of Japanese cinema's attention. An opposite tendency is rearing its head, however. Advances in computer graphics technology have made studio shooting attractive again—the use of blue screens instead of sets saving producers a good amount of the expenses of yore. Hand in hand with an imitation of the Hollywood formula of entertainment spectaculars and an inflation of budgets thanks to co-productions between up to a dozen financial partners, blockbuster filmmaking is on its way back. In this arena where fantasy rules, something as earthy as a city and its inhabitants would inevitably seem to take a back seat to digital monsters and big explosions. However, there would be no Godzilla without a city to stomp on. One of the big moneyspinners of recent time was *The Great Yokai War* (*Yokai Daisenso*, 2005), directed by none other than former Kabukicho chronicler Miike Takashi. Though digitally enhanced, Tokyo takes center stage as it becomes the victim of a gargantuan, monstrous heap of discarded waste— the combined, mutated contents of the urbanites' own trashcans coming back for revenge. And yes, it is Shinjuku's Metropolitan Government Building that is the first to bite the dust.

This tidal wave of new disaster epics shows signs of washing away. The monster hit of the summer of 2006 was Toho studio's remake of its own 1973 blockbuster *The Sinking of Japan* (*Nihon Chinbotsu*). Based on Komatsu Sakyo's novel, it chronicles the destructive results of massive geological rumblings that literally cause the archipelago, and the tectonic plate on which it rests, to gradually but surely submerge into the Earth's fiery core. Director Higuchi Shinji, a former effects man, relishes the opportunity to show Tokyo and other cities crumbling to dust from force-8 earthquakes and burned to a crisp by volcanic eruptions.

Where *The Sinking of Japan* tells its story and its cast emotes with the same subtlety as the film's CGI catastrophes, a timely cash-in takes a far more interesting approach. *The Sinking of the World Except Japan* (*Nihon Igai Zenbu Chinbotsu*) may sound like a quick cash-in, and certainly the reputation of its director Kasawasaki Minoru— guiding hand behind such less-than-subtle comedies as *The Calamari Wrestler* and *Executive Koala*—suggests something akin to a Zucker Brothers parody, but there is more than meets the eye. Based on a short story by non-conformist science fiction writer Tsutsui Yasutaka—a contemporary of Philip K. Dick and J.G. Ballard—it voluntarily positions itself on the opposite end of the political spectrum; where *The Sinking of Japan* makes heavy-handed and less than thoughtful comparisons between the efforts of its rescue worker protagonists (played by impossibly fresh-faced pair of Kusanagi Tsuyoshi and Shibasaki Kou) and the sacrifices of World War II kamikaze pilots, Kawasaki's film portrays a country suddenly forced to cope with a massive influx of refugees from other parts of the world—and the dilemmas of feeding, housing, and integrating them into society.

For that very reason, the sinking of the rest of the world didn't go down nearly as well at the local box office than the sinking of Japan itself.

Nostalgia for the "old days"—or to be more precise, an obstinate and negationist vision of Japan just before, during and immediately after the war—has been selling well. Witness a plethora of jingoistic war movies such as Yamato (*Otokotachi no Yamato*, 2005), *Lorelei* (2004) and *Aegis* (*Bokoku no Iijisu*, 2003), and, in the wake of Yamada Yoji's Oscar-nominated *Twilight Samurai* (*Tasogare Seibei*, 2002), a renewed genteel take on the age-old *jidai geki* samurai dramas that is leagues away from the bloody, anti-feudalistic, left-wing *chanbara* of the 1960s and 70s.

What most of these films share is a view of history that prefers to ignore the intricacies of political dealings and reduce past events to human-interest dramas, devoid of political resonance or any attempt to investigate underlying reasons. All that matters is the milking of human emotions in the interest of drawing the largest possible crowds. Few better examples exist of this than *Always: Sunset on Third Street* (*Always: Sanchome no Yuhi*, 2005), a rose-tinted look at life in a small Tokyo neighborhood in the early 1950s, a stone's throw from the construction of Tokyo Tower. Instead of large-scale devastation, computer graphics here serve to give a warm hue to this city crawling back to its feet, culminating in the titular sunsets that silhouettes the new landmark against an overwhelmingly colorful sky. Here too, a former special effects technician, Yamazaki Takashi, is at the film's helm and it is obvious that he is more familiar with his software than with the films of Terrence Malick. But why worry about being truthful when raising the flag, tugging at the heartstrings, and bombarding an audience with visual effects is the surest recipe for filling cinema seats?

Notes

[1] Richie, Donald. *A Hundred Years of Japanese Film* (revised and updated edition). Tokyo: Kodansha, 2005, pp. 108, 109

[2] http://www.unijapan.org

[3] Schilling, Mark. *Contemporary Japanese Film*. Trumbull: Weatherhill, 1999, p. 15

[4] Mes, Tom and Jasper Sharp, *The Midnight Eye Guide to New Japanese Film*. Berkeley: Stone Bridge Press, 2004, p. 173

[5] Novielli, Maria Roberta. "V-shinema: l'atra industria", in: *Il cinema giapponese oggi—Tradizione e innovazione*, Giovanni Spagnoletti and Dario Tomasi (ed,). Torino: Lindau, 2001. pp. 35-40

[6] Mes, Tom. *Iron Man: The Cinema of Shinya Tsukamoto*. Godalming: FAB Press, 2005

KOREEDA HIROKAZU

Left, clockwise from top left: Naito Takashi, Arata, Terajima Susumu, Oda Erika, and Tani Kei in After Life *(1998); right, Oda Erika in* After Life. *Opposite page: Yagira Yuya, Shimizu Momoko, Kitaura Ayu, and Kimura Hiei (l-r) in* Nobody Knows *(2004); Arata, Natsukawa Yui, Terajima Susumu, Iseya Yusuke, Asano Tadanobu (l-r) in* Distance.

Koreeda Hirokazu's work has always shown a strong affinity for landscape. In his debut film *Maborosi* (*Maboroshi no Hikari*, 1995) he attempted to avoid portraying his characters' emotions in too obvious and conventional a fashion. Eschewing close-ups and keeping his camera at a distance from his players, he let the natural elements and the characters' surroundings do the talking: inky black skies, rain, tunnels, bare rooms. Interaction between man and his environment has featured prominently in Koreeda's work, even in his days directing television documentaries in the early 1990s. These TV productions include films on environmental pollution and Narita airport, always made from a human point-of-view, without falling into the trap of providing inane "human interest."

It was with his second feature that Tokyo began to play a sizeable part in the director's cinematographic landscape. *After Life* (*Wandafuru Raifu*, 1998) is set at a way station between the worlds of the living and the dead, a sort of limbo where souls come to choose their single most impressive memory before moving on to the titular afterlife, where they will eternally relive that one moment of happiness. Koreeda chose to film at an abandoned school building and this structure is the film's single most dominant feature, its walls slightly dilapidated and overgrown with ivy, its interiors austere and institutional. Not unlike Kurosawa Kiyoshi, Koreeda captures something on film that belongs to the past. Since such rundown buildings tend to quickly fall prey to the bulldozer in a country where space is limited,

members belonged to. Strongly informed by the national tragedy that was the 1995 Aum cult subway attack, *Distance* is not an easy film to watch. Joined by an ex-member, they spend the night in the woods to make their peace with the memories of their loved ones before returning to Tokyo the following day. The transition from the green countryside to a wide shot of the West exit of gargantuan Shinjuku station is abrupt: suddenly, the five men and women we've been so close to are swallowed up by the crowd that, captured in a bird's eye view, look like so many ants bustling about anonymously. The rest of the city settings is made up of cramped apartments and narrow streets, the polar opposite of the spacious freedom of the woods.

This idea of the anonymity of city life resurfaces in *Nobody Knows* (*Dare mo Shiranai*, 2004), in which a mother abandons her four children, who are left to fend for themselves in their small apartment. Their predicament is lost on neighbors and passers-by, despite the odors emitting

ISHIOKA MASATO

Top: Ishioka Masato on the set of Tokyo Noir *(2004). Opposite page, top: Scoutman (2000).*
Bottom: Yoshino Kimika in *Tokyo Noir: Night Lovers *(2004).

Most directors who shoot in Tokyo really only use the city as a backdrop in which to set their stories. It is a rare few who pick up on the kind of everyday real-life dramas that unfold within the anonymity of the city. Ishioka Masato takes a painful look at aspects of metropolitan life that most turn a blind eye to. The two titles to bear his name so far both take place within the closed-off, hidden world of the sex industry.

Ishioka's debut in 2000, *Scoutman* (a.k.a. *Pain*) focused on the all-but-illegal activities of some of the lowliest workers in the business, the pony-tailed hustlers whose job it is to accost young girls in the street to find fresh flesh to fuel the country's vast hardcore Adult Video industry. The hook into the film is provided by two guileless young ingénues freshly arrived from the provinces and drawn into this sordid milieu through financial desperation. Atsushi immediately finds his niche among the ranks of the eponymous predatory talent-spotters, while his lame girlfriend Mari is forced to make ends meet by handing out flyers for underground sex parties.

Ishioka continued to lay bare the unglamorous day-to-day banality of sex workers' lives in the omnibus movie *Tokyo Noir* (2004). The second segment of the film, *Girl's Life,* centers around Miyuki, one of the ranks of college students earning money by doling out blowjobs and kindly words to lonely businessmen in the compartmentalized "look but don't touch" world of the *fuzoku* sex club, while for the third, *Night Lovers,* he joins forces with the first segment's director, Kamazawa Naoto, to tell the tale of a high-class hooker who arranges her secret hotel-room hook-ups with clients via the internet while driving around Tokyo by night.

In both films, Ishioka adopts a lowkey, naturalistic approach, often shooting on location with handheld cameras to give his subject matter a more dynamic immediacy. In *Scoutman* in particular, this technique provides an instantly-recognizable snapshot of the Ikebukuro district. Stripping this

seductive and mysterious environment of all window dressing while portraying the extraordinary lives of the ordinary people who populate it, his films ultimately show how the sex industry soils and debases all who those come into contact with it.--*Jasper Sharp*

ISHII SOGO

Left to right: Minami Kaho in Angel Dust *(1994); Ichikawa Mikako (l.) and Asano Tadanobu in* Dead End Run *(2003); opposite page: Nakajima Yosuke in* Shuffle *(1981).*

Although he has always kept a strong bond with his home ground of Hakata, Kyushu, Ishii Sogo's cinema is deeply interconnected with the city of Tokyo. Emerging from the punk music scene of the late 1970s, Ishii was a pioneer of the independent 8mm movement that would go on to rejuvenate the Japanese film industry through the 1980s. His made his first Tokyo-set feature while still a student, becoming something of a celebrity when it was picked for nationwide distribution by major studio Toei. *Crazy Thunder Road* (*Kuruizaki Sanda Rodo*, 1980) followed a clash between biker gangs and the right-wing street soldiers that are such a common sight around the capital. The film was a raucously energetic piece of work, set mostly in the more rundown parts of town: fields, empty lots, and deserted warehouses. His follow-up *Burst City* (*Bakuretsu Toshi*, 1982) continued in a similar vein. Shot in the outskirts of Tokyo, in what has today mostly become suburbia, *Burst City*'s décor is a futuristic industrial wasteland populated by bikers, punk rockers, gangsters, homeless and brigades of riot police.

After 1984's *Crazy Family* (*Gyakufunsha Kazoku*), an attack on the suburban nuclear family, Ishii disappeared from the filmmaking scene for almost a decade, resurfacing in 1994 with a TV omnibus film named *Tokyo Blood*. The four episodes that comprise the 40-minute film all use, as the title implies, the capital as their terrain: *Street Noise* plays like a digest of the films of Tsukamoto Shinya, as a salaryman, crumbling under the pressures of urban life, slowly transforms into a cyborg as he runs through the streets; *Jitensha* [Bicycle] follows two junior high school girls as they walk around Tokyo with their cycles in hand. They take the city as it is, their natural habitat; *Ana* [Hole] sees a construction worker driven mad and drilling holes at random in the soil under the capital in the hope of unlocking a mystery that only exists in his head; *Heart of Stone*, finally, cuts back and forth between wide shots of Tokyo and images of rocky wastelands, taking a metaphysical turn that would announce the tone for the Ishii films that were to follow.

The first of these works was *Angel Dust* (*Enjeru Dasuto*), a murder mystery with an almost hypnotically calm pace, inspired by the works of J.G. Ballard and Philip K. Dick. Here, Ishii had his finger so thoroughly on the pulse of life in the capital that *Angel Dust* effectively predicted the following year's Aum cult drama: the film depicts a series of murders in the Tokyo subway system committed by means of a poison-filled syringe. The director renders Tokyo and its environs almost entirely as geometric shapes, predating the approach Kurosawa Kiyoshi would take to portraying space in the second half of the 1990s.

Subsequent films saw Ishii retreating to the provinces and into the past, but with 2001's *Electric Dragon 80,000V* and its 2003 follow-up *Dead End Run* he plunged right back into the heart of the metropolis. The former follows Asano Tadanobu, in the role of 'reptile investigator' Dragon Eye Morrison, a sort of power-charged pet detective who due to a childhood accident at a power station can absorb and release currents of high-voltage electricity. *Dead End Run* is a compendium of three almost interchangeable stories reminiscent of the *Street Noise* section of *Tokyo Blood*, presenting a trio of men on the run from invisible enemies in the nighttime streets. Both 55-minute experimental works in which sound is of equal important to image, these two films show Tokyo as a labyrinthine procession of identical slabs of concrete and protruding metal tubes, wires and antennas. The city here has lost its function: it is no longer a place where one lives, but where one simply *is*.—*Tom Mes*

NAGASAKI SHUNICHI

Left to Right: Naito Takashi (l.) and Muroi Shigeru in Heart, Beating in the Dark *(1982); Miura Tomokazu, Amami Yuki, and Matsuoka Shunsuke (l-r) in* A Tender Place *(2001). Opposite page, top: Nagasaki Shunichi; bottom: Akiyoshi Kumiko (l.) and Kusakari Masao in The* Enchantment *(1989).*

A contemporary and studio-mate of Ishii Sogo, Nagasaki Shunichi was another of the major figures who emerged from the 8mm scene in the late 1970s. His early works, like *The Summer Yuki Gave up Rock Music* (*Yuki ga Rokku o Suteta Natsu*, 1978) and *The Alley Behind Happy Street* (*Happii Sutoriito Ura*, 1979) are mostly shot in and around the town of Yokosuka, home to a large U.S. naval base and the site of Imamura Shohei's 1963 *Pigs and Battleships* (*Buta to Gunkan*), and derive much of their inspiration from the action films churned out by the Toei and Nikkatsu studios in the previous decade.

It was while tied to a hospital bed for several months in 1979, the result of a serious accident during the filming of his biker film *The Lonely Hearts Club Band in September* (*Kugatsu no Jodan Kurabbu Bando*, 1980), that Nagasaki began to ponder his future as an artist. His release from medical care marked a radical change in the style and substance of his films, turning to a more contemplative tone and a fascination with man's ability to be devoured by his own obsessions—romantic, sexual and otherwise.

From the early 1980s, *amour fou* became the recurring motif of his films. The director now settled in Tokyo, the capital began to provide the backdrop of choice for his work. Subtly manipulated through lighting, lenses, and rudimentary effects like smoke, the city becomes an often dreamlike landscape that provides his characters with a suitably fantastical environment for their derailed psyches. His superb psycho-thriller *The Enchantment* (*Yuwakusha*, 1989) is one of the best examples of this sparse but hugely effective method of transforming the cityscape through basic cinematic means. A throat-grabbing finale uses little more than a rooftop and a flashing Coca-Cola sign to bring the full extent of the characters' delusions into the open, letting it overtake the film's daily reality.

These spaces of the mind reveal themselves in indoor settings too, such as in the two versions of *Heart, Beating in the Dark* (*Yamiutsu Shinzo*, 1982 &

2005), in which criminal couples on the lam find their fears and guilt reflected by the squalid living quarters that serve as their temporary accommodation. Like in *The Enchantment*, a half-opened door to darkness finally makes the delusional spill over into reality. Interiors and exteriors are interchangeable in the shot-on-DV *Dogs* (1998), a film noir whose peculiar gender reversal twist—the detective is a beautiful woman, her paramour an *homme fatale*—hints at its unconventional take on the genre. Nagasaki fills his monochrome images with thick black shadows that seem to express the darker recesses of his protagonist's mind, from which more and more of her actions begin to stem.

Similar shadow play occurs in the earlier *Stranger* (*Yoru no Sutorenja: Kyofu*, 1991), a rare Japanese example of an urban paranoia movie, a genre little seen in the nation's cinema for the simple fact that every corner of Japan's major cities and suburbs alike is lit up at night by the countless neon signs of restaurants, bars, convenience stores and pachinko parlors. In *Stranger*, a female taxi driver with a dark past finds herself stalked by a mysterious, axe-wielding assailant who hides in exactly those normally non-existent shadows. The film mingles this stylized Tokyo with candid, almost documentary-like shots of Shinjuku nightlife, to surprisingly effective result.—*Tom Mes*

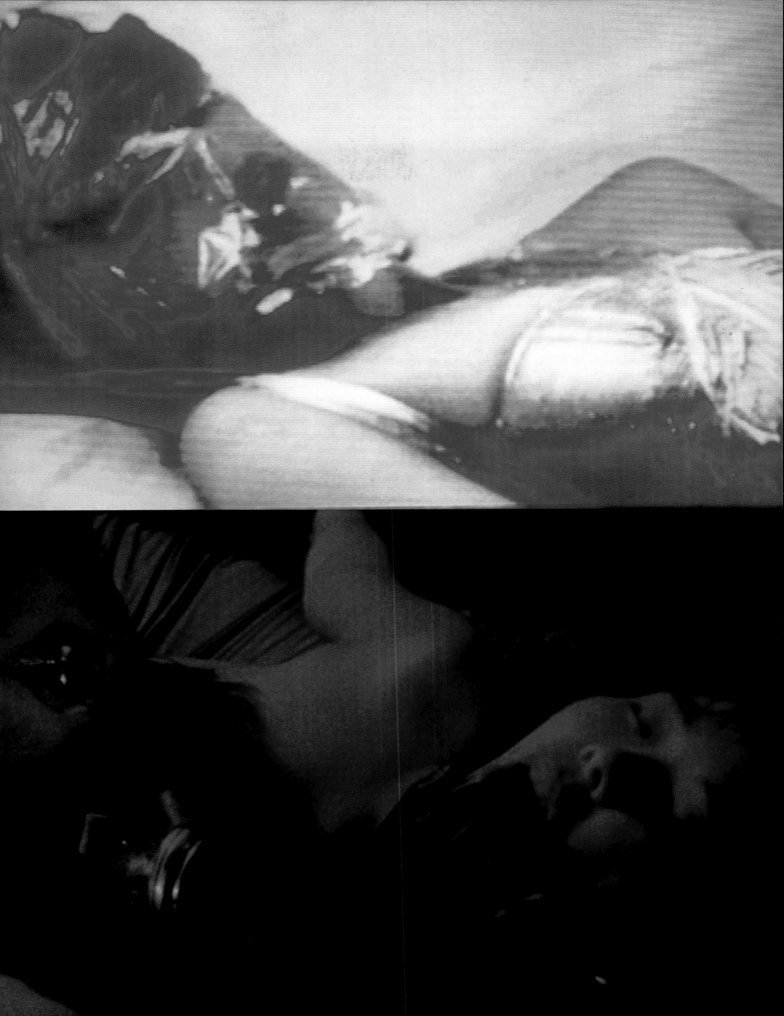

KUDO KANKURO

Left to right: Sakai Wakana, Abe Sadao and Koide Saori in Maiko Haaaan!!! *(2007); Ookura Koji (left) and Kubozuka Yosuke in* Ping Pong *(2002), directed by Sori Fumihiko, screenplay by Kudo Kankuro. Opposite page: Group Tamashii. Standing (left to right): Tomizawa Taku, Miyake Hiroki, Kozono Ryuichi, Kudo Kankuro. Sitting (left to right): Abe Sadao, Minato Kaoru, Murasugi Seminosuke.*

If postmodernity might be said to be the natural state of mind for contemporary Japanese—thanks to its two waves of rapid assimilation of foreign influences, at the start of the Meiji era and the end of World War II—and if this book is a testimony to the versatility, the energy, the creativity, and the artistic gluttony of the Tokyo arts scene today, then one man deserves to be singled out for embodying all these qualities. Kudo Kankuro is the quintessential post-modern, pop-cultural, urban renaissance man, whose work fits the full scope of this volume. He hasn't constructed any buildings yet (except perhaps in the metaphorical sense), but he may well get there one day.

Soft-spoken, hunger-strike skinny, and with a head of unkempt hair, he doesn't seem to fit anyone's definition of a media-courted star. Least of all the Japanese, who tend to prefer the faces on their magazine covers younger, smoother, and a lot prettier. Yet, there he is, regularly gracing the front pages of trendy youth-oriented magazines like Cut and H: "Kudokan," the musician, comedian, actor, playwright, screenwriter, essayist, novelist, radio DJ, and film director, baring his bucktoothed smile, like the reflection in the funhouse mirror of that other multi-disciplinarian and ubiquitous cover boy, AsanoTadanobu.

The Kudokan phenomenon has been in overdrive ever since the then 32-year-old wunderkind won the Japanese Academy Award in 2002 for his screenplay of Isao Yukisada's hit film *GO!*, an adaptation of the Kaneshiro Kazuki novel about the heartaches and tribulations of a second-generation Korean immigrant.. Despite his young age, Kudo already had ten years as a performer and writer under his belt when he ascended the red-carpeted steps to receive his prize. Since then, his dance card has come to look something like this:

2003: ten books, five acting roles, two screenplays for films, teleplays for four weekly TV series;
2004: three books, three screenplays, a five-part manga series, and one album with his rock band Group Tamashii*;*
2005: six books, one acting part, one film script, one series teleplay, one film as a director, and one album;
2006: six books, two acting parts, and one series teleplay.
2007: three acting gigs and a screenplay.

In between, Kudo has continued his work on the stage, undertaken several tours with Group Tamashii, as well as presenting his own weekly radio show, entitled Kick the Kudokan. Plus TV appearances and all those magazine covers. In Tokyo, there is no rest for the wickedly talented.

The Kitano Connection

Such feverish activity inevitably brings to mind Japan's most internationally lauded workaholic, Kitano "Beat" Takeshi, he of deadpan gangster films and sadistic variety shows. The comparison is definitely not without merit: "When Kitano was a TV comedian he had a huge influence, especially on kids of my generation," Kudo recalls. "I grew up watching him on television. When I was a teenager I wanted to be one of his disciples and join the Takeshi Army. I sent them lots of postcards and they actually called me in to the office a couple of times." One of Kudo's early breaks as an aspiring actor and comedian was precisely under the wing of Kitano, in the director's 1995 tale of high school layabouts *Kids Return.* "Being on the set was a strange experience for me, because it almost felt like I was in a documentary: Kitano would never tell me what to do. All of a sudden he would just say 'Start the scene!' It didn't seem like he wanted me to act, but more that he wanted to capture my real reaction, my surprise. It was a very interesting experience for me, to be directed that way."

Alongside absurdist writer/director/actor/TV presenteri Sato Sakichi (of *Ichi the Killer, Gozu, Kill Bill and Tokyo Zombie* fame) and his own mentor Suzuki Matsuo (an almost equally prolific stage

The Ocean Waves (Umi ga Kikoeru, *1993*) © Himuro Saeko/GN

and it is often questionable whether such projects are necessary or in the public interest.

Emblematized by the ongoing construction of the new Olympic Stadium, *Akira* points to the extent that Tokyo's denizens' very social patterns are engineered by government control over their physical environment. Memories of the destruction wreaked by the atomic bomb on the cities of Hiroshima and Nagasaki and the constant threat of earthquakes may have made Tokyo a city constantly aware of its own transience, but the cataclysmic scenes of devastation that form the climax of *Akira* offer more than just the same vicarious thrill of history repeating itself elicited by Godzilla's recurrent rampages across the capital. Instead, *Akira* offers viewers the joyously liberating spectacle of the tearing down of old institutions that stifle the individual as the spurious veneer of modernity is ripped away.

Rather than apocalypse, *Akira* posits renaissance—a wiping clean of the slate—and that the seeds of social change lie dormant in the younger generation, violent forces within Japan rather than outside. It thus harks back to the counter-cultural idealism of the 60s, a decade in which, like his contemporary Oshii Mamoru Ôtomo grew up. The decade of the actual Tokyo Olympics saw students and leftwing radicals taking to the streets to protest the signing of the Japan-U.S.

Security Pact, or Ampo Treaty, which supported the maintenance of American military bases on Japanese soil, ostensibly to protect the Japanese population from the scourge of communism that was sweeping across South East Asia. The failure of the protest movement marked the quashing of effective political dissent within the country and set the course for much of the government's subsequent political obduracy.

This Manichean showdown between the rational forces of progress and technology and destructive forces surging forth from the primitive id finds itself rendered on many occasions within anime. But while the very *mise-en-scène* of *Akira* lends it an explicitly political dimension, on other occasions the subtext is more heavily veiled. The 1987 release of *Wicked City* (*Yôjù Toshi*), directed by Kawajiri Yoshiaki, who would later give the world *Vampire Hunter D* (2001), is typical of the sub-genre of "anime nasties" represented by the OAV titles *Legend of the Overfiend* (*Urotsukidoji*, 1987) and *Demon City Shinjuku* (*Makai Toshi Shinjuku* aka *Monster City*, 1988). With their overtly psychosexual imagery of bodies writhing and splitting in two and sprouting phallic-shaped tentacles, such titles give vent to fears that are more pathological in basis than technological.

The Tokyo of *Wicked City* lies in an uneasy truce with an alternate mirror universe known as the Dark Realm, populated by demons—predominantly depicted in female form, with ivory-white skin, long snake-like black hair, ruby lips, and razor sharp talons—who constantly threaten to overspill into our own dimension to spread a particularly beguiling form of chaos. The setting again owes much to the look of *Blade Runner*, a cold environment besieged by eternal nightfall. The background is depicted with such a hallucinogenic sense of fidelity to the real it feels like a mirage, highlighting anime's potential to draw attention to exactly what it is presenting by the very self-aware nature of its presentation. Floodlights cut through the misty haze and the sky is lit up with twinkling points of light from the fortress-like tower blocks in the skyline. Isolated interiors of love hotels, bars, and brothels are bathed in warmer hues, pockets of light in the darkness, as is the womb-like safe-haven of the car that transports the characters across this stark landscape, similarly to *Solaris* and *Akira*, via the connecting urban highways.

Who or what is symbolized by these dangerous yet highly sexualized suppressed forces is left up to the viewer's interpretation. That one demon attack occurs at Narita airport suggests that, as with the staging of *Blood: the Last Vampire* in a school for foreigners based on the perimeter of the U.S. Yokota airbase during the Vietnam War (which also is pinpointed as the entry point for illegally smuggled military equipment in *Patlabor 2*), the threat comes from outside Japan, much in the same way that Count Dracula's middle-European contagion found its way into England via the port of Whitby.

As well as holding up a dark mirror to modern "civilized" society, films like *Wicked City* and *Akira* can be read as the vicarious expression of a barely-repressed wish for the destruction of this immaculately-ordered yet decadent modern-day Babylon. Interestingly, the Biblically-scaled scenes of devastation by fire and clouds of billowing smoke that conclude *Akira* would later be echoed in the director's later Jules Verne-esque "steampunk" epic, *Steamboy* (2004). In this case Victorian London at the height of the Industrial Revolution serves as Tokyo, with the annihilation of the Olympic dome replaced by the vaporizing of the site of the Great Exhibition.

Towers of Babel

The Babylon reference is significant, as it crops up again and again in anime, though its antecedent lies further back in cinema history. As a center of economic production in the era of late-period capitalism, Tokyo bears similarities with the vision of the future city put forward in Fritz Lang's prophetic *Metropolis* (1926), co-written with his then-wife Thea von Harbou (who penned the novel). Despite boasting a pleasure quarter named Yoshiwara, which draws its name from the old Red Light district situated in Asakusa, the Tokyo of the 20s had little bearing on the design of Lang's conurbation. *Metropolis* was actually conceived during a visit to New York, which the German director undertook at the beginning of the decade.

Metropolis's majestic setting was composed along allegorical lines as an extrapolation of contemporary ideas about the form and function of the city of tomorrow. The city is divided into two, with the technocrats and controllers of all activity, embodied by the ruthless capitalist and city-builder Joh Fredersen overlooking all he controls from the towering higher echelons of the Upper City, while the workers joylessly toil away in the lower depths, manning the machines that ensure the clockwork efficiency of the city's operation. This rigid deadlock between capital and labor, the "head" and the "hands" of the urban body, comes to a dramatic head when Fredersen's son, Freder Fredersen, entranced by the beautiful Maria (who sees to the workers' spiritual welfare), finds himself cast in the role of "heart," the mediator between the two. The climactic rise of the workers is accompanied by the flooding of the lower levels of the city as the harsh, vertical spaces are subsumed by elemental forces akin to those of *Akira*.

Lang's film proved phenomenally influential on subsequent depictions of "the city of the future," with its depiction of human elements mechanically bound to their location to represent the alienating effect of machine age technology. In Charlie Chaplin's *Modern Times* (1936), for example, the automization of the assembly line worker was played to comedic effect, with Chaplin's exaggerated bodily movements, like those of the workers of *Metropolis*, subservient to the machines he is employed to operate and which ultimately take control of him.

The most obvious example from the world of anime to employ certain images and ideas expressed in Lang's film was Rintarô's feature of the same name, produced and written for the screen by *Akira*-creator Ôtomo and released in 2001. With its more rounded character designs reminiscent of the Tintin comics of Hergé, and its focus on story over subtext, the new *Metropolis* represents one of anime's most accessible entry points. Rather than a straight animated remake of the original, it is based on a manga comic by Tezuka Osamu published in 1949, which used the location and characters of Lang's film as its starting point. With robotic slaves substituted for human labor, the film calls for a greater union between man and his machine servants, and as one of the robotic characters develops human emotions, it departs even further from the original to explore similar themes to those of Steven Spielberg's *Artificial Intelligence: AI*, released the same year.

Fredersen finds his parallel in Duke Red, the city's powerful industrialist ruler and a secret benefactor to the Marduks, a violent anti-robot political group who believe these automated slaves are stealing human jobs. (Marduk was an ancient Mesopotamian god and the patron deity of the city of Babylon. He also gives his name to the alien race at war with mankind in the animated universe of *Macross*.) The film opens with the destruction of a robot who has inadvertently strayed from its allocated zone during the inauguration of the newly-constructed Tower of Babel, a testament to the glory of this modern city just like the identically-named construction in Lang's film. Lang's ziggurat served a more allegorical purpose, revealed in a filmed reconstruction of the Biblical myth: "But the minds that conceived the Tower of Babel could not build it. The task was too great, so they hired hands for wages. But the hands that built the Tower of Babel knew nothing of the brain that had conceived it." In Tezuka's story, the Tower has a more sinister function than a monument to the vanity of its builders, masking a huge cannon that has the possibility to harness the radiation of the sun to destroy whole continents. However, it lacks one final component.

Rintarô's *Metropolis* is not Tokyo. In fact, the character of the private detective Ban Shusaku who arrives in the city with his adolescent nephew Kenichi in search of Dr. Laughton, a mad scientist wanted internationally in connection with illegal organ smuggling, announces early on that he has just come from Japan. Dr. Laughton has also been covertly employed by Duke Red to fashion the missing keystone of the ziggurat, a pinnacle of android engineering fashioned in the form of Rock's dead daughter Tima (just as Rotwang was entrusted with the robotic reconstruction of Federersen's dead wife Hel in Lang's film). When Red's adopted son and Marduk activist Rock discovers he is about to be replaced in his father's affection by a machine, he sets out to destroy Laughton's laboratory. But the mechanized Tima is inadvertently rescued by Kenichi, and the two take flight among the robot-populated underground sewer levels of the city, with Tima dressed in Chaplinesque oversized pants for much of the film.

Opening with a quote from French historian Jules Michelet, "Every époque dreams of its successor," Rintarô draws much inspiration from Lang's original designs for *Metropolis*. The modernist, art-deco architecture of the buildings flanking the central square at the foot of the Tower of Babel harks back to the New York of the 20s, emphasized by the evocative Dixieland Jazz on the soundtrack, reminding us of the role architect Frank Lloyd Wright played in the modern face of Tokyo: Wright stayed in Japan from 1916 to 1922 after being commissioned to design Tokyo's Imperial Hotel (sadly demolished in 1968), among other buildings which proved highly influential on the city's skyline. Other areas used in the film—the neon-lit pleasure area, the noisy thoroughfares and bustling pedestrian concourses, and a sign in the background marked "Ginza-7"— more explicitly evoke contemporary Tokyo, serving as a reminder that its own skyline is an eclectic mish-mash of architectural fashions and that the city's essence lies more in its structure than its individual buildings. Lacking a single cohesive

center around which everything else revolves (a great source of interest for Barthes, who wrote that "Quadrangular, reticulated cities (Los Angeles, for instance) are said to produce a profound uneasiness: they offend our synesthetic sentiment of the City, which requires that any urban space have a center to go to, to return from, a complete site to dream of and in relation to which to advance or retreat; in a word, to invent oneself."), it is more like a collection of villages or neighborhoods, each with their own distinct flavor and atmosphere: the oasis of Western-styled cosmopolitanism that is Ginza; the time-capsule of traditional Asakusa; or the vibrant hubs of contemporary youth culture at Shibuya and Harajuku.

Inner Worlds / Outer Worlds

Allusions to the Tower of Babel story are frequent within Japanese animation. *Patlabor: The Movie* (*Kidô Keisatsu Patorebâ*, 1990), a theatrical spin-off from the popular *Patlabor* OAV series directed by Oshii Mamoru, one of the medium's most articulate practitioners, was another to invoke the Babylon myth. In the world of *Patlabor*, Tokyo's ceaseless construction is undertaken by large humanoid "Labor" robots crewed by human workers sitting within the hollow cabs of their skulls, a visual reification of the "head" and "hands" motif of *Metropolis*. The series belongs to the sub-genre known as *mecha-anime*, which also includes the morphing fighter plane/robots of the *Macross* stories and which evolved in no small measure due to the fact that blocky humanoid machines are far less tricky to animate than realistic human figures.

Patlabor centers around the members of Special Vehicles Division 2, a law-enforcing unit formed to combat crimes committed using these Labor machines. They do so using their own police-issue Patrol Labors, or Patlabors. The stories are set in a recognizable near-future Tokyo, which, quaintly, has already come to pass. The first movie takes place in 1999, where rising sea and population levels have prompted mammoth urban redevelopment in the form of a large manmade island in Tokyo Bay as part of the controversial Babylon Project (clearly modeled on the construction of Kansai International Airport, built on a sinking seabed 5 kilometers from Osaka and opened in 1994, as much as the redevelopment of Tokyo's Odaiba area during the 90s). Several incidents of newly-commissioned Labor machines taking on a life of their own and running amok prompt a widespread panic. The fault is tracked down to a bug within the machine's Operating System, triggered off by a specific high-pitch frequency inaudible to human ears that is created by the sound of the wind whistling through the skyscrapers constructed as part of the project. As a large typhoon whips across the ocean towards Tokyo, the prospect of these giant mechanical construction workers tearing the city down to its very foundations is revealed to be a conscious act of sabotage by the now-vanished programmer of the Labors' instruction code.

Oshii's films present a Russian Doll-like conception of the world in which man is not only embedded within the environment he has himself created, but within the very mechanical apparatus with which he constructs and transforms it also. Furthermore, the film expresses a view that has remained at the heart of cyberpunk fiction, and which seems particularly well-suited to the self-consciously "constructed" nature of animation itself; that man's consciousness and spirit is embedded, intentionally or not, in the tools he creates. In Oshii's most internationally famous work, the US-Japan co-pro-

Above: Pom Poko *(Heisei Tanuki Gassen Pompoko, 1994).Takahata Isao.* © *Hatake Jimusho/GNH*

duction *Ghost in the Shell* (*Kôkaku Kidôtai*, 1995) adapted by Oshii's regular writer Kazunori Itô from the manga by Shirow Masamune, he takes this idea into the internet age.

Ghost in the Shell is set in 2029, where expansive electronic networks through which all economic transactions are conducted have radically transformed the notion of physical space and made the world an effectively borderless domain. The world is populated by both humans and robots, and all manner of man-machine hybrids that inhabit the gray area between. Advances in technology have transformed the world of *Patlabor*, in which the Labors act as externalizations of their human laborers, to produce ever more human-looking cyborgs, whose ameliorations range from prosthetic limbs to computer-augmented brains to assist interfacing with the new environment.

However, just as the advanced mechanization of the individual human body has yet to extinguish entirely the human soul that lies at the heart of these man-machine integrated systems (the "ghost" of humanity within this artificial "shell" to which the title refers), so too do human-derived concepts such as ethnicity and the nation state persist. To combat the rise in international cyber-terrorism, a covert Government run unit named Section 9 has been formed, comprised of such "enhanced" cyborgs as Major Motoko Kusanagi, whose body is completely cybernetic, leaving only the vestiges of her human mind. In this first film, Section 9 is pitted against an opponent who is neither human nor machine, but an ethereal consciousness inhabiting the net that has evolved from a rogue computer virus and refers to itself as the Puppet Master. The virus manifests itself in the material world by "ghost-hacking" the brains of the city's inhabitants, altering their memories for its own needs.

Ghost in the Shell and its 2004 sequel *Ghost in the Shell 2: Innocence* draw upon sophisticated concepts of life in the electronic age that take their cue from the newly emerged computer-based academic discipline of Artificial Life. Taking Darwinian ideas to their extremes, Artificial Life posits that any organism, be it organic (carbon-based), or inorganic (either machine or electronic) exhibits the qualities of being alive if it has the ability both to self-perpetuate and to subtly alter its structure over subsequent generations to make it more adequately suited for survival in a constantly changing environment: the life-form's medium is unimportant, and indeed by this definition it need not even exist in physical space at all. The discipline emerged from the earlier school of Artificial Intelligence due to philosophical problems inherent in defining what exactly constitutes "intelligence." Does a computer specifically programmed to play chess, for example, manifest intelligence, or is intelligence better defined in terms of its possessor's ability to adapt to new environments and new problems, regardless of whether it is ever conscious of doing so? The idea that computer code can evolve to manifest certain "lifelike" qualities is convincingly argued in a pivotal paper published in 1994 by Eugene Spafford entitled *Computer Viruses as Artificial Life*.

The major challenge in staging *Ghost in the Shell's* philosophical teasers is in visualizing the invisible; the world of cyberspace, an abstract domain that sits alongside the concrete world in a manner similar to the Dark Realm of *Wicked City*. Like so

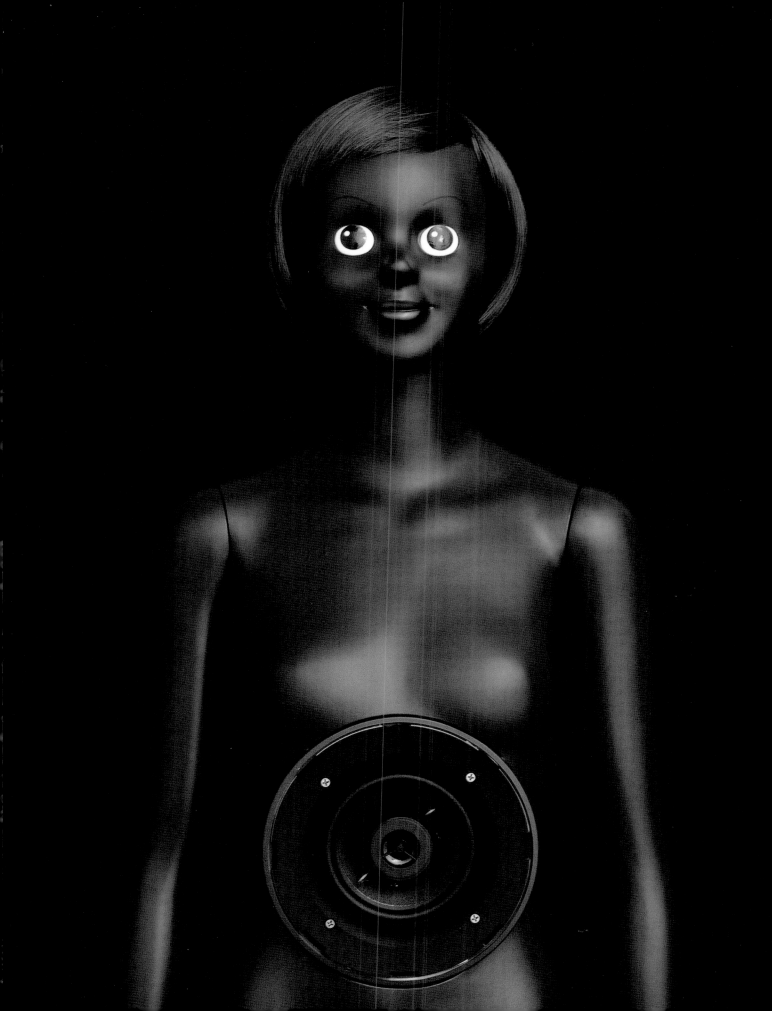

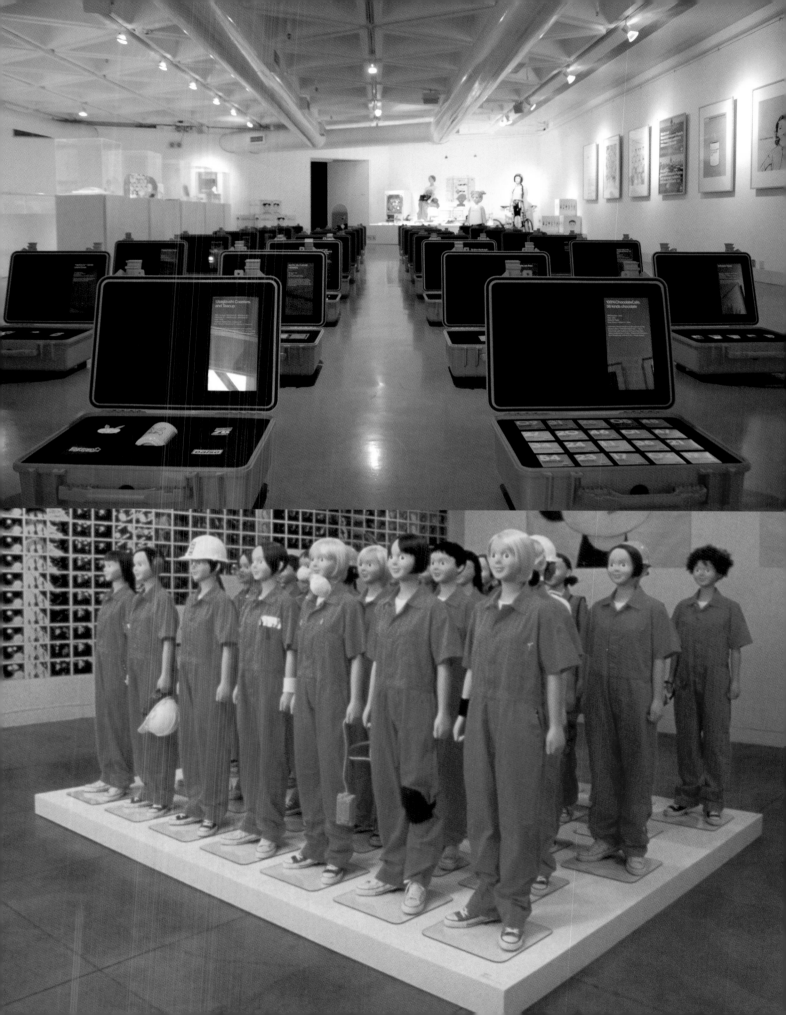

This spread: PET Bottle (2003).

0 "54917

Below: Packaging for 100% Chocolate Cafe in Kyobashi, Chuo Ward, for Meiji Seika Kaisha, Ltd. (2003);
opposite page: promotional material and merchandise for pop group RIPSLYME, Warner Music Entertainment (2002).
Following spread, page 324; Brockmann figures; page 325: still from GRV2284 Music Video (2005).

Clockwise from top left: Polyrhythm *(1991). Synthetic resin, iron, plastic Tamiya 1/35 scale models of U.S. infantry (West European Theater), 227 x 55 x 90 cm;* Kase Taishuu Project *(1994). Chromogenic prints (4 parts), 82 x 62 cm each;* Randoseru Project *(1991). Children's backpacks in various animal skins, 30 x 23 x 20 cm each.*

This page, clockwise from top left: The World of Sphere *(2003), Acrylic on canvas, 350 x 350 cm; Stills from "*SUPERFLAT MONOGRAM*" (2003) Created by Murakami Takashi; producer: Takashiro Tsuyoshi; co-producer: Himi Takeshi; director: Hosoda Mamoru; executive producer: LVMH/ Louis Vuitton. Opposite page: Murakami Takashi. Following spread: 727(1996). Acrylic on canvas mounted on board, 300 x 450 x 7 cm.*

Above: Acupuncture Painting "Opening Wide, Squeezing Tight"—Terre Verte *(Squeezing Tight), (2006).*
Acrylic on canvas mounted on board, 120 x 120 x 5 cm; opposite page: Reversed Double Helix *(2003-2005).*
Installation in Rockefeller Center, New York City.

A Night in Ueno, 50th Year of Showa (2004). Acrylic on canvas, 200 x 230 cm.

Land of Sodom and Gomorrah *(2006). Acrylic on canvas, 181.8 x 227.3 x 38 cm.*

Untitled *(2002). Acrylic on canvas, 162 x 130 cm.*

Above: Noshi & Meg, on Earth, year 2036*(2002). Acrylic on Canvas, 91 x 73.5 x 2 cm.*
Opposite page: Crosswalk *(2002), Acrylic on Canvas,* 145.5 x 112 x 3 cm.

AOSHIMA CHIHO

Opposite page: Building *(1999). Inkjet print on paper, 190 x 75 cm.*

The products of an entirely self-taught and self-assured aesthetic, Aoshima Chiho's art—both in the form of digital and traditional media—embodies all of the hyper-articulated and obsessive qualities associated with the Superflat movement's maturing visual language. First receiving acclaim as one of a handful of young female artists in the Murakami Takashi-organized Tokyo Girls Bravo exhibition from 2002, her work also gives meticulous expression to a willful agenda to emancipate women *otaku* and give voice to their divergent and often revisionist perspectives. Simulacra of the city, rendered with soaring anthropomorphic skyscrapers or with realistic tower blocks, become the foundation for a menagerie of swirling vegetal forms, slippery creatures and tribes of emaciated, luminous sylphs and schoolgirls. Often gloomy but emitting an irrepressible buoyancy at times, her day-glo, computer-generated universes are then outputted in large-format by heavy-duty printers onto paper and on a variety of materials—some destined as one off-installations and still others as museum-shop novelties.

Despite an early childhood love of drawing, Aoshima was discouraged from pursuing the arts and majored in economics at Hosei University in Tokyo. During her senior year, she discovered computer graphics while working a part-time job, and she has become a unique CG artist who creates her signature work through the manipulation of Bezier curves, a feature of Adobe Illustrator. Her work has won international acclaim, especially since Aoshima's inclusion in 2003's Tokyo Girls Bravo group show held in Tokyo and New York. She collaborated with Miyake Issey the same year, having her work featured in his Spring/Summer collection. Aoshima was also invited to take part in the 54th annual Carnegie International at the Carnegie Museum of Art in Pittsburgh in 2004, where she displayed her largest piece to date, measuring 106 feet wide by 15 feet high. In May 2005, she took part in the Little Boy project with her ecologically-themed "City Glow" and "Paradise" series, which filled ad spaces throughout the Union Square subway station in New York City. Aoshima presented her first sculpture in a solo show in 2005, which also featured a five-screen, seven-minute animated film.

...hima Chiho.

...ge, top: **City Glow, Mountain Whisper** *(2006). Multi-panel graphic installation in Glouc...*
...don Underground, dimensions variable; bottom: **City Glow & Paradise series** *(2005). Mul...*
...allation in Union Square Station, New York City Subway, dimensions variable (bottom).

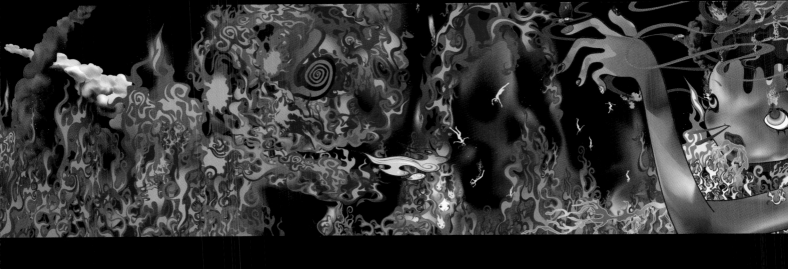

Top: Magma Spirit Explodes: Tsunami is Dreadful *(2004). Chromogenic print, 87.172 x 589 cm.*

Bottom: We like the night *(2006). Pen, color pencil, watercolor, acrylic and wood glue on Japanese paper, 41 x 120 cm.*

Clockwise from top left: City Glow *(2005). Chromogenic print, 170 x 170 cm;* Blessing *(2006).*
Acrylic gouache, watercolor, color pencil, pen, wood glue and fixative on paper, 225 x 260 mm;
Good Evening *(2006). Watercolor, color pencil, pen, wood glue and fixative on paper,*
255 x 255 mm;

Above: (left) "Penyo-henyo" Myomyonmyo Edition (2004). Fiberglass, steel, acrylic resin, various fabrics, 419 cm. high; (right), MR; opposite page: Penyo-henyo" Nyonyo Edition "Good Morning, Good Morning" (2004-06). Fiberglass, steel, acrylic resin, various fabrics, 272 x 100 x100 cm.

Mr., who takes his *nom de guerre* from the nickname of "Mister" Nagashima Shigeo, the legendary third-baseman of the Tokyo Yomiuri Giants in the 1960s, began his creative career assembling pieces from trash he had collected. Inspired by mid-century Pop Art and Arte Povera, the decision to do "found art" was not one motivated by avant-gardist or similarly progressive impulses. It was instead largely dictated by penury, as the young Mr. could barely afford to buy art supplies.

The output of his early toil was highly derivative, at least until he decided to exploit his all-consuming obsessions within *otaku* culture. Shamelessly afflicted with the "Lolita complex," Mr. started doodling characters on the backs of a decade's worth of receipts from supermarkets and *kombini*—24-hour convenience stores. This experience led him to seriously engage painting, with a significant interest in drawings, sculpture video and performance art as well. Described by the artist Paul McCarthy as having "an unbearable irresistibility in its tiny, innocent world," his sexualized compositions are peopled by the sort of wide-eyed and long-limbed denizens typical of contemporary anime. They have even acquired the dimensionality of its cartoon antecedents. Often with their hair dyed pink, his repertory of characters resemble the flatly rendered cells of traditional animation, and are set against the deep perspective of urban landscapes redolent of matte paintings.

After several failed attempts at entering Tokyo National University of Fine Arts and Music—the alma mater of his later mentor Murakami Takashi—Mr. eventually got a degree from Sokei Art School in Tokyo in 1996. Patterning himself fully on his idol Nagashima, who retired from baseball first as player and then manager to be a TV personality, Mr. additionally sees himself as a multimedia entertainer. Brandishing a *katana* which he'd inherited from an ex-girlfriend, the openings of his solo shows used to feature a ritualized "sword performance." The resident *lolicon* and arguably the executive *otaku* in the Kaikai Kiki collective after Murakami himself, Mr.'s work is shown widely in North America and Western Europe. In Christmas of 2004, four of Mr.'s anime-inspired sculptures were installed in Miyake Issey's Roppongi Hills boutique. Since then, he has held solo exhibitions at the Musée d'Art Contemporain in Lyon in 2006 and at Lehmann Maupin Gallery in New York in 2007.

Takoyakisukiya (2004). Acrylic on canvas, 51.5 x 72.8 cm.

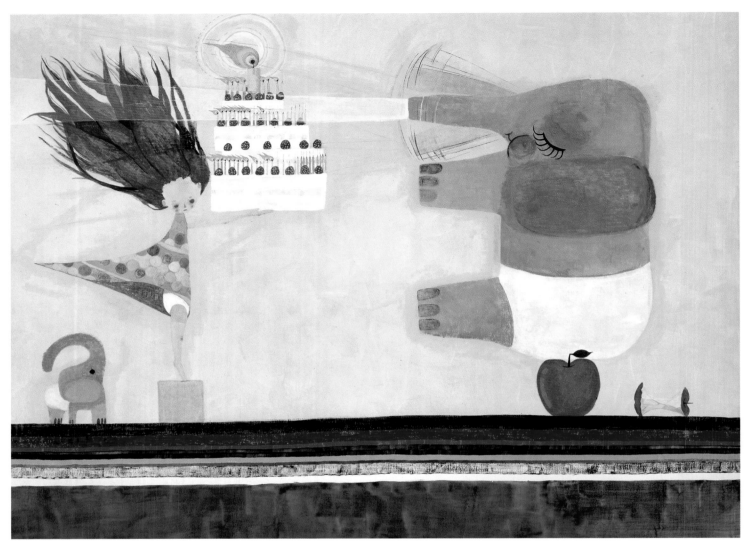

Happy Birthday *(2003). Acrylic on canvas, 194 x 259 cm.*

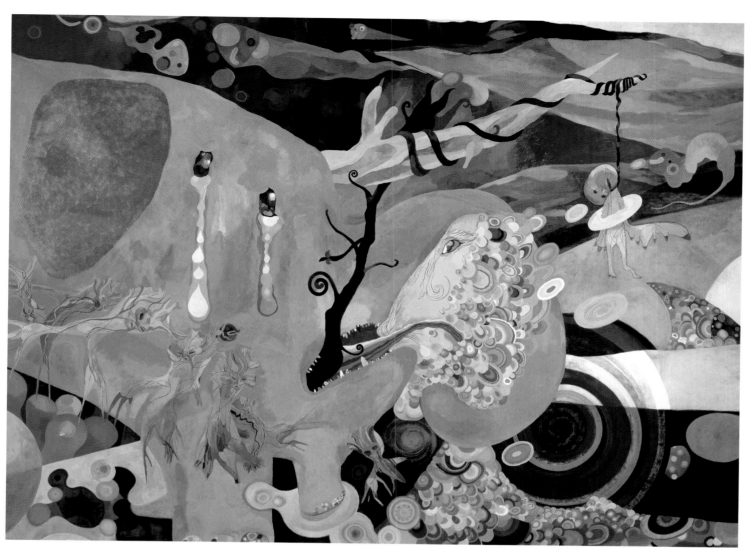

Re: The Song of Passing *(2006). Acrylic on canvas, 248.5 x 333.3 cm.*

KUNIKATA MAHOMI

Above: Butcher Shop *(2004). Acrylic on canvas, 10 x 15 cm.*
Opposite page: The Reality of the Roppongi Bar Hosts, Part I *(2004). Acrylic on canvas, 45.5 x 38 cm.*

Kunikata Mahomi's work comes from a place of deep hurt, informed by her social marginalization as a female *otaku,* an eating disorder, frustrated attempts at being a professional *manga* writer, and the effects of a family tragedy. When her older brother died—the sole supporter of her family—she was forced to take charge and care for her developmentally challenged younger brother. Her resulting art is exceedingly raw and unmitigated, and the painful sensations her work elicits are heightened by the frequent, ironic inclusion of colorful and cheery images.

At first viewing, her pieces appear to be entirely devoid of context, the dislocated or isolated parts of a greater, notional whole, like the leaves of a comic or journal violently ripped from their bindings. The episodic quality of the work is completely intentional, and is rooted in her education as an artist. Although Kunikata went to art school and aspired to become an animator, she soon found that the genre required far more than technical dexterity. In short order, she realized that she lacked a writer's gift for narration and plot resolution, skills highly prized in the cutthroat business of *manga* and anime in Japan. These shortcomings tempered her ambition somewhat but in no way impeded her determination to create an art that became less and less invested in commercial utility. She upends the localized conventions of *otaku* media to examine larger issues of gender and psychology. Her horrific depictions of

self-mutilation and other forms of transgression are deeply personal and raw, and are at odds with the fetishistic violence of sexually explicit anime, *manga* or *ero-games* (erotic video games) intended for male audiences.

Kunikata was among eleven finalists chosen by Murakami Takashi at his GEISAI art fair in 2000. Since her introduction to the art world, she has shown her work at Little Boy at the Japan Society and in New York, and at J'en Reve at the Fondation Cartier in Paris. Her first solo show took place in 2005 at the Kaikai Kiki booth at the NADA Art Fair in Miami, Florida.

Crayon *(2004). Acrylic on canvas, 10 x 15 cm.*

379

Shining *(2006). Chromogenic print, dimensions variable.*

Below: Ms. Kanata, Konata, Izuko, and Itsuka of outer space *(2003). Acrylic on canvas, 60 x 60 cm. (4 parts).*
Opposite page: Ano ne no ne *(2002). Acrylic on canvas, 91 x 4 cm.*

NINAGAWA MIKA

The assertion in Ninagawa Mika's official website of being "Japan's most popular photographer" is no mean boast. She is certainly the most prolific in one crucial respect: tapping into many segments of the huge market for photo books, her pictures are very much tied to a publishing program that is without peer in the field. With the publication of one or two bestselling monographic or topical volumes of her work every year for the past eight years, and with an impressive backlist of reprinted titles, over 200,000 copies of her art books have been sold. Formally represented by Koyama Tomio's influential gallery, Ninagawa's images have been widely exhibited in Japan and abroad since 1999. Key installations at Colette Paris and Arndt and Partner, Berlin, both in 2007, and frequent participation in Art Basel Miami coincide with up to three significant shows—individual or group—annually in Japan. Commercial demand for her editorials is high among Japan's fashion glossies, and in addition to leading magazines like the local editions of *Vogue, Elle, Harper's Bazaar, GQ, Figaro,* and *Marie Claire,* her work extends to an equally influential web of teen publications.

The broad appeal of Ninagawa's photography can best be summed up by a signature approach that is bathed in excoriatingly vivid colors and dreamlike in its manipulation of depth of field. Adaptable to portraiture, landscape and still life, at the heart of her published work is a number of themed books that rotate between four subject categories: travel photography, flora, fauna and young women—and matrices of either of the four. Photographs of local and international personalities from Kuriyama Chiaki to the Hilton sisters constitute some of the louder prints in her portfolio, but it is books like *Sugar and Spice* (2000) and *Pink Rose Suite* (2001) that the work achieves a calm, pictorial mastery. In the latter, a series of photographs following holidaymakers on a cruise ship along the Gulf coast from Miami to Cozumel, Ninagawa's camera is occasionally diverted from the surreal scenes on deck to shoot on dry land. Images of folk religious statuary and striking tableaux of artificial flowers create contrasts in scale that are united by impossibly blue skies and surf.

A joint recipient of the Kimura Ihei Award in 2001—the one and only time honor was bestowed on three artists—Ninagawa's selection with Hiromix and Nagashima Yurie also heralded the arrival of critically and commercially successful women in art photography, a field that for much of the modern period was an all-male preserve. At the head of the *onnanoko shashinka*—literally girlie photographers, Ninagawa takes special pleasure in shooting her

ornately clad human subjects against baroque stylings that suggest a firm grasp of practical scenography. This is not at all surprising as she is the daughter of leading theater director and sometime actor Ninagawa Yukio; and the young Mika's exposure to her father's enormous body of work is of vital import. Combined with the knowledge gained from her own professional experience, this patrimony has equipped her recent move to cinema.

In her directoral debut *Sakuran* (2007) a tale of rival *oiran* set in the cathouses of a luridly reimagined Yoshiwara pleasure district in old Edo, Ninagawa introduces a full range of movement and sound to her familiar compositions. Featuring the tough, punkish charms of the performer Tsuchiya Anna, whose association with the photographer began with a number of "idol" books nearly a decade ago, the film brandishes a visual language animated from the entirety of Ninagawa's stills. Slashing at the screen in impossibly saturated colors, the ceremonial kimonos of the protagonists are even silkscreened with Ninagawa's floral photography from books like *Acid Bloom* (2003), *Everlasting Flowers* (2006), and *A Piece of Heaven* (2002), their once two-dimensional forms sheathed over the principal characters.—*Ian Luna*

Talent credits, opposite page: Aso Kumiko; page 388, top left: Matsumoto Sora; page 388, top right: Tsuchiya Anna; page 388, bottom left: Fukada Kyoko; page 388, bottom right: Kuriyama Chiaki; page 389, top left: Erena; page 389, top right: Kuriyama Chiaki; page 389, bottom left: Unoki Shinya, Katia and Lateeef Motohashi; page 389, bottom right: Ishi Maki; page 393: Saito Hanae.

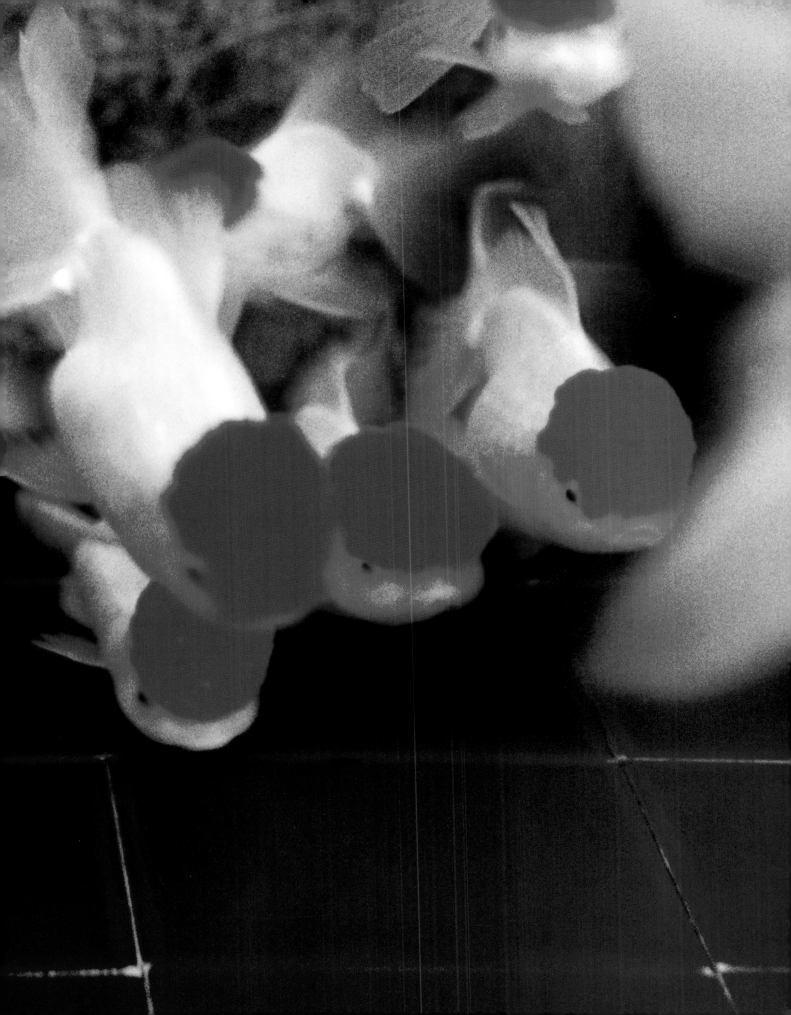

TAJIMA KAZUNALI
MILD INC

A voluptuary with a patient, technical efficiency and a keen nose for business, Tajima Kazunali achieved considerable fame in the mid 1990s to become one of the city's busiest commercial photographers. His profuse output is a vivid and extravagant demonstration of traditional mass media's continuing, persuasive appeal, with a current portfolio that melds extensive editorial work for high fashion glossies and photography books with a substantial foothold in TV commercial and music video direction. Tajima commands an office and studio with a panoramic view of Daikanyama, practicing his many trades under the aegis of Mild Incorporated.

Known to his public as Tajjiemax, his is a visual idiom that draws heavily on contradiction, and whether ironic or straightforward, nuanced or ham-fisted, populist or esoteric, lighthearted or severe, rigidly prescribed or experimental, the effect is always impeccably and opulently realized. Often appearing in thr pages of magazines like the Japanese editions of *Elle*, *Harper's Bazaar* and *Vogue*, these images suggest a flexible aesthetic with insistent and recognizable traits. Role-playing is an important anchor in his compositions, and these histrionics transition seamlessly into his videography. His music videos for artists like Tei Towa, Kahimi Karie and Nakatani Miki alternate spontaneity with calculation, and project cinematic identities on their subjects that are sometimes at variance with their more familiar personas. His TV advertisements are more widely seen and are decidedly more "anonymous," but they do communicate recognizable authorship. In the last decade or so, he has produced 30-second spots for companies such as Uniqlo, Cannon, Shiseido, Sony, and most memorably, a string of surreal advertisements for that most Japanese of institutions, Kewpie Mayonnaise.

Fame-obsessed Tokyo is fecund territory for someone not at all ashamed at greasing the wheels of celebrity. Tajima's close associations with a number of key cultural figures have maintained a steady demand for his all-seeing eye. In their most accessible forms, these relationships have led to a number

of slick "idol" books, cultivating the image of personalities such as Sakamoto Ryuchi, the legendary composer and former frontman of Yellow Magic Orchestra, whose many changeable guises Tajima commemorated in a number of volumes over a ten-year period.—*Ian Luna*

Opposite page: editorial from Harper's Bazaar Japan *(2005); page 396-397:* HUgE W Magazine *(2006); page 398: image of Tei Towa from the release of the album* Flash, *(2005); page 399: Asano Tadanobu,* CUT Magazine *(1999); page 400: editorial for* SOEN Magazine *(2003); page 401: Sakamoto Ryuchi for Yamaha (2003); page 402, top to bottom: Kuriyama Chiaki,* Nylon Japan *(2004) &* Nakashima Mika *(2005); page 403: "Be Flower" editorial,* Studio Voice Magazine *(2003); page 404: Kitano "Beat" Takeshi,* Sight Magazine *(2004); page 405: "Metropolitans" editorial,* Dazed & Confused Japan *(2003).*

MAKINO TOMOAKI

All images from the unpublished series Etudes of Mother and Son *(2006-2007).*

The ability to reveal the interior life of a sitter in one image—bringing to the surface their desires and aspirations, met and unmet—is the special province of a select number of professional portraitists. It also helps to have topical and comic premises. Makino Tomoaki's first book of photographs, *Tokyo Soap Opera* (2005), is a frank portrayal of 116 mature women captured in the intimate spaces of their own homes, reenacting overheated scenes from domestic or Korean daytime soaps. Contorted into exaggerated and often hilarious poses, any real discontent in these homemakers' lives is masked by their innate grace and hammy aplomb. But in the picture of a woman wielding a kitchen knife, or of another woman in a closet hiding behind her husband's hanging neckties, menace and painful regret lurk in equal frequency.

In like manner, Makino's 2007 "Etudes of Mother and Son" demonstrates his reverence for his mother's generation. Honoring the female closest to him in a series of scathingly funny and somewhat disconcerting visual dialogues, Makino is ever the dutiful child in absurdist scenes that variously take place in a cemetery, or in the bathroom of their one-family home in the suburbs. The odd beauty of these pictures inflate the already indispensable role his mother plays in his life, just as his *Soap Opera* queens overstate the role of fantasy in theirs. And whether he's snapping the woman he's known his whole life or those he encounters for only an afternoon of shooting, Makino's gift lies in his ability to seek their instant and complete corroboration and collaboration in his wry games. His muses are simultaneously beatified by his preoccupation with their otherwise hidden lives and made especially fragile under his lens' sensitive gaze.

This curious mix of strength, humor and frailty that emerges in Makino's portraits is a direct result of an intuitive and experiential approach to craft. A photographer at weddings and other events, his work is a subversion of his commercial activities. And his industry has not gone unnoticed. Upon graduating from the Tokyo Polytechnic University's Department of Photography he was honored early in his career with Fuji Photo Salon's "New Face Prize" award in 2002, and went on to become a finalist in Takei Masakazu's Foil Awards in 2004 and the Kimura Ihei Memorial Award in 2005. The effects of a childhood among many strong women and a childlike need to receive and bestow attention provide the nucleus for an inimitable and perceptive body of work. Although Makino intentionally reveals the tricks of the trade at times (his images from "Etudes," for example, make no attempt to hide the remote switch for the shutter), these instances do not diminish an undeniable ability to leave the eye unnerved, and the heart touched.—*Lauren A. Gould/Ian Luna*

HATAKEYAMA NAOYA

Above: Hatakeyama Naoya. Opposite page: River Series I *(1993-1994).*

The dialogue between the natural world and the city has rarely had as attentive a as listener than Hatakeyama Naoya. Hatakeyama scours Japan's (post) industrial heart to capture passages that reveal in their dreamlike—and often breathtaking—beauty the uneasy relationship between the urban environment and the remnants of the condition it supplanted or continues to exploit. This notional exchange attains a stark, literal quality in *Lime Works* (1996), a series of photographs of limestone pits from which much of the aggregate used to build modern Japan is extracted. "If the concrete buildings and highways that stretch to the horizon are all made of limestone dug from the hills," Hatekeyama deduces, "the quarries and the cities are like negative and positive images of a single photograph."

Lauded with the Kimura Ihei Memorial Award for Photography in 1997, the 42nd Mainichi Art Award in 2001, representing Japan at the 49th Venice Biennale, and with solo exhibitions in North America and Western Europe, Hatakeyama projects his sublime, intimate conversations onto an expanding international stage. More than most, he seems to relish the role of witness, employing qualities of light and color with the intention of shedding light on—rather that merely aestheticizing—the tensions that exist between any number of essential dualisms: man and nature, light and dark, stillness and movement, sight and perception, concealment and exposure. Hatakeyama derived inspiration from these oppositional states since his creative infancy, finding a ready source in an upbringing in rural Iwate Prefecture and later at Tsukuba University's School of Art and Design, where he had an incipient career shooting landscapes of the small city and its surroundings. But the move he credits with sustaining his interest in photography was to Tokyo— a landscape, he remarked, "where every space was crowded with things," and where he found sure purpose as an artist.

Taken as a whole, the artist's Tokyo work describes a transcendent love for the city and an appreciation for its many estrangements. In the quiet of the city's liminal spaces, Hatakeyama goes about a mission wholly his own, content to depict the ephemeral and reveal the transitory in a rapid-fire culture often much too busy to stop and truly take notice. Whether documenting the gradual metamorphosis of the city from high above or illuminating the dark tunnels beneath the city in the *Underground* series (1999), his images maintain a near-accidental feel despite a meticulous attention to the usual rules governing composition and color. The views of a waterway coursing through Shibuya in his first *River* series (1993-94) reveal glimpses of the familiar hitherto unseen. Shot mostly at night and bathed in the full spectrum of colors, the tableau describes a naturally occurring feature long ago tamed by human hands. As if to underscore this, the vertical field of view is cut literally in two registers, with a false horizon set along the concrete shoulders that now line both banks of the stream. This sublime effect is heightened when all the prints are shown in sequence.—*Lauren A. Gould/Ian Luna*

River Series I *(1993-1994).*

MI-ZO
MINORI
ZOREN GOLD

The finely honed artifacts of a relationship that is equal parts vocational and personal, the pictures of Murakami Minori and Zoren Gold present the viewer with inimitably postmodern puzzles. Halfway between photography, hand-drawn illustration and computer-generated graphic design, their compositions—peopled by alluring, phantasmal figures and set against dreamlike cityscapes—impart a studied knowledge of the visual arts of the 20th century. Drawn from the worlds of film, painting and photography—their work is a miscellany of the modern movement. Symbolist, surrealist, cubist, constructivist and social-realist influences populate their artificial and meticulously composed environments.

But theirs is also a universe that is firmly grounded in the multicolored carnival of present-day Tokyo, and as they harness the unique, associative qualities and the flat dimensionality of collage into an unmistakable, razor-sharp 21st century iteration, many of their altered worlds betray a local, temporal residency. Neighboring train stations, a traffic median, the nearby ATM, the nondescript exteriors and the cramped, intimate spaces of traditional one-family homes, these all become the likely settings for an exalted form of street theater caught on film. Primarily but not wholly envisioned for a fashion clientele, these compositions even lend themselves to moving images, as the duo occasionally branches out to do high-concept music videos for the likes of Shibuya-*kei* diva Kahimi Karie and J-pop crooner Hirai Ken—and some very lo-fi ones done with a mobile phone camera for their own page on myspace.com.

Calling themselves a "creative photography unit" Mi-Zo is formally a German photographer and a Japanese illustrator and graphic designer, whose passage to creative partnership hints at some of the origins of their truly collaborative and hybridized art. The pair first met on a chance encounter in 1997 while pursuing separate career paths in Los Angeles, and after a less than auspicious beginning, established Mi-Zo as a joint enterprise in 2000. Relocating to Tokyo and now based in the hipster village of Nakameguro, much of their early work involved Zoren behind the camera—and Minori in front of it, with the Adobe Photoshop and Illustrator work shared evenly between them. In their recent monograph, *The Object that Dreams* (2006), Minori quipped that "being the subject is part of artistic expression. I become the subject with objectivity, and cherish the chance to feel free in a photograph." She has stepped out of frame as of late, however to accommodate other talent, and as their global profile grows, their images have begun to assimilate new vistas and climes. Ten years since that fateful season in Southern California, 2007 saw the couple engage a photographic tour of the western United States, snapping pictures through Nevada and crossing the wide ocean to Hawaii.—*Ian Luna*

MORIMOTO MIE

Morimoto Mie's reputation is indelibly linked with a number of Superflat practitioners, and her documentary photography for Nara Yoshitomo, and to a lesser extent, Kaikai Kiki stalwart Takano Aya, suggests a little of the young Hans Namuth flitting between the irritable gods of mid-century American abstract expressionism. But she is very much a creator in her own right, and her perception of the world is as refined, exacting and tenacious as those of her painter friends.

The enduring effects of late 1990s Japanese photography, with its emphases on spontaneity, extreme candor and compositional minimalism, are very much present in her work. But her own particular refinements denote a strong nostalgia for a more traditional storytelling. Her fashion editorials and six months she spent following Nara around his studio provided a framework for logical narrative. The many lessons learned from these experiences imbue her "candid" work with the attachment of a photojournalist on assignment, who has begun to care deeply for her subjects. She's left clues of their interior lives in her pictures. And in details like a cigarette lighter and flowers deliberately placed on a blanket, the barely visible wire fence enclosing a pair of African wild dogs, the distance between two children making it up a hill with familiar views of the city behind them, Morimoto's emotional investment and its depth of feeling is made plain.

Consequence and mystery, dynamism and a studied calm, all figure in a perception of modern, urban life that is hardly despairing but is certainly ambivalent even in its most reassuring moments.

Morimoto resides in Tokyo, and in addition to the acclaimed *Studio Portrait: Nara Yoshitomo* from 2003, her most recent book, *The Missing Piece/Peace,* for the antipoverty NGO 2025 has her following the sibling actors Miyazaki Aoi and Masaru as they reach out to indigent children in Kolkata, India. Most recently, Morimoto was selected to participate in the prestigious VOCA 2007 exhibition at the Ueno Forest of Art. Also in 2007, a retrospective of her work was held at graf media gm in Osaka, and her new, urbanistic work was shown in Misako and Rosen Gallery in Tokyo.—*Ian Luna*

Pellentesque pretium nulla posuere purus. Nullam quis tellus vel leo nonummy suscipit.

KAWAUCHI RINKO

Above: Kawauchi Rinko

The fragmentary nature of Kawauchi Rinko's work draws certain force from the details of everyday life. Envisaged as interrupted narratives—flowering weeds growing along a crack in the sidewalk, a heaping teaspoon of tapioca, swings at a playground, vines creeping up links of chain, streaks of sunshine across a windowsill, an animal caught in the tactical haze of a lens flare, snowflakes against a night sky, and a half-eaten watermelon slice—a deep sense of anticipation surrounds these disparate scenes. Invariably taken with her favorite 6 x 6 Rolleiflex, her square, uncropped pictures—which she deprecatingly calls "ordinary snapshots"—are delicate without being precious, seducing the eye as they certainly give voice to a distracted, tinkering and sometimes sullen inner child. She fully owns up to this nostalgic sensibility, and admits being attracted to things that caught her eye as a little girl. The image of an eviscerated bird in one of her books, for all its grisly and somber contemplation of mortality, may well have been the product of a child's insatiable curiosity.

The square format suits her images just fine as she prefers a world that is neither vertical nor horizontal, but as her interests have now expanded to full-on documentary photography, the aspect ratio of her negatives have widened to accommodate a broader range of subject matter. Her 2007 book, *Semear*—Portuguese for "to sow"—is a very personal record of the huge Japanese diaspora in Brazil, and has her taking pictures from a greater distance as well as a few low to the ground. But in views of revelers in the stands of a samba stadium, garlands of paper cranes, children climbing a fruit tree, a recumbent ant, the peeling of a mango, and the juxtaposition of a lilac-colored *cattleya* orchid and a similarly hued tunic of a toddler on her belly, this new series eloquently rephrases all the universal themes already put forward by her Japanese work. The emotional restraint in her pictures have even migrated to stills for Koreeda Hirokazu's award-winning film *Nobody Knows* (*Dare mo Shiranai*, 2004) which contrasts plaintively with the intensity of feeling in a story of abandoned children left to fend for themselves in Tokyo.

An activity she describes as natural as shopping or cooking or drinking tea, photography for Kawauchi is not something merely reflexive, and she has gone so far as to describe it as a primal "hunting instinct." Born in Shiga prefecture, Kawauchi was first introduced to photography while studying graphic design at Seian Junior College of Art and Design in Kyoto. Working as a photo assistant in Osaka and later relocating to Tokyo, her decision to abandon a wholly commercial career was hastened by her contact with Takei Masakazu, who was then publisher of the art press Little More and is now president of Foil Publishing. Takei's simultaneous release of three photo books of her work *Utatane* (catnap), *Hanabi* (fireworks), and *Hanako* in 2001 proved the critical breakthrough she needed. Kawauchi would garner the 27th Kimura Ihei Memorial Award for *Utatane* and *Hanabi* the next year, and published a new title every year thereafter. Her backlist now includes *Blue* (2003), *AILA* (2004), *the eyes, the ears* and *Cui Cui* (both from 2005).

Kawauchi's pictures have traveled the globe, finding welcome reception in North America and Europe, with exhibitions of her work at Cohan and Leslie Gallery in New York, the UCR/California Museum of Photography in Riverside, California, and a key exhibition in Paris' Fondation Cartier in 2005. She is a favorite at group exhibitions as well, having taken part in the Lonely Planet show held at Art Tower Mito and Martin Parr's Rencontres Internationales de la Photographie d'Arles in the same year. In 2007, her work was shown at the Museu de Arte Moderna in Sao Paulo and the Hasselblad Center in Goteborg, Sweden.—*Lauren A. Gould/Ian Luna*

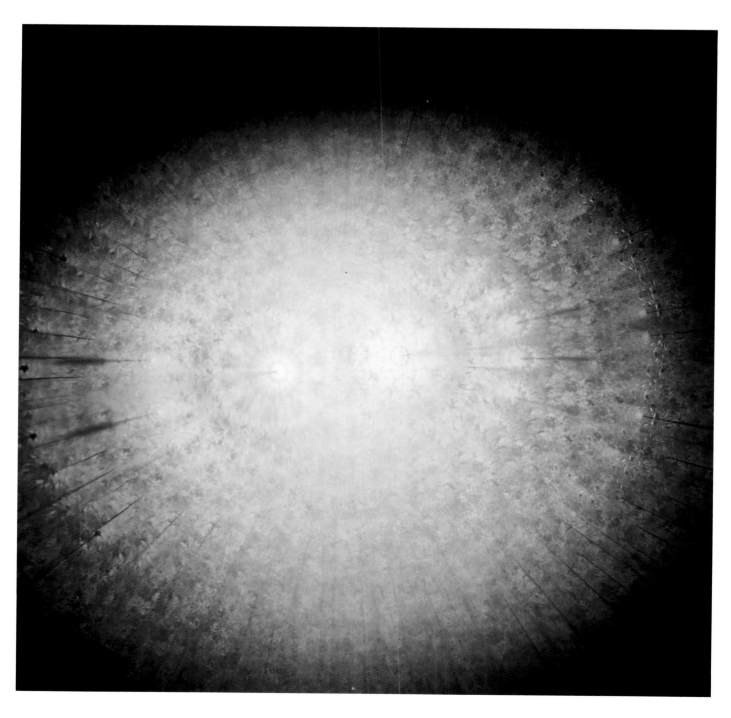

HOMMA TAKASHI

There is critical consensus that no one person in the last decade has exerted more influence on the photographic arts of contemporary Japan than Homma Takashi. Equipped with a thorough and relentless understanding of the place he calls home, his accumulated images of Tokyo and its people present an exhaustive portrait of a city at century's end, as the polity it supports tentatively crosses into any number of possible futures. The far-ranging material effects of the "lost decade" following the implosion of the bubble economy in 1991, the social ills brought about by the postindustrial transition, the myriad pleasures of the modern life, and the swagger and the seduction of youth have found quiet yet undeniable expression in his body of work.

Homma's thwarted ambition to become a baseball player under the unremitting demands of the national high school varsity system and its *Koshien* tournament, his work in advertising with the seminal firm Light Publicity while still in university, and a brief but disappointing stint in London all contributed to a tenuous but disciplined photographic career in the early 1990s. Paying his dues in any number of mind-numbing journeyman gigs and shooting "idols" Homma found his true voice later in the decade, by framing the urban ennui of the *kogai*—mid-rise housing developments—that dominate the sprawling prefectures surrounding Tokyo.

Miles away from the throb and din of Shibuya, Asakusa or Shinjuku, Homma uncovers a threatening disquiet among the boring tower blocks, windswept public spaces, and the sullen, apathetic children of these suffocating "feeder" communities. Nothing is imposed. There is no dramatic lighting or tedious compositional deliberation. The art here lies in Homma's reflexive use of the camera, capturing all before him in the harsh daylight, often with the same intangible detachment that the objects/subjects themselves embody. Simply called *Tokyo Suburbia* the 1997 book and exhibition exercised a profound effect on the public imagination, catapulting Homma into local and international acclaim. With the show traveling to the Netherlands, Switzerland and the United States in 2000, the photographer received the 24th Kimura Ihei Memorial Photography Award at home.

Leaving for New York to photograph the aftermath of September 11 in *Stars and Stripes* (2002) for *Casa BRUTUS* magazine, Homma's latest book shot in Japan revisits well-trod urbanistic themes. But in *Tokyo and My Daughter* (2006), the artist returns to the heart of the city with not a little conceit. Scenes of an anonymous, almost cloying domesticity starring Homma and his toddler "daughter"—really an actress—are juxtaposed with the somber exteriors of buildings bereft of passersby. But these are no longer the gaudy-grim structures of *Tokyo Suburbia*. They are rather key architectural passages from the last few years, and include Sejima Kazuyo's House in a Plum Grove, Aoki Jun's G House and Mori Minoru's Roppongi Hills complex. Shot from dusk until dawn, Homma conveys the environment around him in the most passive way possible, allowing the spontaneity of his eye to capture images instead of his calculating mind. The task of assigning meaning comes afterwards, flooding every photo with each interpretation, and inevitably striking a chord in the process.—*Ian Luna/Lauren A. Gould*

A JAPANESE RENAISSANCE IN ART & FASHION PHOTOGRAPHY
ESSAY BY HAYASHI FUMIHIRO

In Japan today there are but a scant few fashion photographers in any true sense. In the realm of Japanese photography, where the advertising industry holds the greatest sway, most photographers focus on the narrow fields of commercial advertising and entertainment in which to establish their success. Generally speaking, fashion photography is looked at as a means of presenting oneself on the way to a career in advertising. It can honestly be said that there are virtually no photographers today restricting themselves solely to fashion photography.

Additionally, the Japanese fashion photography scene is dominated by a pronounced inferiority complex toward Western culture and its celebrities, despite the fact that the shooters' own culture is presently being observed with rapt attention overseas. In this scene, shallow mimicry of Western photographers will not be abided. It's plain, when you view the billboards and advertising posters for fashion houses that paper the city of Tokyo, that the Japanese inferiority complex with regard to the West is quite strong and deep-rooted.

Rather than seek out unique emerging talent in fashion photography, fashion publications these days seem to revolve around C-list celebrities, or rely on the name value of trend-setting arbiters of taste simply referred to as *stylists* in Japanese-English. (When the name of one such *stylist* appears on a magazine cover, it is said to increase sales by tens of thousands of copies.) In concentrating solely on the pursuit of profit, most Japanese magazines appear to have lost their aesthetic compass, and instead turned into crass catalogues of juxtaposing egos on display.

What I am describing here took place largely during what should rightly be called the "Japanese Lost Generation," one that was primarily affected by a downbeat economy, and proceeded from the burst of the economic bubble in the mid- to late-nineties. During this decade the aesthetics, ethics, and values of the Japanese have been radically altered and corrupted. Nihilism and venality have come to prevail throughout the country. Just now, at the crest of this devastating collapse of morality into anarchy and chaos, Japanese culture is witnessing the beginning of a new era of change – a renaissance. The strongest current in this sea change is a breach from the "Caucasian complex." Creative individuals educated in Western countries, especially Europe, saw that those overseas were being swayed by Japanese culture. Not just in its traditional forms, but their contemporary iteration in *otaku* culture, which encompasses *manga*, anime, computer games, and so on, as well as in a Western attention to whole health that embraces Japanese foods, Zen meditation and the like. What those creative types did upon

their return to Japan served as a collective trigger for this change. When Japanese people leave Japan and thus depart Japanese society, they are forced to contend with an entirely unaccustomed cognitive process—they must find and come to grips with their individuality. When confronted with the image of their essential originality they are forced to consider the realization that they are, in fact, Japanese. In their contemplation they recognize that the source of their creativity is fundamentally different from that of their Western-acculturated counterparts, and is not found in either longing for or imitating that culture. It is from this moment that the Post-Lost Generation commences, when the impact of those creators becomes evident.

When viewed in retrospect, the Lost Generation can be seen as an era in which the Japanese fashion scene fell enormously under the spell of both sampling culture (in the sense of DJ sampling) and American mass consumerism. In the guise of stylish, smooth-sounding English words like *sanpuringu* (sampling) and *koraboreeshon* (collaboration) the Japanese fashion scene was willing to abandon all reservations about imitation and casting originality to the wayside. In this, the community adopted, whole hog, a mutated, childish form of materialism.

Please keep in mind this set of circumstances surrounding Japanese fashion photography when considering the following assertion: The great change in Japanese fashion photography actually did take place in the 1990s. It was Homma Takashi who defined the image of Tokyo in the '90s, and in so doing, more than anyone, influenced all of subsequent Japanese photography. His fashion photos, which took the form of naturalistic portraits that drew out the peculiarly Japanese *lolita* look, infused fashion photography with documentary import. The nihilism that his